Epica Book 17
Europe's
Best Advertising

EDITOR
Andrew Rawlins

ART DIRECTOR
Frédéric Ansermet

SYNOPSES
Mark Tungate

EDITORIAL ASSISTANTS
Maureen Lynch
Jill Sayles
Patrick Taschler

COVER DESIGN
Getty Images Creative Studio

COVER IMAGE
Stephen Stickler/Getty Images

PUBLISHER
AVA Publishing S.A.
enquiries@avabooks.ch

DISTRIBUTION
North America
Sterling Publishing Co.
www.sterlingpub.com
All other countries
Thames & Hudson Ltd.
sales@thameshudson.co.uk

PRODUCTION
AVA Book Production Pte Ltd.
production@avabooks.com.sg

Printed in Singapore

© COPYRIGHT 2004 EPICA S.A. ALL RIGHTS RESERVED

Under no circumstances can any part of
this book be reproduced or copied in any
way or form without prior permission
of the copyright owners.
EPICA S.A.
65 rue J.J. Rousseau,
92150 Suresnes, France
Tel: 33 (0) 1 42 04 04 32
Fax: 33 (0) 1 45 06 02 88
www.epica-awards.com
info@epica-awards.com

Epica S.A. has made every effort to publish full
and correct credits for each work included in
this volume based on the information provided
on the Epica entry forms. Epica S.A. and
Applied Visual Arts Publishing S.A. (AVA) regret
any omissions that may have occurred, but
hereby disclaim liability.

Contents

INTRODUCTION

Foreword by John Pallant	5
2003 Winners	6
The Jury	8
Annual Report	10

EPICA D'OR 2003

"Play to Win" by Lewis Blackwell	12
"Designed for Impact" by Patrick Burgoyne	14

FOOD & DRINK

Food	16
Confectionery & Snacks	26
Dairy Products	34
Alcoholic Drinks A	42
Alcoholic Drinks B	46
Non-Alcoholic Drinks	54

CONSUMER SERVICES

Transport & Tourism	68
Retail Services	80
Financial Services	94
Public Interest	106
Communication Services	142

THE HOME

Homes, Furnishings & Appliances	154
Household Maintenance	162
Audiovisual Equipment & Accessories	170

HEALTH & BEAUTY

Toiletries & Health Care	176
Beauty Products	186
Prescription Products & Services	190

AUTOMOTIVE

Automobiles	194
Automotive & Accessories	218

BUSINESS TO BUSINESS

Office Equipment	226
Business Services	230
Industrial & Agricultural Equipment	240

FASHION

Clothing & Fabrics	246
Footwear & Personal Accessories	256

MISCELLANEOUS

Media	266
Recreation & Leisure	284

TECHNIQUES

Advertising Photography	300
Media Innovation	308
Direct Marketing	318
Publications	330
Packaging Design	338
Illustration & Graphics	348

INTERACTIVE

Internet Sites	354
Online Ads	366
Online Films	369
Integrated Campaigns	374

John Pallant, European Creative Director, Saatchi & Saatchi.

THIS BOOK WILL TEACH YOU **HOW TO DO** ADVERTISING
THIS BOOK WILL TEACH YOU **HOW NOT TO DO** ADVERTISING

This is the least interesting page in this book.

(Feel free to turn over now, if you wish. I completely understand.)

Much, much, much more interesting are just about all the others.

For there you'll find some of the best ideas from some of the most talented advertising writers and art directors in Europe.

And fabulous they are, too.

(The ideas, that is. The writers and art directors are a pretty odd bunch.)

Study them closely. And when you have studied them, keep this book by your side and study them again.

Because while there are many 'how to' books on just about everything else, this is the closest you'll get to a 'how to' book on creative advertising.

If you are just starting out in this business, there is much to learn here.

And even if you are not, there is much to be reminded of. The power of simplicity, the importance of......(well, I won't go on, you can find out for yourself).

You will see, too, that these principles apply everywhere in Europe.

There are no great cultural differences when it comes to advertising.

Look closer still, and you may even start to detect some techniques which could be borrowed and applied to your own work.

A layout design. The way a headline is constructed, perhaps. A clever image.

Please resist this temptation. (Hard to do, I know, in these days of less people having to do more work in less time.)

And please resist it again in a few years from now when you think nobody will remember.

Because although this book will teach you how to do advertising, it will be advertising like the advertising in this book.

And as great as it is, the advertising in this book is now the great advertising of the past.

The great advertising of the future will be nothing like it. That's why it will be great advertising, of course.

And where will you find your inspiration for that? Well, fortunately, just about everywhere else apart from this book.

In other words, don't just spend your life thumbing through advertising annuals. And don't spend your life sitting in your office looking out at the world through the window either.

Go out and actively search out new experiences to feed your imagination. You'll have more fun, for one thing, and it will show in everything you do.

And then when you create an idea that bears the unique stamp of your personality and experiences, that's when other people will say, 'I wish I'd done that'. Because they couldn't possibly have done it in a million years.

(And guess what, some of those people will be sitting on awards juries.)

But before you do all that, of course, please do enjoy the wonderful work here and absorb everything it has to give you.

And be inspired, too.

But be inspired not to imitate, but to go and inspire us all back in return.

Which is all from me.

So now you can turn to the most interesting pages in this book.

John Pallant, European Creative Director, Saatchi & Saatchi.

Epica d'Or (print): adidas

Epica d'Or (film): Nike

EPICA WINNERS 2003

EPICA D'OR (FILM)	WIEDEN + KENNEDY (AMSTERDAM)	NIKE "MUSICAL CHAIRS"
EPICA D'OR (PRINT)	180 AMSTERDAM (AMSTERDAM)	ADIDAS RUGBY WORLD CUP "IMPACT" CAMPAIGN

PRINT & INTERACTIVE WINNERS

FOOD	CAYENNE (MILAN)	ITALIAN FOOD COLLECTION CAMPAIGN
CONFECTIONERY & SNACKS	TANDEM DDB (MADRID)	CHUPA CHUPS "COWBOY"
DAIRY PRODUCTS	LOWE BRINDFORS (STOCKHOLM)	YOGGI YOGHURTS "PICK YOUR OWN"CAMPAIGN
ALCOHOLIC DRINKS (A)	JWT+H+F (ZÜRICH)	SMIRNOFF ICE "PIANO"
ALCOHOLIC DRINKS (B)	GRAFFITI BBDO (BUCHAREST)	GUINNESS BEER "THINK POSITIVE"
NON ALCOHOLIC DRINKS	J WALTER THOMPSON (BARCELONA)	MORENO COFFEE CAMPAIGN
TRANSPORT & TOURISM	BETC EURO RSCG (PARIS)	AIR FRANCE "FLYING CHEAPLY" CAMPAIGN
RETAIL SERVICES	.START (MUNICH)	BURGER KING "BAND AID"
FINANCIAL SERVICES	CONTRAPUNTO (MADRID)	SANITAS MEDICAL INSURANCE "FAMILY" CAMPAIGN
PUBLIC INTEREST	LEO BURNETT (PRAGUE)	AMNESTY INT'L "THANK YOU" CAMPAIGN
COMMUNICATION SERVICES	LOWE (ZÜRICH)	ORANGE NETWORK QUALITY CAMPAIGN
HOMES, FURNISHINGS & APPLIANCES	HASAN & PARTNERS (HELSINKI)	IKEA "LIVE A LITTLE MORE" CAMPAIGN
HOUSEHOLD MAINTENANCE	LOWE (LISBON)	SKIP BLACK VELVET CAMPAIGN
AUDIOVISUAL EQUIPMENT & ACCESSORIES	TBWA\PARIS (PARIS)	SONY PLAYSTATION 2 "SUPERMARKET"
TOILETRIES & HEALTH CARE	GREY (LONDON)	REMINGTON BIKINI TRIM AND SHAPE
BEAUTY PRODUCTS	MAGIC HAT (LONDON)	E45 BODY LOTION CAMPAIGN
PRESCRIPTION PRODUCTS	ADVICO YOUNG & RUBICAM (ZÜRICH)	INTERPHARMA RESEARCH CAMPAIGN
AUTOMOBILES	TBWA\PARIS (PARIS)	NISSAN 4X4 RANGE "EXPLORE" CAMPAIGN
AUTOMOTIVE & ACCESSORIES	LEO BURNETT(WARSAW)	FIAT AUTHORIZED SERVICE STATIONS CAMPAIGN
OFFICE EQUIPMENT	KOLLE REBBE (HAMBURG)	BISLEY OFFICE FURNISHINGS CAMPAIGN
BUSINESS SERVICES	LG&F (BRUSSELS)	AXA RECRUITMENT CAMPAIGN
INDUSTRIAL & AGRICULTURAL EQUIPMENT	POULTER PARTNERS (LEEDS)	BRITISH GLASS, GLASSPAC CAMPAIGN
CLOTHING & FABRICS	STORÅKERS McCANN (STOCKHOLM)	LEE JEANS "BEHIND THE SCENES" CAMPAIGN
FOOTWEAR & PERSONAL ACCESSORIES	180 AMSTERDAM (AMSTERDAM)	ADIDAS RUGBY WORLD CUP "IMPACT" CAMPAIGN
MEDIA	FCB/TAPSA (MADRID)	TVE NEWS CAMPAIGN
RECREATION & LEISURE	LOUIS XIV DDB (PARIS)	WORLD ATHLETICS CHAMPIONSHIPS CAMPAIGN
ADVERTISING PHOTOGRAPHY	MARC GOUBY for TBWA\PARIS (PARIS)	SONY PLAYSTATION 2 "VETERANS" CAMPAIGN
MEDIA INNOVATION	SAATCHI & SAATCHI (VIENNA)	MOBILKOM AUSTRIA A1 MMS PROMOTION
DIRECT MARKETING	HARRISON TROUGHTON WUNDERMAN (LONDON)	IBM: FINANCIAL TIMES MAILING
PUBLICATIONS	ZAPPING (MADRID)	BUENA VISTA"THE JUNGLE BOOK 2" PRESS BOOK
PACKAGING DESIGN	LOWE BRINDFORS (STOCKHOLM)	TIGER OF SWEDEN PACKAGING & BAGS
ILLUSTRATION & GRAPHICS	K2 DESIGN (ATHENS)	2004 OLYMPIC GAMES PICTOGRAMS
INTERACTIVE: WEBSITES	FRAMFAB DENMARK (COPENHAGEN)	NIKE FOOTBALL/PANNA K.O. SITE
INTERACTIVE: ONLINE ADS	TBWA\GERMANY (BERLIN)	SVF/ SELF-DEFENSE CLASSES FOR WOMEN
INTERACTIVE: ONLINE FILMS	HOSS GIFFORD (GLASGOW)	EDINBURGH INTERNATIONAL FILM FESTIVAL
INTERACTIVE : INTEGRATED CAMPAIGNS	FORSMAN & BODENFORS (STOCKHOLM)	VOLVO XC 90 LAUNCH CAMPAIGN

FILM WINNERS

FOOD	DDB (BUDAPEST)	McDONALD'S "HI"
CONFECTIONERY & SNACKS	CLM BBDO (PARIS)	SNICKERS "THE FOUNTAIN"
DAIRY PRODUCTS	NEW DEAL DDB (OSLO)	DREAM ICE CREAM "PREGNANT"
ALCOHOLIC DRINKS (A)	DDFH&B/JWT (DUBLIN)	SMIRNOFF BLACK ICE "PARENT TRAP"
ALCOHOLIC DRINKS (B)	TBWA\LONDON (LONDON)	JOHN SMITH'S BITTER CAMPAIGN
NON-ALCOHOLIC DRINKS (2 WINNERS)	CLM BBDO (PARIS)	PEPSI "ELEPHANT TOWER"
	CLEMMOW HORNBY INGE (LONDON)	TANGO SOFT DRINK "SEAL"
TRANSPORT & TOURISM	NEW DEAL DDB (OSLO)	NOR-WAY BUSSEKSPRESS "EGGS I" & "EGGS 2"
RETAIL SERVICES	ROBERT/BOISEN & LIKE-MINDED (COPENHAGEN)	INTERFLORA"POWER OF FLOWERS" CAMPAIGN
FINANCIAL SERVICES	DDB (AMSTERDAM)	CENTRAAL BEHEER INSURANCE "HORSE"
PUBLIC INTEREST	LEO BURNETT (PRAGUE)	UAMK ROAD SAFETY "FUNERAL"
COMMUNICATION SERVICES	FORSMAN & BODENFORS (GOTHENBURG)	TELE 2 "MAILSLOT" & "MAILBOX"
HOMES, FURNISHINGS & APPLIANCES	LEO BURNETT (WARSAW)	IKEA WINTER SALE "LET IT SNOW"
HOUSEHOLD MAINTENANCE	SAATCHI & SAATCHI (PARIS)	ARIEL STYLE "THE EVERYDAY LIFE OF CLOTHES"
AUDIOVISUAL EQUIPMENT	MARINI DOTTI E ASSOCIATI (MILAN)	FUJIFILM DIGITAL CAMERAS "ESCAPE"
TOILETRIES & HEALTH CARE	FORSMAN & BODENFORS (GOTHENBURG)	LIBERO DIAPERS "TIME FOR A WEE"
AUTOMOBILES	WIEDEN + KENNEDY (LONDON)	HONDA ACCORD "COG"
AUTOMOTIVE & ACCESSORIES	CLM BBDO (PARIS)	TOTAL PETROL STATIONS "THE TELEPHONE"
BUSINESS SERVICES	KOLLE REBBE (HAMBURG)	INLINGUA LANGUAGE SCHOOL "EUROLINGO"
INDUSTRIAL & AGRICULTURAL EQUIPMENT	EURO RSCG C&O (PARIS)	AIRBUS A340 AEROPLANES "COUPLES"
CLOTHING & FABRICS	WIEDEN + KENNEDY (AMSTERDAM)	NIKE "STREAM"
FOOTWEAR & PERSONAL ACCESSORIES	WIEDEN + KENNEDY (AMSTERDAM)	NIKE "MUSICAL CHAIRS"
MEDIA	CLEMMOW HORNBY INGE (LONDON)	THE DAILY TELEGRAPH "BIRTHDAY"
RECREATION & LEISURE	GORGEOUS for RKCR/Y&R (LONDON)	THE TIMES LONDON FILM FESTIVAL "DIRECTOR"

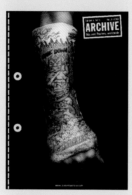

The Jury

The Epica jury is made up of journalists and editors from Europe's leading advertising magazines.

AUSTRIA
Extra Dienst

BELGIUM
Pub

CZECH REPUBLIC
Strategie

DENMARK
Markedsføring

FINLAND
Markkinointi & Mainonta

FRANCE
CB News

GERMANY
Lürzer's International Archive
Werben und Verkaufen

GREAT BRITAIN
Creative Review
Marketing Week
The Drum

GREECE
+ Design

HUNGARY
Kreatív

IRELAND
IMJ

ITALY
Pubblicitá Italia
Pubblico
Strategia

NETHERLANDS
Marketing Tribune

NORWAY
Kampanje

POLAND
Media & Marketing Polska

PORTUGAL
Prisma

RUSSIA
Advertising Ideas
Kreativ.Creativity

SLOVAKIA
Stratégie

SLOVENIA
MM
New Moment

SPAIN
El Publicista

SWEDEN
Resumé

SWITZERLAND
Persönlich
Werbewoche

TURKEY
Marketing Türkiye

9

Photos: James Carr (Bark), Peter van Woensel Kooy (Marketing Tribune) and Epica.

Annual Report

The awards ceremony took place on January 23rd, 2004, at Clontarf Castle in Dublin. The event was hosted by IMJ, Ireland's leading marketing magazine, and sponsored by Guinness. IMJ also celebrated its 30th anniversary at the ceremony and inaugurated its Hall of Fame.

In 2003, for the first time, the Epica jury awarded two grand prix; an Epica d'Or for the best film entry and one for the best entry in other media. These top awards both went to Dutch agencies, and they were both for well-known sports brands.

Wieden + Kennedy Amsterdam won the film Epica d'Or with the Nike "Musical Chairs" commercial directed by Ulf Johansson of Traktor.

180 Amsterdam won the second Epica d'Or with their 2003 Rugby World Cup print and poster campaign for adidas entitled "Impact".

2003 also marked the creation of four distinct interactive categories with winners from Copenhagen, Berlin, Stockholm and Glasgow. The advertising photography prize, traditionally one of Epica's most prestigious awards, went to French photographer Marc Gouby for the PlayStation 2 "Veterans" campaign.

A total of 62 winners and 315 finalists were announced in 2003. These figures compare with 58 winners and 271 finalists the previous year. All the winners and finalists are shown in the Epica Book, together with a selection of other high-scoring entries.

Work from 609 companies and 39 countries competed in the awards. Forsman & Bodenfors, Gothenburg, was the most successful entrant with 3 winners and 9 finalists. The UK and France led the country rankings with 10 winners each, followed by Sweden and the Netherlands with 6.

Romania celebrated its first-ever Epica winner, while Lithuania appeared on the list of finalists for the first time.

	Entrants	Entries	Winners	Finalists
Austria	21	106	1	3
Belarus	1	2	-	-
Belgium	26	209	1	11
Croatia	8	19	-	2
Czech Republic	7	99	2	9
Denmark	21	121	2	8
Finland	16	236	1	12
France	31	327	10	31
Georgia	1	1	-	-
Germany	82	790	4	44
Greece	7	49	1	-
Hungary	15	37	1	1
Iceland	2	7	-	-
Ireland	8	63	1	3
Israel	14	69	-	7
Italy	30	221	2	8
Latvia	1	1	-	-
Lebanon	5	18	-	-
Lithuania	5	20	-	1
Luxembourg	3	10	-	-
Macedonia	2	9	-	-
Morocco	1	4	-	-
Netherlands	26	164	6	17
Norway	9	68	2	10
Poland	14	87	2	5
Portugal	9	107	1	5
Romania	7	37	1	1
Russia	13	48	-	-
Saudi Arabia	1	1	-	-
Serbia	1	2	-	-
Slovakia	5	42	-	1
Slovenia	15	73	-	-
Spain	29	282	5	15
Sweden	69	510	6	50
Switzerland	24	237	3	14
Turkey	17	85	-	3
Ukraine	3	12	-	-
United Arab Emirates	4	43	-	4
United Kingdom	56	338	10	49
TOTAL	609	4.554	62	315

For more information on the Epica awards, and to see all the 2003 film winners in real time, visit www.epica-awards.com.

The Reunion arena and the spectators who filled it.

Play to Win
by Lewis Blackwell

There was no escape from competition for the winners of the 2003 Epica d'Or film award. Not only did they have to compete with a history of memorable commercials for Nike, they also had to create a spot based on the idea of competitiveness in everyday life. But there is nothing cut-throat about their film, Musical Chairs, which focuses on the playful aspects of a game that unites people rather than setting them against each other.

Copywriter Carlo Cavallone and art director Alvaro Sotomayor of Wieden + Kennedy Amsterdam, were asked to connect their spot to Tag, the previous commercial in the campaign. Early ideas included making a sport out of activities like babysitting or hide and seek. But the final combination of musical chairs at a basketball game had the advantage of universal familiarity and a backdrop which was grand in scale but controllable - they hoped.

Authenticity was essential for their idea to work, so they headed for Texas where basketball, like so much else, is huge. They negotiated a location that represents the real, all-American setting they were after: Reunion arena, former home of the Dallas Mavericks, with a capacity of around 18,000 spectators. They also cast the Mavericks' real-life mascot and musician to play their own roles in the commercial and the referees are genuine Dallas professionals. Only the players' shirts were specially fabricated, as the game's governing body, the NBA, would not permit the use of an existing team's shirts.

The Reunion arena after post-production.

The cheerleaders with the Wieden + Kennedy creative team and their clients.

Alvaro Sotomayor playing ball with Douglas Caballero.

Musical Chair? A souvenir at Dallas airport on its way to Amsterdam.

The players were cast from a pool of college team members, including the Spaniard Pau Gasol, now a major US star playing for the Memphis Grizzlies. His rival for the last seat in the game of musical chairs is played by 23-year old Douglas Cavellero. The creatives and director saw immediately that he had the kind of looks - attractive and cool, but typically young American sports fan - and, equally important, the stamina they were looking for.

Although the vast Reunion stadium possessed the giant scale Cavallone and Sotomayer had visualised, it also posed a huge filming challenge: the spot was based on a sold-out game, but there was obviously no question of employing thousands of extras. Consequently, the director Ulf Johansson, had to figure out how to maintain the illusion of an 18,000 capacity crowd while working with just 200 extras. "It was a bit of a nightmare," confesses Johansson's producer Philippa Smith. "Throughout an intense two-day shoot, we had three units working constantly as the crowd kept shifting around, changing their clothes as they went." They were filmed standing up, sitting down and each take was shot from every possible camera angle.

London's Moving Picture Company, who did the seamless post production, had plates made of every shot before compositing them together. The result is a spontaneous, mini-action movie with no visible hint of manipulation. It opens on a scene of fast and furious action on the court, with the stadium musicians playing the kind of music used to rouse the crowd during an attacking phase of the game. When the music comes to an abrupt stop, both teams dash into the stands where the entire audience has erupted in a spontaneous game of musical chairs.

In each corner of the stadium, people dash for every available seat, including a baby stroller, locker room benches and the driver's perch in a fork-lift truck. Eventually, the game narrows to a two-man race between player 43 and a young fan on his way back to his seat with drinks. Simultaneously, both men glance at the overhead screen showing the position of the very last free seat and hurtle towards it. The fan vaults into the seat, Nike Air-Max shod feet first, beating his rival by a hair's breadth. An instant later, the music strikes up and the game recommences.

As a sign-off, the word "play" appears on screen alongside a Nike swoosh. The low-key brand projection reflected the creative team's emphasis on the overall feeling rather than the product. Johansson also believed that the best way to get a convincing scenario was just to let people play and this was his major directorial command. The only casualties of the cast's enthusiasm were a few sprained ankles. In general, however, the enjoyment and stamina of the whole team made the shoot, "the most inspiring and exhilirating we have worked on," says Smith.

The reaction of their client at Nike Europe, Paulo Tubito, was equally enthusiastic. "We had great feedback with this spot, I even had old friends calling up about it. But it was also doubly successful in terms of brand-building and new product awareness."

Given its success on so many levels, an alternative title for Musical Chairs might have been 'Play to Win' - or maybe that was just a useful betting tip for the Epica d'Or.

Lewis Blackwell is the creative director of Getty Images, having previously been editor-in-chief and publisher of Creative Review for many years.

13

Designed for Impact
by Patrick Burgoyne

All Black Jonah Lomu signing his self-portrait.

Jonah Lomu.

England's hero, Jonny Wilkinson.

Talk about suffering for your art: when 180 art director Stuart Brown had an idea for an adidas rugby campaign, he decided to test it out at home first. So, he covered himself in black poster paint, wrapped his mattress in cellophane, stuck on a sheet of paper and charged. "The results were pretty good but I had a migraine for a day and it took two weeks to get the paint off," he remembers.

Nevertheless, Brown's efforts persuaded the client to go for an idea which has ended up winning this year's Epica d'Or for print. "Adidas asked us how they could make an impact during the Rugby World Cup – we took that brief quite literally," remembers Alex Melvin, partner and head of strategic planning at the Amsterdam-based agency. Like most other sports brands, adidas is often seen as a company that just make shoes you can do sport in. But, Melvin believes, the truth is that they're more of a multi-specialist. "They've been involved in hundreds of sports at highly technical levels," he says. "So we were quite keen to drill down a little bit deeper knowing that as a brand they're inside the sport working with players: they'll develop different boots for forwards and for backs, different shirts depending on the player and his position. We wanted to do really impactful stuff but also be insightful of the game, demonstrating that this brand is one that understands the players and their capabilities."

The resulting concept was to cover adidas-sponsored players in paint and ask them to hurl themselves at white canvases. Hopefully, the resulting marks would convey the power of the game and its athletes, putting the viewer in the midst of the action. These images would then form the artwork for the brand's major campaign around the tournament.

Jonah Lomu before impact.

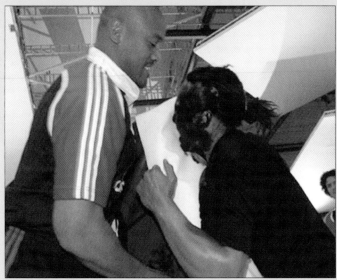
Tana Umaga hits the tackle bag.

Jonah and England's Martin Johnson.

Having convinced the client, 180 then had to persuade 15 of the world's top rugby players to have themselves covered head to foot in paint. Eventually, they managed to gather the whole of the New Zealand All Blacks team, plus assorted adidas-sponsored players from other countries, in a studio near Wimbledon dog track in London. The players were covered in Vaseline and a special body paint, then given ear plugs (another of 180's "testers" had unfortunately developed an ear infection during the early trials). They were then asked to run at, dive on and tackle canvases held by team-mates.

"What we really wanted to know was, when you get two huge guys, and they go 'whack!' what does that feel like?" says Brown. "This was a way of recording the moment but also the scale of the impact as well." The agency also got the players to adopt a particular move or position which they were associated with. When the English players got their turn for the campaign, Martin Johnson jumped against a canvas as if catching a ball in a line-out while Jonny Wilkinson went for a mid-stride profile as if just about to kick the ball for a conversion. "There's a few of Jonah Lomu doing his classic hand-off move," adds Brown, who was impressed with the way the session brought out the artistic side in the All Black star. "Kees Meeuws and Jonah were telling us that they were both going to do foundation courses at art college," says Brown. "Kees actually went and did it while Jonah left to go and play rugby. Kees was directing Jonah and we just stood back and watched the two of them get on with it."

Peter McHugh, partner and executive creative director on the campaign, believes that this close relationship that the players had with one another was one reason why the campaign came out so well. "They were all very cooperative with each other and you can see it in what we made. People get to a certain level at something and they all appreciate what each other does. They wanted to make the most dramatic prints they could." Extra details on the player's faces were obtained from stock footage and subtly added in post to strengthen the images.

And what originally began as a poster campaign grew organically to include TV commercials, giant bus wraps, a calendar and, something the team were particularly excited about, a touring exhibition entitled Impact: The Art of Rugby with an accompanying art book to be published in the UK, Australia and New Zealand.

"We tried to tap into a particular aspect of each player's performance that the knowledgeable fan would respect about them," says McHugh. "What it was about the player that's unique or special. Some are truisms about rugby, while some just acknowledge the fact that this is not a person that you want to get in the way of."

The finished work is an innovative spin on the tired world of the sports celebrity endorsement: in this case each athlete was actively involved, donating their own image as a unique self-portrait. It was that rare thing in advertising – a generally original concept that perfectly matched the brand and really connected with consumers. A campaign with real impact, you might say.

Patrick Burgoyne is the editor of Creative Review.

Agency:	DDB, Budapest	A young guy walks the city streets, heading for work.
Creative Director:	Zoltán Simon	He seems extremely popular – even he seems surprised
Copywriter:	Zoltán Simon	by how many people wave hello during the short journey.
Art Director:	Tibor Varga	A couple on a motorbike, a businessman, a group of
Production:	Argus Film	teenagers on pushbikes, a pretty girl who gives his hand
Director:	Jonas Zachrisson	an affectionate squeeze, an elderly lady in a café – they all
Client:	McDonald's, "Hi"	greet him like an old friend. The reason is revealed when
		he dons a cap and takes his place behind the counter –
		at McDonald's. The burger chain and its staff have been
		cheerfully serving customers in Hungary for 15 years.

The Italian food collection.

The Italian food collection.

The Italian food collection.

The Italian food collection.

Agency: Cayenne, Milan
Creative Director: Giandomenico Puglisi
Art Directors: Giandomenico Puglisi
                   Debora Mighali
Copywriters: Federico Bonriposi
                   Mario Gardini
Photographer: Fulvio Bonavia
Client: UNIPI
                   (Unione Industriale Pastai Italiani),
                   The Italian Food Collection

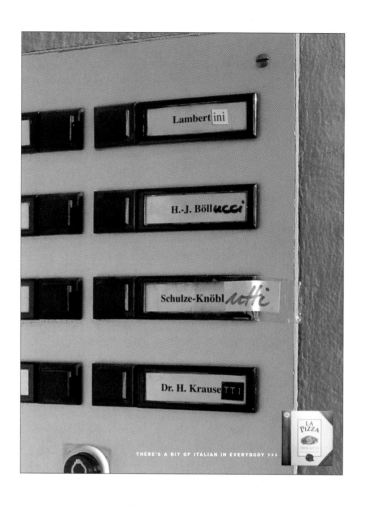

THERE'S A BIT OF ITALIAN IN EVERYBODY >>>

18 **Food**

Agency:	Young & Rubicam, Frankfurt	Agency:	McCann-Erickson, Frankfurt
Creative Director:	Norbert Graf	Creative Director:	Erich Reuter
Copywriter:	Lothar Mueller	Copywriter:	Jens Sabri
Art Director:	Thorsten Steeg	Art Director:	Suzanne Förch
Photographer:	Thorsten Steeg	Photographer:	Jean-Pascal Günther
Client:	Wagner La Pizza	Client:	Happy Dog Petfood

Food   **19**

Agency:	Lowe, Amsterdam	A boy with a football emerges onto an
Creative Director:	Pieter van Velsen	apartment block balcony. He tosses the ball
Copywriter:	Zwier Veldhoen	onto the balcony of the penthouse above.
Art Director:	Ivar van der Zwan	Then he scurries downstairs and presses
Production:	Hazazah	the intercom buzzer. "Sir, I've kicked my ball
Director:	Yani	onto your balcony. May I have it back?" The
Producers:	Suzanne Huisman	man drops the ball to the boy far below. He
	Peter Burger	looks amazed that a kid could kick a ball so
Client:	Calvé Peanut Butter,	high. Chortling Dutch viewers see that the
	"Dick Advocaat"	man is the national football team coach –

and that the little wannabe soccer star has caught his attention. Calvé Peanut Butter – how big do you want to be?

Agency:	Lowe, Amsterdam
Creative Director:	Pieter van Velsen
Copywriter:	Jeroen van de Sande
Art Director:	Jorn Kruijsen
Production:	Ocean View
Director:	Paul Ruven
Producers:	Clarisse Venekamp
	Nathalie Moser
Client:	Mora, "Spring Roll"

Father and son sit at the kitchen table, tucking into their supper. Dad has just taken a bite of his spring roll when his wife walks in with the post. "So which one of you ordered this?" she asks disgustedly, holding up an erotic lingerie catalogue. The boy clearly thinks he's been caught out – until he notices that his father's face has become flushed and sweaty, as if with embarrassment. Mother's eyes narrow. Those Mora spicy spring rolls can really get you into trouble…

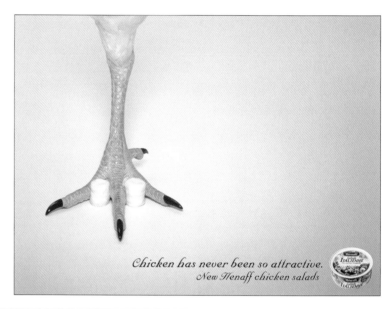

Chicken has never been so attractive.
New Henaff chicken salads

Pork has never been so attractive.
New Henaff pork salads

Agency:	BBDO, Denmark	**Agency:**	BDDP & Fils, Paris
Creative Directors:	Jesper Hansen	**Creative Director:**	Olivier Altmann
	Ulrik Michelsen	**Copywriters:**	Laurent Duvoux
Copywriter:	Jesper Hansen		Eric Thome
Art Director:	Ulrik Michelsen	**Art Directors:**	Laurent Duvoux
Client:	Whiskas Cat Food		Eric Thome
		Client:	Henaff Meats

Atria
Good food, better mood.

Agency:	Taivas, Helsinki
Copywriter:	Kari Puumalainen
Art Director:	Nestori Brück
Production:	Filmitalli
Director:	Markus Virpiö
Producers:	Hanna Salminen
	Kaj Wasastjerna
Client:	Atria Foods,
	"A Man's Mind"

"Looks like the roads were packed with morons again," a woman thinks to herself, as her husband strides angrily into the kitchen. "Those roads are packed with morons!" he exclaims. His grumbling continues as he unpacks the shopping – half of which he has forgotten – and rummages through kitchen drawers looking for cutlery. But once he has something to eat, he literally becomes a different person – transforming from bearded and moody to clean-shaven and suave. "Darling," this new personage asks charmingly, "would you like to go to the theatre?" Atria foods – with good food comes a better mood.

Agency:	H2E Hoehne Habann Elser,
	Ludwigsberg
Creative Directors:	Jens Schmidt
	Peter Herrmann
Art Director:	Nana Poehner
Client:	Trill Birdseed

Nautilus. Pure crab.

22 **Food**

Agency:	Leo Burnett, Paris	**Agency:**	The Union Advertising Agency, Edinburgh
Creative Directors:	Christophe Coffre		
	Nicolas Taubes	**Creative Directors:**	Andrew Lindsay
Copywriter:	Jean-Guillaume		Simon Scott
	Pascaud	**Copywriter:**	Stuart Anderson
Art Director:	Delphine Bojago	**Art Director:**	Ruth Yee
Photographer:	Pascal Hirsch	**Photographer:**	Jean Cazals
Client:	Nautilus Canned Crab	**Client:**	Quality Meat Scotland

Agency:	Advico Young & Rubicam, Zürich	Agency:	KNSK, Hamburg
Creative Director:	Daniel Comte	Creative Directors:	Anke Winschewski
Copywriter:	Peter Rettinghausen		Katja Winterhalder
Art Directors:	Dennis Schwarz	Art Director:	Roland Schäfer
	Mauko Iten	Photographer:	Michaela Rehn
Photographer:	Nicolas Monkewitz	Client:	Winterhalder
Client:	Gerlinea		Low Fat Corned Beef

Happy Easter

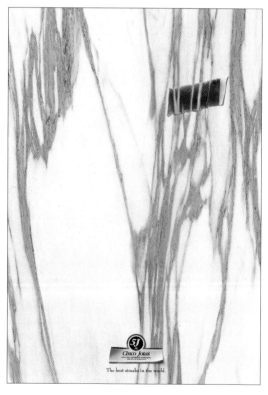

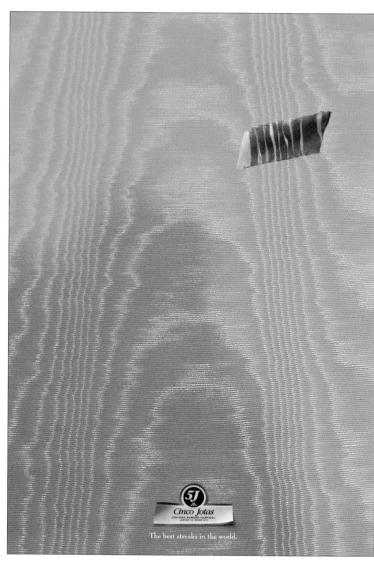

Agency:	Bruketa & Žinić, Zagreb	Agency:	Tandem DDB, Madrid
Creative Directors:	Davor Bruketa	Creative Directors:	Manuel Montes
	Nikola Žinić		Alberto Astorga
Art Directors:	Davor Bruketa	Copywriter:	Elena Hernando
	Nikola Žinić	Art Director:	Cesar Lanaquera
Client:	Podravka Food Company	Photographer:	Santiago Boil
		Client:	5J Cinco Jotas, Cured Ham

Agency:	Skandaali/Leo Burnett, Helsinki		At dawn in the forest, a man puts some raw meat on a rock as bait for an unidentified wild beast. Then he sits with his colleague in a camouflaged hideout. They wait in vain for hours, telephoto lenses trained on the bait. Finally, at nightfall, they venture out to eat a snack around a camp fire. One of them unwraps some juicy sausages from HK Sininen. Twigs crackle behind them, and an almighty roar rents the air. Sounds like something else wants to bite into those delicious sausages…
Creative Directors:	Paula Rosti		
	Mirva Viitanen		
Copywriter:	Markku Haapalehto		
Art Director:	Erkki Mikola		
Production:	Rudolf Konimois, Talinn		
Director:	Kaido Veermäe		
Producer:	Katrin Kissa		
Client:	HK Sininen Sausages, "The Bait"		

Agency:	Sek & Grey, Helsinki		"This is William," says the voiceover. A harmless-looking middle-aged man sits at a restaurant table. "And this is William's salad." A half-empty plate of mixed leaves is placed in front of him. Unexpectedly, William flies into a rage, head-butting the plate and then smashing it to pieces. "It seems that William doesn't like salad," the narrator observes. So William is brought the new calzone pizza – containing salad – from Home Pizza. He takes a big, contented bite. In this form, salad is more fun.
Copywriter:	Niklas Lilja		
Art Director:	Risto Sihvo		
Production:	Hacienda		
Director:	Jappe Päivinen		
Producers:	Johanna Valasti		
	Petteri Lehtinen		
Client:	Home Pizza, "William"		

Agency:	CLM BBDO, Paris	A surfer dude is lying flat-out beside his
Creative Director:	Anne de Maupeou	board in a busy city street. He gets up,
Copywriter:	Olivier Durand	dazed and soaking wet. But how can this
Art Directors:	Xavier Brissard	be? He's miles away from the sea. Passers-
	Vaïnui de Castelbajac	by look bemused. The surfer takes an
Production:	Gang Films	energy-giving bite of his Snickers chocolate
Director:	Josh Taft	bar, and takes his board to a greenish pool
Producers:	Jean-Marc Tostivint	of water, tightly shot so we can't see what it
	Pierre Marcus	is. As a huge geyser of water springs into the
	Laurence Dupuy	air, the camera pulls back – and we see that
Client:	Snickers Chocolate Bar,	it is a fountain, which the surfer rides like a
	"The Fountain"	giant wave. Game on!

Come back to where the flavor is.

SURGEON GENERAL'S WARNING: Quitting Smoking Now Greatly Reduces Serious Risks to Your Health.

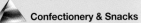 **Confectionery & Snacks** **27**

Agency: Tandem DDB, Madrid
Creative Director: Mario Gascon
Copywriter: David Perez
Art Director: Bernat Sanroma
Client: Chupa Chups

28 **Confectionery & Snacks**

Agency:	Staal, Oslo	Agency:	Staal, Oslo
Copywriter:	Arne Schau-Knudsen	Copywriter:	Arne Schau-Knudsen
Art Director:	Nico Wahl	Art Director:	Nico Wahl
Production:	Moland Film Company.	Production:	Moland Film Company.
Director:	Jens Lien	Director:	Torstein Bieler
Producer:	Magnus Waal	Producer:	Magnus Waal
Client:	Kim's Snacks, "Paprika"	Client:	Kim's Sharable Hearts, "Shadow"

In a clothes shop, a man selects a grey shirt. But when he enters the changing room, he spots a left-behind glittery red bra and thong. For a lark, he decides to try them on. As he is admiring himself in the mirror, the fire alarm rings. He can't struggle out of the tight undies, and is forced to flee the store dressed in this compromising manner. Needless to say, his family see him on the TV news. If you're looking for something to spice up your life, it's best to stick to Kim's X-tra spicy paprika crisps.

We're in a cinema, and on the screen a nauseatingly nice campaign about love and understanding is accompanied by a cheesy voiceover urging us to share with others. But the silhouettes in front of the screen tell a different story, as the unmistakeable shadows of a boy and his girlfriend battle for possession of a packet of sweets. Finally, we see her strike him with a giant hammer and steal the snack. Kim's Sharable Hearts – try to share.

David Copperfield's private collection

Bruce Lee's private collection

Federico Fellini's private collection

Frankenstein's private collection

Agency:	BBDO, Düsseldorf
Creative Director:	Marco Pupella
Copywriters:	Verena Koschel
	Hans-Holger Pollack
Art Directors:	Klaus Meurisse
	Katja Luckas
Photographer:	Jost Hiller
Client:	M&M's Private Collections

30   **Confectionery & Snacks**

Agency:	FHV BBDO, Amstelveen
Creative Directors:	Chris Bailey
	Joeri Jansen
Copywriters:	Marieke Schellart
	Michel van Duyvenbode
Art Directors:	Marieke Schellart
	Michel van Duyvenbode
Photographer:	Johannes Schwartz
Client:	Snickers Chocolate Bar

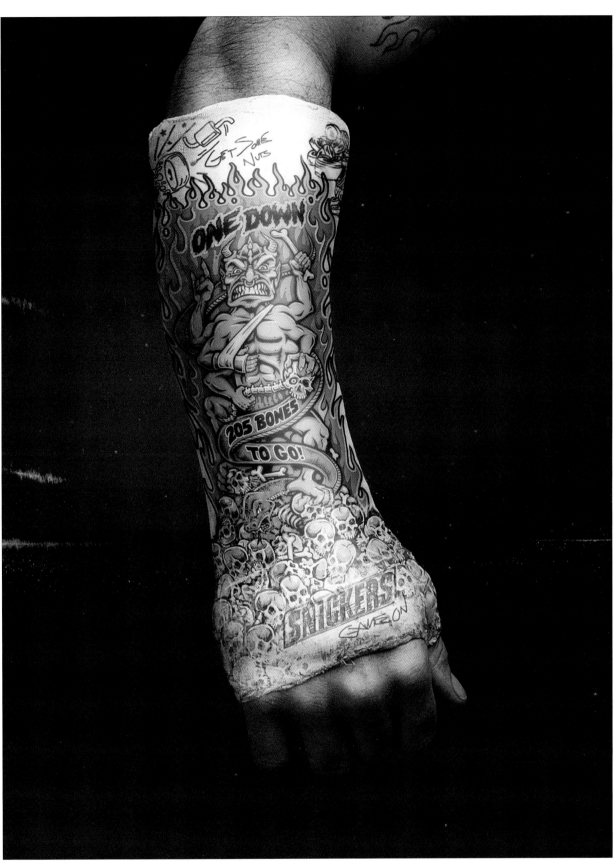

Agency:	Abbott Mead Vickers
	BBDO, London
Creative Directors:	Paul Belford
	Nigel Roberts
	Peter Souter
Copywriter:	Ben Kay
Art Director:	Cam Blackley
Photographer:	Brock Elbank
Illustrators:	Jimbo Phillips
	Vince Ray
Client:	Snickers Chocolate Bar

32   **Confectionery & Snacks**

Agency:	Duval Guillaume, Brussels	Agency:	Well Advertising PR Agency, Budapest
Creative Director:	Jens Mortier	Creative Director:	Peter Harsagyi
Copywriter:	Olivier Roland	Copywriter:	Andrea Kantor
Art Director:	Sabine Botta	Art Director:	Marton Karsai
Photographer:	Christophe Gilbert	Photographer:	Viktor Galos
Client:	Jacques Chocolate	Client:	Chio Tortilla & Fritties Dips Postcards

"Cowards."

Agency:	Publicis, Frankfurt
Creative Director:	Ljubomir Stoimenoff
Copywriter:	Ronja Ketterer
Art Director:	Katja Rowold
Photographer:	Martin Url
Client:	Maggi Texicana Salsa

Agency:	Lowe & Partners, London
Copywriter:	Tony Barry
Art Director:	Damon Collins
Production:	MJZ (Morton Jankel Zander)
Director:	Kuntz & Maguire
Producers:	Kate Collier
	Debbie Turner
	Russell Benson
Client:	Rowntrees Fruit Pastilles, "Exam"

"Dad, I'm having real trouble with my revision," complains a sensitive-looking student, surrounded by text books in his bedroom. "Nobody said becoming a doctor was going to be easy," says his father. By way of encouragement, the man proffers a packet of sweets. "Have one of these – they're fruity, they're chewy, and they'll guarantee you'll pass those exams." The son takes one happily. Cut to a few years later, and the son is a loser working in a fish and chip shop. Rowntrees Fruit Pastilles – they're fruity and chewy. What more do you want?

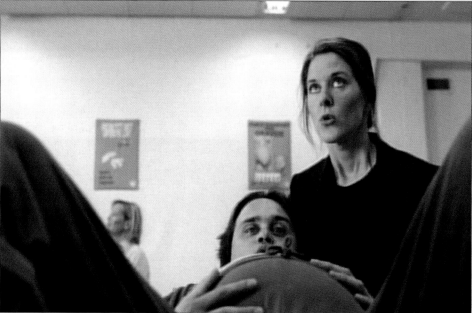
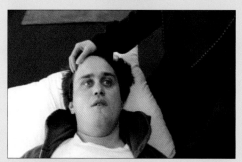

Dream on...

Dream
Ice cream

34 **Dairy Products**

Agency:	New Deal DDB, Oslo
Copywriter:	Eirik Hovland
Art Director:	Morten Varhaug
Production:	4¹/2
	Big Deal
Director:	Bent Hamer
Producers:	Vigdis Roset
	Per-Henry Knudsen
Client:	Dream Ice Cream,
	"Pregnant"

Here s a bizarre scene: a group of pregnant men practising breathing exercises at an antenatal class, coached by their patient wives. As they take a tea break, the men look terribly uncomfortable waddling around with their protuberant bellies. Meanwhile, their wives make mobile phone calls or work on portable computers. We cut to the reality of a pregnant woman, eating Dream ice cream in her kitchen while her husband taps away on his computer at the breakfast bar. She was having a nice dream.

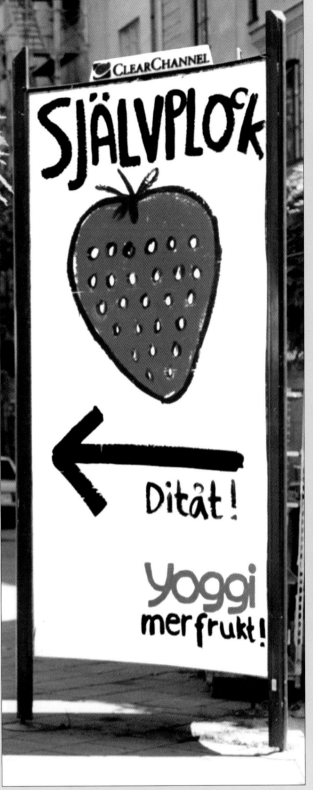

 Dairy Products 35

Agency:	Lowe Brindfors, Stockholm
Creative Director:	Johan Nilsson
Copywriter:	Monica Hultén
Art Directors:	Mitte Blomqvist Joakim Blondell
Illustrators:	Mitte Blomqvist Joakim Blondell Monica Hultén
Client:	Yoggi Fruit Yoghurts

This campaign mimic's the type of handmade signs that farmers often put up along the roadside – "Pick your own" signs with some sort of fruit painted on them. The posters were placed close to specific grocery stores, some with arrows pointing the way.

Pick your own at Blekingegatan 1.

Pick your own – 50m.

Pick your own – this way!

Pick your own (in Fältan Grocery Store).

Turn around! Pick your own. 50M Yoggi - more fruit.

Agency:	McCann, Malmö	
Creative Director:	Magnus Ohlsson	
Copywriter:	Klas Tjebbes	
Art Director:	Albin Wendel	
Production:	Acne Film, Stockholm	
Client:	Lätta Light Margarine, "Wasp"	

Tranquilly watering his flowers, a gardener is shocked when a young man dashes across his lawn, leaping the paddling pool. The camera follows the runner as he rampages across a suburban housing estate – charging through houses, jumping gates, fences, a snarling dog and even a toddler. Finally he rushes into a supermarket car park, where he vaults a line of shopping trolleys. We see that he is being pursued by a wasp – which falls to the ground, exhausted. Lätta Light Margarine: you can do a bit more, if you weigh a bit less.

Agency:	McCann, Malmö
Creative Director:	Magnus Ingestedt
Copywriter:	Klas Tjebbes
Art Director:	Albin Wendel
Production:	Traktor, Santa Monica, CA
Client:	GB Ice Cream, "Roadkill"

Two macho lorry drivers get together for an ice cream. "How are things, Åke?" asks the toughest of the pair. Åke looks shell-shocked. He replies despondently: "That squirrel in Düsseldorf – it came out of nowhere." His friend pats his shoulder consolingly. "I know. Munich, '92." He gulps back tears: "A hedgehog." Åke gives a melancholy smile, grateful for this confession. "It feels so good talking to you, Micke." Like them, GB Ice Cream is hard on the outside, but soft inside.

Agency:	Advico Young & Rubicam, Zürich
Creative Director:	Hansjoerg Zuercher
Copywriter:	Johannes Raggio
Art Director:	Willem Baumann
Photographer:	Julien Vonier
Client:	Swiss Milk Producers

38   **Dairy Products**

Agency:	New Deal DDB, Oslo	A macho-looking guy remembers to lower the toilet seat after he has used it. He even pauses to straighten out the tube of toothpaste and stand it up neatly. Cut to the reality of a sensitive gay man, eating Dream ice cream in his bathrobe, while the big hairy bloke – his boyfriend – watches football. Well, it was a nice dream.
Copywriter:	Eirik Hovland	
Art Director:	Morten Varhaug	
Production:	4½	
	Big Deal	
Director:	Bent Hamer	
Producers:	Vigdis Roset	
	Per-Henry Knudsen	
Client:	Dream Ice Cream, "Toilet Seat"	

Agency:	Leo Burnett, Stockholm	Extraordinary scenes in a domestic kitchen, as a woman practises free climbing by using shelves, cupboards, the fridge, the door lintel and finally the microwave to move around the room without touching the floor. Her little girl seems oblivious to the "spider woman" act – presumably she is used to her mother's hobby. The microwave pings, announcing that dinner is ready. When Kelda's convenient soups and sauces are on the job, you have to think of other ways to use the kitchen.
Creative Director:	Lars Hansson	
Copywriter:	Ulf Eriksson	
Art Directors:	Mattias Frodlund	
	Axel Isberg	
Production:	Acne	
Directors:	Henrik Sunderen	
	Max Vitali	
Client:	Kelda Ready Made Soups & Sauces, "Climber"	

BURSTING WITH **BIG** FRUIT

BURSTING WITH **BIG** FRUIT

BURSTING WITH **BIG** FRUIT

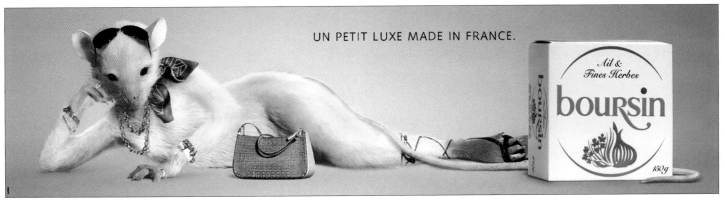

UN PETIT LUXE MADE IN FRANCE.

Agency:	McCann-Erickson, London	Agency:	Lowe, Brussels
Creative Director:	Luke White	**Creative Director:**	Georges Lafleur
Copywriter:	Rick Chant	**Copywriter:**	Véronique Sels
Art Director:	Barney Hobson	**Art Director:**	Herlinde Cornelis
Photographer:	Mike Parsons	**Photographer:**	Frank Uyttenhoven
Client:	Yoplait Yoghurt	**Client:**	Boursin Cheese

40   **Dairy Products**

Agency:	Hasan & Partners, Helsinki	A man and a woman are eating lunch in a
Creative Director:	Timo Everi	posh restaurant. To the visible exasperation
Copywriter:	Eka Ruola	of his companion, the man makes all the
Art Director:	Juha Larsson	classic faux pas: talking on his mobile
Production:	Hansel Productions	phone, reading the newspaper between
Director :	Colin Nutley	courses, noisily slurping his food, and flirting
Producers :	Anna Wallmark	outrageously with the waitress. Losing her
	Mary Lee Sjönell	temper, the woman – obviously his wife –
Client:	Arla Light Cheese	tugs violently at her wedding ring, about

to throw it in his face. But it is stuck. Has
she put on a bit of weight? Arla Adam
Light Cheese – eat light.

Agency:	McCann-Erickson, Tel Aviv	At a football match, a teenager is about to
Creative Director:	Alon Seifert	tuck into his Yop yoghurt. His attention is
Copywriter:	Ida Markovitch	distracted by a beautiful girl, and as he stares
Art Director:	Zohar Neman	at her his neighbour jogs his arm, splashing
Production:	Ulpanot	his nose with a fleck of yoghurt. The kid
Director:	Shahar Segal	wipes it off with an index finger, which he
Producers:	Avner Peled	licks. By chance the stadium's cameras
	Shira Ben Dov	capture the action, but from afar it looks like
Client:	Yop Yoghurt,	he is picking his nose and eating the result.
	"Don't Eat That"	Watching the big screen replay, the other

spectators are disgusted. The kid is confused
– Yop Yoghurt is delicious, after all.

Milk makes bones strong.

Milk helps you grow. It also makes you strong – and keeps it that way. The calcium it contains builds and maintains bones in young and old alike. So if you want to be as strong as Lovely your entire life, take 3 portions of milk or dairy products every day: for example 1 glass of milk, 1 cup of yogurt and 1 piece of cheese. For more nutritional information, go to www.swissmilk.ch.

Just good milk.

Agency:	Advico Young & Rubicam, Zürich	**Agency:**	Kolle Rebbe, Hamburg
Creative Director:	Hansjoerg Zuercher	**Creative Directors:**	Andreas Geyer
Copywriter:	Johannes Raggio		Ulrich Zünkeler
Art Director:	Willem Baumann	**Copywriter:**	Peter Liptak
Photographer:	Julien Vonier	**Art Directors:**	Peter Liptak
Client:	Swiss Milk Producers		Franziska Raether
		Photographer:	Daniel Schröder
		Client:	Weihenstephan Alpen Milk

A SHARPER BITE

Agency:	DDFH&B/JWT, Dublin	A young woman says goodbye to her parents,
Creative Director:	Tom Butler	about to go on holiday with her boyfriend for
Copywriter:	Tim Das	the first time. The father says sternly to the
Art Director:	Brendan O'Reilly	boyfriend: "Do you think you can manage to
Production:	Speers Film	return this lady in the same condition you
Director:	Tom Merilion	found her?" The cheeky young man replies:
Producers:	Johnny Speers	"Mr Johnson, my intentions are just as
	Dave Brady	honourable as yours were the first time you
Client:	Smirnoff Black Ice,	took your wife away on holiday." The father's
	"Parent Trap"	face darkens at the implication, but his wife
		merely says: "Isn't that sweet?" Our hero
		smirks at the camera. Smirnoff Black Ice has a
		sharper bite.

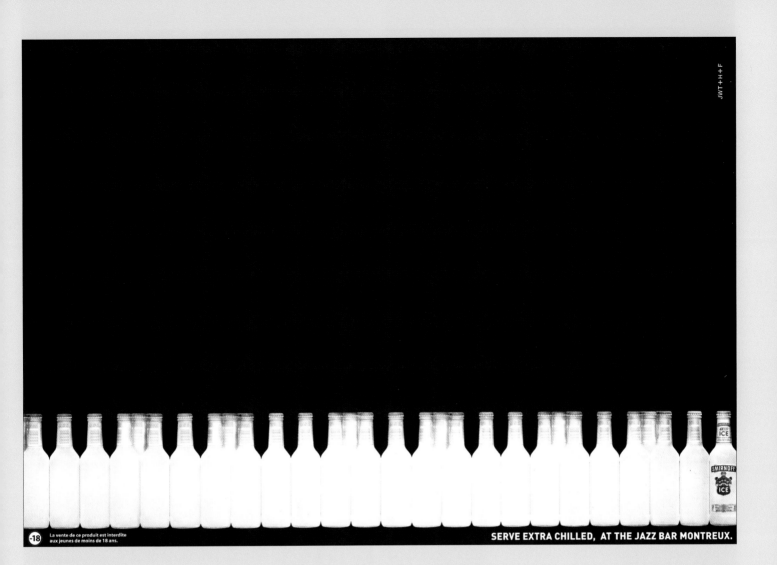

SERVE EXTRA CHILLED, AT THE JAZZ BAR MONTREUX.

La vente de ce produit est interdite aux jeunes de moins de 18 ans.

 Alcoholic Drinks A 43

Agency:	JWT+H+F, Zürich
Creative Director:	Remy Fabrikant
Copywriter:	Henning Von Vogelsang
Art Director:	Nicolas Vontobel
Photographers:	Stefan Minder
	Felix Schregenberger
Client:	Smirnoff Ice

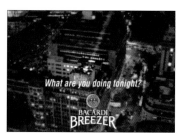

Agency: McCann-Erickson, Amstelveen
Creative Director: Rob van Vijfeijken
Copywriters: Menno Schipper
Martyn Smith
Art Directors: Nils Taildeman
Mark Hurst
Production: Radical Media, London
Director: Greg Nicholas
Producers: Dominic Delaney
Luke Beauchamp
Marcel Ossendrijver
Client: Bacardi Breezer, "Rooftop"

Where are all the tennis balls coming from? They land on a fruit stall, in a swimming pool, and bounce onto a café terrace. One hits a man at a cash dispenser. It's raining tennis balls. As people pick them up, they notice a message written on them. The camera pans to the roof of an apartment block, where fun-loving types are writing invitations to a party on the balls and thwacking them into the city using tennis rackets. The DJ is setting up and the drinks are already on ice. Bacardi Breezer – what are you doing tonight?

Agency: Publicis Conseil, Paris
Creative Directors: Antoine Barthuel
Daniel Fohr
Denis Rognon
Copywriter: Laure Ferry Sauvaire
Art Directors: Catherine Thery
Emeric Chapuis
Photographer: Marc Gouby
Client: Bacardi Rum

Alcoholic Drinks A   **45**

Agency:	BDDP & Fils, Paris
Creative Director:	Olivier Altmann
Copywriter:	Olivier Couradjut
Art Director:	Remy Tricot
Photographer:	Vincent Dixon
Client:	Clan Campbell Whisky

46 Alcoholic Drinks B

Agency:	TBWA\London
Creative Directors:	Trevor Beattie
Copywriters &	Paul Silburn
Art Directors:	Chris Kelly
	Rob Webster
	Chris Bovill
	John Allison
Production:	Spectre
Director:	Daniel Kleinman
Producers:	Johnnie Frankel
	Diane Croll
Client:	John Smith's Bitter,
	"Mum", "Diving" & "Babies"

This campaign introduces a chubby and refreshingly direct anti-hero. In the first execution, he tells his mother that she will have to go into an old people's home. "But I'm only 55!" she protests. "Why should I go into a home?" He replies: "Because I want to put a snooker table in your bedroom – and the kids are afraid of your moustache."

In version two, we're at a diving competition, where competitors perform backward somersaults and other feats of athleticism. But our beer-drinking pal merely grabs his knees and drops into the water like a bomb, drenching the judges in the process for maximum points.

The third ad shows our friend at a curry house – his natural environment – with his wife and friends. He is telling them about his daughter, Britney. "The other day, she asked me where babies come from." Fearing the worst, his wife inquires: "And what did you tell her?" With the aid of a sausage, he relates: "I told her that when her daddy loves her mummy very much, he inserts his erect penis into her vagina. He ejaculates sperm, which travels through the womb, fertilises the egg, and develops into a baby over nine months." John Smith's Bitter – no nonsense.

GUINNESS

Think positive!

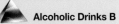 Alcoholic Drinks B   **47**

Agency:	Graffiti BBDO, Bucharest
Creative Director:	Adrian Preda
Copywriter:	Cosmin Ezaru
Art Director:	Cosmin Ezaru
Client:	Guinness Beer

48   **Alcoholic Drinks B**

Agency:	Leo Burnett, Prague
Creative Director:	Basil Mina
Copywriter:	Jiri Pleskot
Production:	Stillking Films
Director:	Anthea Benton
Producer:	Premysl Grepl
Client:	Pilsner Urquell Beer, "Jungmann"

The Czech language has been driven underground by the Austro-Hungarian Empire. In 1845, freedom fighter Josef Jungmann and his followers are on the streets, handing out pamphlets and encouraging a German-speaking nation to rediscover Czech. Discouraged, they regroup over Pilsner Urquell beers in a nearby bar. Suddenly Jungmann stands and gives an impassioned speech about the beauty of the beer in his mother tongue. Inspired, the other customers praise him in Czech. When the next round appears, Jungmann automatically replies: "Danke." There is a disapproving silence.

Agency:	Mother, London
Copywriter:	Joe De Souza
Art Director:	Sam Walker
Production:	MJZ (Morton Jankel Zander)
Directors:	Tom Kuntz
	Mike Maguire
Producers:	Kate Collier
	Debbie Turner
	Charlie Gatsky
Client:	Hoegaarden Beer, "The Town"

"Welcome to Hoegaarden, Belgium," says a roadside sign. In a series of tableaux, we see that Hoegaarden must be one of the most boring towns on earth. The solitary policeman has nothing to do, the hospital is empty, the undertaker practises on a dummy, the local priest addresses a congregation of thinly disguised tennis rackets and balloons – even the local prostitute is bored. A caption says: "Hoegaarden – home of the famous beer. And not much else." The final frame shows a hitchhiker, leaving the town, with a sign reading: "Anywhere".

My precious

Bar Code

Agency: Grey Worldwide, Dubai
Creative Director: Joseph Maalouf
Copywriter: Tertia Du Toit
Art Director: Xerex Faustino
Illustrator: Xerex Faustino
Client: Heineken Beer

Advertising alcohol in the Middle East is quite a challenge. Because of cultural sensitivies, showing brand names and pack shots in press ads is not permitted. These ads are part of an ongoing print campaign that uses the Heineken crown cap as a mnemonic device to get around these constraints.

Agency: Young Advertising, Dublin
Copywriter: John Cullen
Art Director: Gerard Roe
Photographer: Dave Campbell
Client: Bulmers Cider

This large outdoor concept was strategically positioned on an overhead railway hoarding across two main Dublin city arteries, one side leads to Dublin's northside, the other to the southside. It highlights the ongoing good-humoured rivalry and banter that has existed between 'Northsiders' and 'Southsiders' for years.

Nastro Azzurro - The Godfather of Italian beer has now arrived in Sweden.
It's an offer you can't refuse.

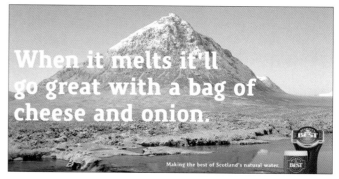

Agency:	John Doe Worldwide, Stockholm	Agency:	Arc, London
Copywriter:	Christoffer Lundström	Creative Directors:	Graham Mills
			Jack Nolan
Art Director:	Fredrik Blomberg	Copywriter:	Martin Duckworth
Photographer:	Juan Luis Sanchez	Art Director:	David Bradbury
Client:	Nastro Azzurro Beer	Photographers:	Colin Prior
			Paul Wakefield
		Client:	Belhaven Best Beer

Agency: CLM BBDO, Paris
Creative Director: Anne de Maupeou
Copywriter: Benoît Sahores
Art Director: Cédric Haroutiounian
Photographer: Marc Gouby
Client: Guinness Beer

OUT.

STELLA ARTOIS
TENNIS CUP

ATP tennis tournament, Budaörsi Teniszcentrum, Terrapark
14-19. July 2003

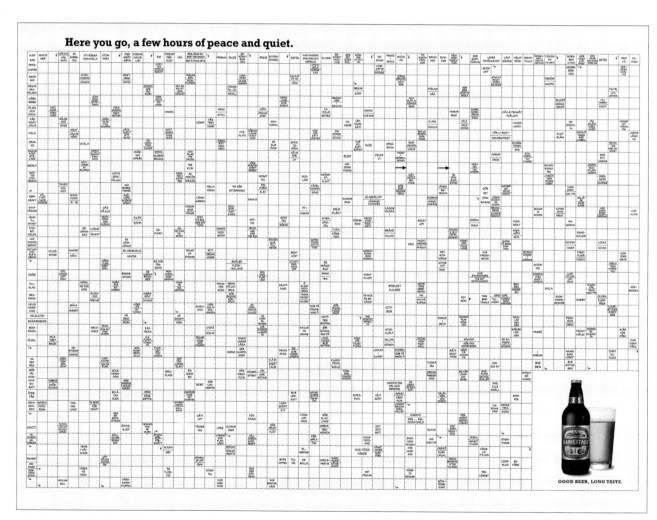

Here you go, a few hours of peace and quiet.

GOOD BEER, LONG TASTE.

Agency:	Lowe GGK, Budapest	Agency:	Paradiset DDB, Stockholm
Creative Director:	Attila Bujtàs	Copywriter:	Anders Lidzell
Copywriters:	Klaudia Rosenkranz	Art Director:	Kjell Doktorow
	Andrea Toth	Illustrator:	Patrik Andersson
Art Director:	Jozsef Kohan	Client:	Mariestads Beer
Photographer:	Gabor Mate		
Client:	Stella Artois		
	ATP Sponsorship		

SHOULD HAVE STAYED WITH YOUR MATES.

MADE FOR MATES.

Agency:	Aimaq Rapp Stolle, Berlin		Agency:	LDV/Red Cell, Antwerp
Creative Director:	André Aimaq		Creative Director:	Werner Van Reck
Art Director:	Ramona Stöcker		Copywriter:	Paul Van Oevelen
Client:	Heineken		Art Director:	Paul Popelier
			Photographer:	Herman Poppelaars
			Client:	Maes Beer

54   **Non-Alcoholic Drinks**

Agency:	Clemmow Hornby Inge, London	
Creative Director:	Charles Inge	
Copywriter:	Laurie Smith	
Art Director:	Matt Pam	
Production:	Partizan	
Director:	James Pilkington	
Producers:	David Stewart	
	Ben Clark	
Client:	Tango Soft Drink, "Seal"	

We appear to be watching a wildlife documentary, as the narrator describes killer whales toying with a seal. "Nature is revealed in all its savage glory, as the seal tonking begins." The seal is tossed from tail to tail, and lands back on the beach with a splat! Hang on – that's not a seal at all, but a man who has zipped himself into a seal costume with a pile of fresh oranges. Now he's covered in juice. Some people will do anything to experience the hit of whole oranges! But it's much easier to drink Tango.

They say coffee is a stimulant. And how?

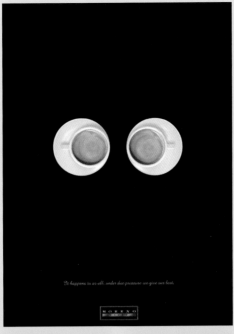

It happens to us all, under due pressure we give our best.

There are only two pleasures that keep you awake all night.

The best alarm-clock in the world has never been a clock.

Bitterly. Is there any better way to start the day?

 Non-Alcoholic Drinks 55

Agency:	J. Walter Thompson, Barcelona
Creative Director:	Àlex Martínez
Copywriters:	Àlex Martínez
	Jaime Chávarri
Art Director:	Carles Puig
Photographer:	Ramón Serrano
Client:	Moreno Coffee

They say coffee is a stimulant. And how?

It happens to us all, under due pressure we give our best.

There are only two pleasures that keep you awake all night.

The best alarm-clock in the world has never been a clock.

Bitterly. Is there any better way to start the day?

Non-Alcoholic Drinks

Agency:	CLM BBDO, Paris
Creative Directors:	Anne de Maupeou
	Vincent Behaeghel
Copywriters:	Anne de Maupeou
	Vincent Behaeghel
Art Director:	Vincent Behaeghel
Production:	Radical Media, London
Director:	Tarsem
Producers:	Tommy Turtle
	Pierre Marcus
	France Monnet
Client:	Pepsi,
	"Elephant Tower"

An Indian boy has a hypnotic power over elephants – although it may have something to do with his can of Pepsi, which the pachyderms will follow anywhere. Using his trusty can, the young man creates a legendary circus act: the elephant tower. But his career is ruined when a kid in the audience opens a can of Pepsi, and the elephants run amok. Sitting on a rock above the Ganges, our hero reflects on his fate, opening a consoling can of Pepsi. The hissing sound delights a watching hippo, which performs a back flip. "I think I'm back!" exclaims the deluded animal trainer.

Agency:	CLM BBDO, Paris
Creative Directors:	Vincent Behaeghel
	Bernard Naville
Copywriters:	Bernard Naville
	Justin Andrews
Art Director:	Vincent Behaeghel
Production:	Radical Media, London
Director:	Tarsem
Producers:	Tommy Turtle
	Pierre Marcus
Client:	Pepsi, "OK Corral"
	& "Wanted"

Five strangers ride into a dusty Western town. They are none other than David Beckham and his (now former) Manchester United team mates. Striding into a saloon, they are eyed moodily by the locals – played by the Real Madrid team. When Real's goalkeeper takes an arrogant gulp of Beckham's Pepsi, he is challenged to a penalty shootout. In true Western style, Beckham's trusty horse comes to his aid. In a short sequel, Rivaldo steals a crate of Pepsi from the saloon, but is knocked off his horse by an impossibly long drop-shot from Roberto Carlos.

Agency:	CLM BBDO, Paris
Creative Director:	Anne de Maupeou
Copywriter:	Leo Berne
Art Director:	David Bertram
Production:	Radical Media, London
Director:	Tarsem
Producers:	Tommy Turtle
	Pierre Marcus
	France Monnet
Client:	Pepsi X,
	"Longer Nights"

Thousands of ravers at an all night party are disappointed by the sight of the rising sun. After swigging from bottles of Pepsi X energy cola, they race en masse over the horizon, arriving at another time zone where it is still night. But there are only a few moments of ecstasy before the inevitable occurs, and they are forced to move again.

58   **Non-Alcoholic Drinks**

Agency:	Clemmow Hornby Inge, London	
Creative Director:	Charles Inge	
Copywriter:	Brian Turner	
Art Director:	Micky Tudor	
Production:	Partizan	
Director:	Traktor	
Producers:	Anthony Falco	
	Phillippa Smith	
Client:	Tango Soft Drink, "Postman"	

"Is it just me, or are things getting a little bit tense?" The ever-earnest sports commentator describes the scene as a man lies in his basement, drips falling onto his face from the hallway above – which is flooded with apple juice. Outside, the postman arrives, dropping a stamped and addressed apple through the letter box. It falls into a blender. The tiny extra volume of apple juice forces the hallway floor to give way, drenching the man below in juice. For an easier way to enjoy whole apple juice, try Tango.

Agency:	Clemmow Hornby Inge, London
Creative Director:	Charles Inge
Copywriter:	Brian Turner
Art Director:	Micky Tudor
Production:	Rogue
Director:	Nick Jones
Producers:	Libby Davies
	Ben Clark
Client:	Tango Strange Soda, "Pronunciation"

A stern-looking official arrives outside Tango House to announce the launch of a new soft drink to the expectant press corps. "We at Tango are very proud to be bringing you Tango Strange Soda," he says, seriously. "And to make things more interesting, we'll be pronouncing it like this: Tango Strraaange SoDahh!" His demonstration is accompanied by suitably odd facial expressions and hand movements. "Thank you." The journalists look baffled – and feel ridiculous as they try to copy his pronunciation. The new drink really is strange!

YOU KNOW WHEN YOU'VE NOT BEEN TANGO'd
WWW.TANGO.TV

YOU KNOW WHEN YOU'VE BEEN TANGO'd
WWW.TANGO.TV

BRACE YOURSELF FOR NEW FRUIT FLING. Tango
WWW.TANGO.TV

Agency: Clemmow Hornby Inge,
                   London
Creative Director: Charles Inge
Copywriter: Brian Turner
Art Director: Micky Tudor
Production: Partizan
Director: Traktor
Producers: Anthony Falco
                   Phillippa Smith
Client: Tango Soft Drink,
                   "Barrel Miss" & "Barrel"

This ad features another unlikely sporting event from the Tango team. Using compressed air and an office chair on wheels, a man transforms himself into a human rocket – and hurtles headlong into a barrel of oranges. A first attempt to hit the oranges fails dismally – but the commentator is delighted in a companion spot when a second try leaves the man covered in orange juice. Surely drinking Tango would be a better way to experience the hit of whole oranges?

Agency: Clemmow Hornby Inge,
                   London
Creative Director: Charles Inge
Copywriter: Alex Ball
Art Director: Christer Andersson
Photographer: Andy Green
Client: Tango Fruit Fling
                   Soft Drink

 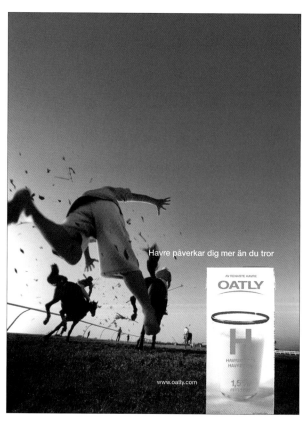

Agency:	Ekros:Block, Helsingborg	A tennis player taking a break is troubled by a pesky fly. As the insect buzzes around her head, she snorts and swipes at it with her long pony tail – just like a horse. In fact, her pony tail seems to have a life of its own. Could she have been drinking Oatly, the healthy oat beverage?
Copywriter:	David Andersson	
Art Director:	Per Ekros	
Production:	Tre Vänner, Stockholm	
Director:	Stefan Nipstad	
Producer:	Martin Persson	
Client:	Oatly Oat Drink, "Pony Tail"	

Agency:	Ekros:Block, Helsingborg	Oats will make a difference in you.
Creative Director:	Per Ekros	
Copywriters:	David Andersson Christian Hultberg	
Art Director:	Melker Henningsson	
Photographer:	Andreas Kindler	
Client:	Oatly Oat Drink	

Agency:	BETC Euro RSCG, Paris		**Agency:**	BETC Euro RSCG, Paris
Creative Director:	Rémi Babinet		**Creative Director:**	Rémi Babinet
Copywriter:	Luc Rouzier		**Copywriter:**	Sylvier Minier
Art Director:	Eric Astorgue		**Art Directors:**	Florence Bellisson
Production:	Bandits			Yuki Kani
Director:	Pedro Romahanyi		**Photographer:**	John Akerhust
Producers:	Emmanuel Guiraud		**Client:**	Evian Mineral Water
	Fabrice Brovelli			
Client:	Evian Mineral Water, "Voices"			

Let's observe the effects of Evian on your body. A series of unlikely characters sing Queen's "We Will Rock You" in distinctly babyish voices. A middle-aged business-man, rowers, a surfer, a secretary, an elderly lady and a pregnant woman all sing the hit song with the innocent voices of children. That's because drinking pure mineral water keeps your body young. Evian – live young.

It's a relief.

It's a relief.

62 **Non-Alcoholic Drinks**

Agency:	Young & Rubicam, Paris	Agency:	Skandaali/Leo Burnett, Helsinki
Creative Director:	Hervé Riffault	Creative Directors:	Paula Rosti
Copywriter:	Fabien Teichner		Mirva Viitanen
Art Director:	Nicolas Harlamoff	Copywriter:	Markku Haapalehto
Photographer:	Francis Azemaro	Art Director:	Erkki Mikola
Client:	Orangina Light	Illustrators:	Andrew Farley
			Warren Madill
			Brian James
		Client:	Kevyt Olo Mineral Water

Agency:	Young & Rubicam, Paris
Creative Director:	Hervé Riffault
Copywriter:	Ugo Fossa
Art Director:	Gilles Menet
Production:	Quad
Director:	Remy Belvaux
Producer:	Isabelle Escat
Client:	Orangina Light, "Orangina Light Party"

In this surreal spot, people dressed as oranges, bubbles and sugar cubes queue up for an Orangina Light party at a dome-shaped orange nightclub. But the mean-looking bouncers won't let the sugar cubes into the club. "Sorry, no sugar tonight – it's a 'light' party." Meanwhile, those dressed in orange stride confidently into the club. One rebellious sugar cube attempts to barge his way inside with an attractive orange, but is ejectcd. Orangina – now available without sugar.

Agency:	Publicis, Frankfurt
Creative Directors:	Michael Boebel
	Harald Schmitt
	Tom Tilliger
Copywriter:	Peter Kaim
Art Director:	Nico Juenger
Photographer:	Johannes G. Krzeslack
Client:	Coca-Cola Light, 20th Anniversary

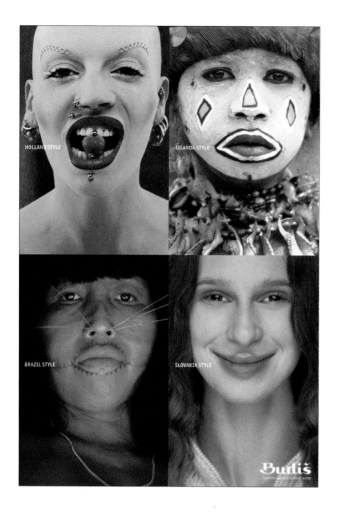

Non-Alcoholic Drinks

Agency:	Wiktor Leo Burnett, Bratislava		**Agency:**	Grey, Copenhagen
Creative Director:	Raffo Tatarko		**Copywriter:**	Peter Dinesen
Copywriter:	Vlado Slivka		**Art Director:**	Rasmus Moltke
Art Director:	Raffo Tatarko		**Photographer:**	Jimmy Hansen
Photographer:	Martin Frinder		**Client:**	Ribena
Illustrator:	Vlado Korcek			
Client:	Budis Mineral Water			

Agency:	Jean & Montmarin, Paris	Agency:	Rafineri, Istanbul
Creative Director:	Gérard Jean	Creative Directors:	Ayse Bali Sarc
Copywriter:	Pierre-Marie Faussurier		Murat Çetintürk
Art Director:	Sébastien Zanini	Copywriter:	Demir Karpat Polat
Photographer:	Daniel Schweizer	Art Director:	Ali Bati
Client:	Teisseire Cactus Soft Drinks	Photographer:	Ilkay Muratoğlu
		Client:	Café Del Mondo,
			Flavoured Coffee Blends

66   **Non-Alcoholic Drinks**

Agency:	Vinizius Young & Rubicam, Barcelona	**Agency:**	King, Stockholm
Creative Director:	Javier Villanueva	**Client:**	Linne Still Flavoured Water
Copywriter:	Darío Guberman		
Art Directors:	Víctor Arriazu		
	Luis Moreno		
Photographer:	David Levin		
Client:	Hornimans Infu-Relax Herbal Tea		

New. Now in a bottle.

Agency:	TBWA\España, Barcelona	**Agency:**	Duval Guillaume, Brussels
Creative Directors:	Ramón Sala	**Creative Director:**	Jens Mortier
	Jordi Sebastià	**Copywriter:**	Jens Mortier
	Joan Teixidó	**Art Director:**	Philippe De Ceuster
Copywriters:	Ramón Sala	**Photographer:**	Koen Demuynck
	Gerard Garolera	**Client:**	Spa Reine Water
Art Directors:	Jordi Sebastià		
	David Garriga		
	Meritxell Horts		
Photographer:	Jordi Sebastià		
Client:	Font Del Regàs		
	Mineral Water		

PUNCTUAL DEPARTURES.

LOOK OUT FOR ADDITIONAL DEPARTURES.

Agency: New Deal DDB, Oslo
Copywriters: Stig Bjølbakk
               Bendik Romstad
Art Directors: Henrik Sander
               Anne Gravingen
Production: Moland Film Company
Director: Jesper Ericstam
Producer: Irene Sødal Diethricson
Client: Nor-way Bussekspress,
               "Eggs 1" & "Eggs 2"

In her quaint cottage beside a country road, an elderly lady stands at her window. When a coach passes, she starts to boil an egg. She takes up her place at the window, and when the coach returns with its load of passengers, she takes the egg off the gas and tucks into it. The Nor-way Bussekspress is so punctual you could use it as an egg timer. In the second execution, though, the woman's egg is seriously under cooked because the coach firm has introduced additional departures.

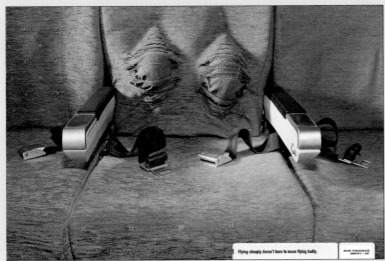

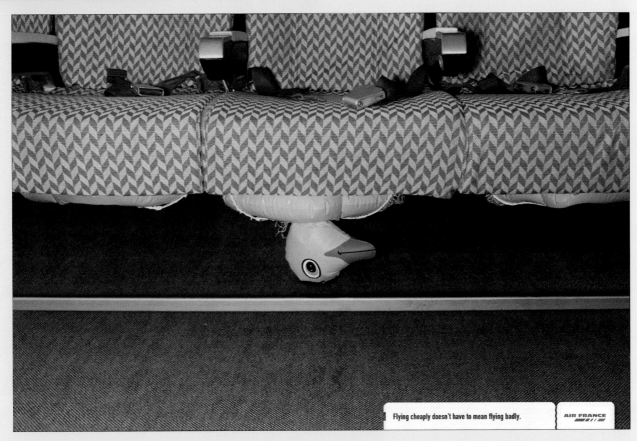

Flying cheaply doesn't have to mean flying badly.

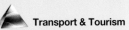

Agency:	BETC Euro RSCG, Paris
Creative Director:	Rémi Babinet
Copywriter:	Bruno Delhomme
Art Director:	Andrea Leupold
Photographer:	Lars Tunbjörk
Client:	Air France

Agency:	Hasan & Partners, Helsinki	**Agency:**	Hasan & Partners, Helsinki
Creative Director:	Timo Everi	**Copywriter:**	Antti Einiö
Copywriter:	Niko Kokonmäki	**Art Director:**	Magnus Olsson
Art Director:	Juha Larsson	**Photographer :**	Thomas Gidén
Photographer:	Markku Lähdesmäki	**Client:**	Scandic
Illustrator:	Jan Rudkiewicz		Conference Hotels
Client:	Silja Line Cruises		

RESPECT. NEVER TRAVEL WITHOUT IT.

Youth and
Student
Travel
Center

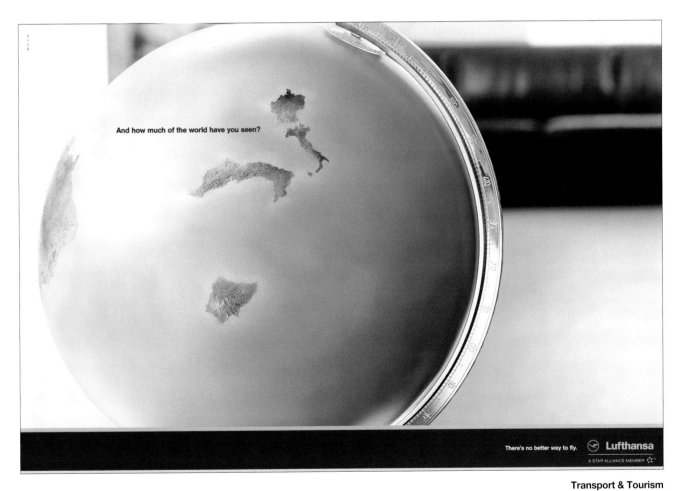

And how much of the world have you seen?

There's no better way to fly. ⊖ Lufthansa
A STAR ALLIANCE MEMBER

Agency:	Leo Burnett Italia, Milan	An African tribesman leaves his unspoiled home in Kenya to catch a plane to Milan. All the way through the long journey, he is carrying a carefully wrapped bundle. Arriving at a Milanese apartment building, he knocks on a door – which is opened by a surprised Italian woman. "Hello," says the tribesman, unrolling the bundle. "You must have dropped it on the safari." He hands her an empty plastic soft drink container. Respect – never travel without it.	**Agency:**	M.E.C.H. McCann-Erickson Communications House, Berlin
Creative Director:	Sergio Rodriguez		
Copywriters:	Emiliano Antonetti	**Executive CD:**	Torsten Rieken
	Gaia Stagnitti	**Creative Director:**	Britta Poetzsch
Art Directors:	Alessia Casini	**Copywriter:**	Britta Poetzsch
	Hilde Capra	**Art Director:**	Carla Schweyer
Production:	The Family	**Photographer:**	Stefan Boekels
Director:	Alberto Colombo	**Illustrator:**	Rosemarie Altmann
Producers:	Stefano Quaglia	**Client:**	Lufthansa
	Alessandro Pancotti		
Client:	CTS Tour Operator, "Masai"		

72 Transport & Tourism

Agency:	Lowe Brindfors, Stockholm	Two bored businessman are sitting next to one another on a plane flight. The largest of the pair grabs the last newspaper in the seat pocket. Seeing that his fellow traveller is annoyed, he offers to swap it for the thin man's book. The man considers this, and indicates the pen in the other's top pocket. The portly businessman reflects, and points at his companion's tie. By the time the plane lands, they've swapped half their clothing in an orgy of deal-making. Looking for a good deal? Save money by travelling with SAS economy tickets in business class.
Creative Director:	Johan Nilsson	
Copywriter:	Totte Stub	
Art Director:	Magnus Löwenhielm	
Production:	Blink Productions, London	
Director:	Dougal Wilson	
Producers:	Bart Yates	
	Anders Gernandt	
Client:	SAS Airline, "The Deal"	

Agency:	Beagle, Amsterdam	In this spot we meet Martha, who works at a café in Barcelona. But as she comes from Madrid, she prefers to tell us all about the Spanish capital, enthusing over its great food and glorious architecture. But she is cut off when her boss walks past, and switches to talking about the café where she works. To find out more about Barcelona, you'd be better off picking up the latest brochure from tour operator Holland International.
Creative Director:	Edward Hissink	
Copywriter:	Michiel Bles	
Production:	Artcore	
Director:	Daniël Norgueira	
Producer:	Monique van Beckhoven	
Client:	Holland International Tour Operator, "Barcelona"	

To London, faster than ever.

Agency:	TBWA\Brussels
Creative Director:	Jan Macken
Copywriter:	Vincent Abrams
Art Director:	Michael Mikiels
Photographer:	Christophe Gilbert
Client:	Eurostar

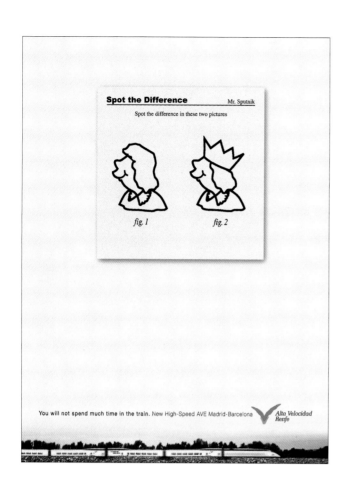

Agency:	Publicis España, Madrid	Agency:	Tandem DDB, Madrid
Creative Directors:	Tony Fernández-Mañés	Creative Directors:	Manuel Montes
	María Jesús Herrera		Alberto Astorga
	Juanma Pérez-Paredes	Copywriter:	Samuel Vazquez
Art Director:	Cristina Baños	Art Director:	Alfonso Villar
Client:	AVE, High Speed Railways	Photographer:	Alejandro Iglesia
		Client:	Halcon Viajes Travel Agency

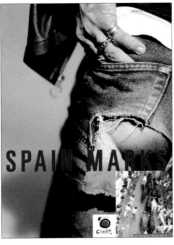

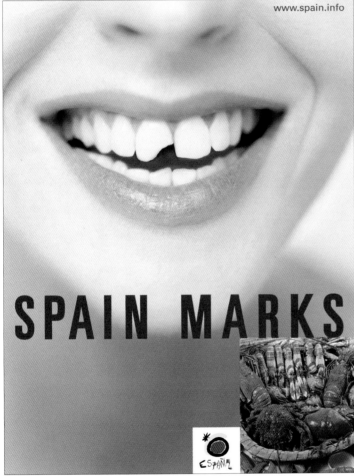

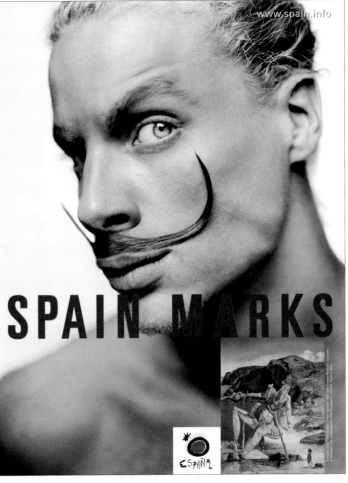

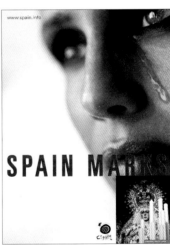

Agency:	Publicis España, Madrid
Creative Directors:	Tony Fernández-Mañés
	Luis M. Solero
	Mari Luz Sánchez
Copywriter:	Mari Luz Sánchez
Art Director:	Luis M. Solero
Photographer:	José Manuel Ferrater
Client:	Turespaña Spanish Tourism

Agency:	Spillmann/Felser/Leo Burnett, Zürich		Agency:	Advico Young & Rubicam, Zürich
Creative Director:	Martin Spillmann		Creative Director:	Hansjoerg Zuercher
Copywriter:	Peter Brönnimann		Copywriter:	Johannes Raggio
Art Director:	Dana Wirz		Art Directors:	Dana Wirz
Photographer:	Julien Vonier			Christian Bobst
Client:	Flims Laax Falera Alpine Resort		Photographer:	Nicolas Monkewitz
			Client:	Flims Laax Falera Alpine Resort

Agency:	Lowe Brindfors, Stockholm	**Agency:**
Creative Director:	Johan Nilsson	
Copywriter:	Martin Stadhammar	
Art Directors:	Carl-Johan Ekberg	
	Carl Dalin	
Client:	SAS Pleasure	

Agency: Lowe Brindfors, Stockholm
Creative Director: Johan Nilsson
Copywriter: Martin Stadhammar
Art Directors: Carl-Johan Ekberg / Carl Dalin
Client: SAS Pleasure

Agency: Lowe Brindfors, Stockholm
Creative Director: Johan Nilsson
Copywriter: Martin Stadhammar
Art Director: Carl Dalin
Client: SAS Pleasure

These "blah blah" posters resembled party-political ads for and against European Monetary Union that were all over Sweden when the referendum took place in autumn, 2003.

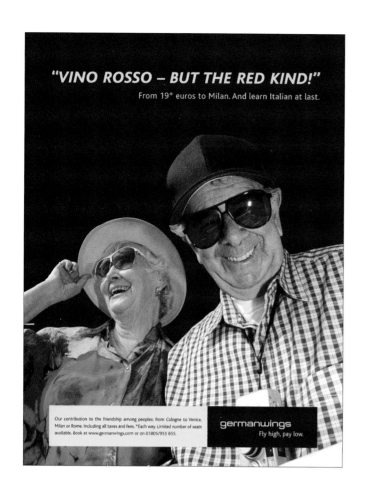

Agency:	.start, Munich	Agency:	.start, Munich
Creative Director:	Stefan Hempel	Creative Directors:	Peter Hirrlinger
Copywriters:	Doris Haider		Andreas Klemp
	Kristina Popp	Copywriter:	Doris Haider
Art Directors:	Stephanie Rauch	Art Director:	Stephanie Rauch
	Eva Schaefer	Photographer:	Hubertus Hamm
Client:	Germanwings Budget Airline	Client:	Germanwings Budget Airline

Agency: McCann-Erickson, London
Creative Director: Luke White
Copywriter: Ivor Jones
Art Director: Gary Woodward
Photographer: John Offenbach
Client: American Airlines

Agency: Publicis, Frankfurt
Creative Director: Gert Maehnicke
Copywriter: Hasso von Kietzell
Art Director: Alan Vladusic
Client: Qantas Airways, Drain Cover Installations

Agency:	Robert/Boisen & Like-Minded, Copenhagen	These are the latest in a series of commercials illustrating what happens when you give flowers to the one you love. A woman painstakingly hangs a magazine rack in the loo, and tenderly places a publication about cars into it. Meanwhile, another man is astonished to receive a beer pump for his birthday. That's the power of flowers.
Creative Director:	Michael Robert	
Copywriter:	Joachim Nielsen	
Art Director:	Michael Robert	
Production:	Moland Film Company	
Director:	Stefan Treschow	
Producer:	Christiern Topsoe	
Client:	Interflora, "Magazine Rack" & "Birthday"	

REAL BIG BURGERS.

BIGGER. BETTER. BURGER KING.

Agency: .start, Munich
Creative Directors: Thomas Pakull
                   Marco Mehrwald
Copywriters: Marcel Koop
                   Beate Bogensperger
Art Director: Sven Achatz
Photographer: Yorck Dertinger
Client: Burger King

The power of flowers

The power of flowers

Now we deliver wine too

Agency:	Robert/Boisen & Like-Minded, Copenhagen
Creative Director:	Michael Robert
Copywriter:	Joachim Nielsen
Art Director:	Michael Robert
Production:	Moland Film Company
Director:	Stefan Treschow
Producer:	Christiern Topsoe
Client:	Interflora, "Shirt", "Lunchpack" & "Road Hump"

Here we meet two more men who are about to discover the power of flowers. One of them gets out of bed early to iron a shirt, only to find that his entire wardrobe has been neatly pressed. And another discovers that his packed lunch is a cordon bleu feast. In a slight twist on the traditional theme, an Interflora van veeeery slooowly negotiates a road hump. The caption reveals: "Now we deliver wine, too."

Agency:	Wirz Werbung, Zürich	**Agency:**	Heimat, Berlin
Creative Director:	Matthias Freuler	**Creative Directors:**	Guido Heffels
Copywriter:	Thomas Kurzmeyer		Jürgen Vossen
Art Director:	Barbara Hartmann	**Copywriters:**	Steffen Pejas
Photographer:	Roth + Schmid		Tobias Löffler
Client:	Tibits Vegetarian Restaurant	**Art Director:**	Michael Milczarek
		Photographer:	Alexander Gnädinger
		Client:	Hornbach Home Improvement Stores

84 **Retail Services**

Agency:	Publicis, Zürich
Creative Director:	Jean Etienne Aebi
Copywriter:	Daniel Krieg
Art Director:	Ralf Kostgeld
Production:	Pumpkin Film
Director:	Kasper Wedendahl
Producers:	Sonja Brand
	Heinrich Reinacher
Client:	Migros Supermarkets,
	"Culture" &
	"Mental Arithmetic"

Art gallery owner Jacqueline Lüthi praises supermarket chain Migros for its decision to sponsor cultural events – encouraging people to go to the theatre, opera and classical concerts. But wouldn't it be great, she muses, if the staff publicised this in the stores? We cut to a dream sequence of staff singing operatically – "This cheese is fully ripe! I must be rid of it by tonight!" – and dancing around the aisles. Jacqueline sighs: she knows her dream will never come true. Anyway, promoting culture is always a good thing.

Mathematician Marco Vanotti appreciates the fact that products in Migros supermarkets are clearly labelled with the price. But he would like to take this a step further by making everyone add up their own bill – thus improving the nation's mental arithmetic skills. We see people in the supermarket adding up their bills, distracting one another, and getting into a terrible pickle. One boy uses the situation to cheat the cashier, buying a mound of sweets for a few pennies. Marco shrugs. Anyway, it's an advantage when you don't have to hide your prices.

Agency:	CLM BBDO, Paris
Creative Director:	Anne de Maupeou
Copywriter:	Fred Lutgé
Art Director:	Dimitri Guerassimov
Photographer:	Mathieu Deluc
Client:	3 Suisses
	Mail Order Catalogue

A Delicate Obsession

Julius Meinl
DELICATESSEN

Corn-fed chicken: €8,30/kg

Christmas lobster: €24,67/kg

86   **Retail Services**

Agency:	Demner, Merlicek & Bergmann, Vienna	**Agency:**	GV\Company, Brussels
Creative Director:	Mariusz Jan Demner	**Creative Director:**	Jan Dejonghe
Copywriter:	Monika Prelec	**Copywriters:**	Peter Slabbynck
Art Director:	Germaine Cap de Ville		Chiara De Decker
Photographer:	Joachim Haslinger	**Art Directors:**	Alex Ameye
Client:	Julius Meinl Delicatessen		Tom Apers
		Photographers:	Jean-François De Witte
			Pascal Habousha
		Client:	Delhaize Supermarkets

Thanks for the good times Roger.

Agency:	King, Stockholm	This series of entertaining commercials for ICA Supermarkets is a mini soap opera. In the latest instalments, we renew our acquaintance with ICA branch manager Stig and his colleagues Sonja, Ulf, Roger and Kasja. Key episodes feature Roger failing to invite the pretty Kasja to the cinema (he ends up going with Stig instead), Stig trying to pluck up courage to declare his love for Sonja, and a stolen food mystery. The finale shows Roger discovering that the supermarket is actually a film set, and escaping into the real world.
Production:	Tre Vänner	
Director:	Walter Söderlundh	
Client:	ICA Supermarkets	

spring is back

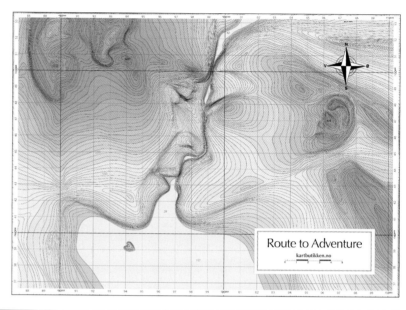

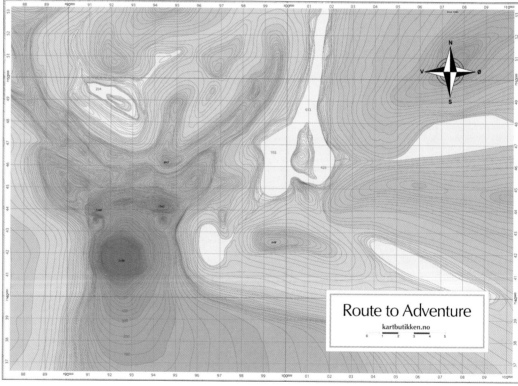

Agency:	Tandem DDB, Madrid	Agency:	Bold\TBWA, Oslo
Creative Director:	Jose Ma Roca De Vinyals	Creative Director:	Ragnar Roksvaag
Copywriters:	Sergi Zapater	Copywriter:	Peter Andersen
	Isahac Oliver	Art Director:	Torgrim Naerland
Art Directors:	Juan Ramon Alfaro	Illustrator:	Torgrim Naerland
	Xavi Sitjar	Client:	Kartbulikken
Photographer:	Javier Pastor Heredia		Online Map Shop
Client:	L'Illa Diagonal		
	Shopping Center		

Agency:	Wirz Werbung, Zürich	Agency:	Jean & Montmarin, Paris	One needed courage in those days.
Creative Director:	Matthias Freuler	Creative Director:	Gérard Jean	
Copywriter:	Christoph von Arb	Copywriter:	Christophe Trouvé-Dugeny	
Art Director:	Sandro Nicotera	Art Director:	Thierry Meunier	
Photographer:	Roger Schneider	Photographer:	Olivier Rheindorf	
Client:	Zürcher Brockenhaus, Second-Hand Store	Client:	Houra.fr. Internet Shopping	

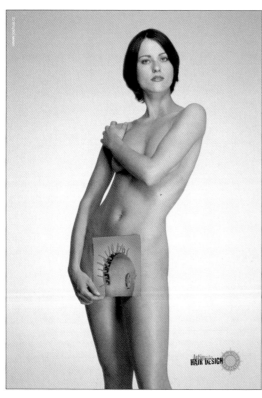

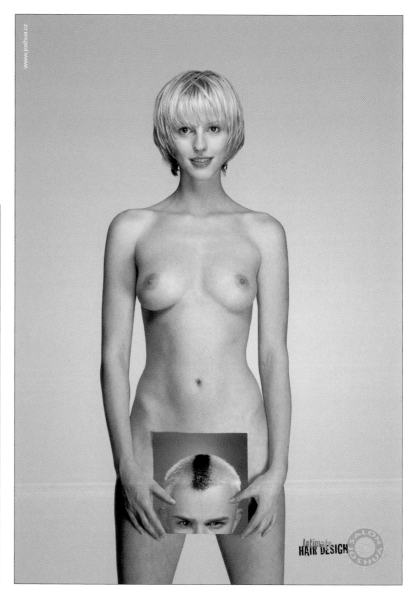

90   **Retail Services**

Agency:	McCann-Erickson, Prague	Agency:	McCann-Erickson, Prague
Creative Directors:	Philip Wilson Philip Pec	Creative Directors:	Philip Wilson Philip Pec
Copywriters:	Juraj Janis Philip Pec	Copywriters:	Juraj Janis Philip Pec
Art Directors:	Anna Mala Tereza Viznerova	Art Directors:	Anna Mala Tereza Viznerova Leos Carda
Photographer:	Vuk Latinovic	Photographer:	Vuk Latinovic
Client:	Joshua Hair Salon	Client:	Joshua Hair Salon, Intimate Hair Design

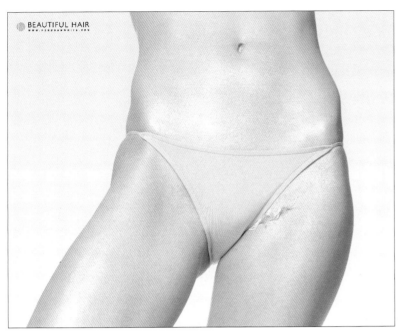

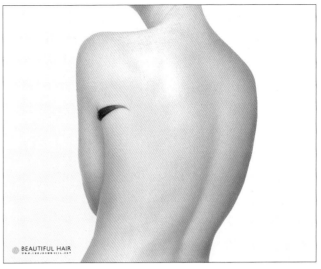

Agency:	Springer & Jacoby, London
Creative Director:	Robin Weeks
Copywriter:	Wayne Guthrie
Art Director:	Azar Kazimir
Photographer:	Leon Steele
Client:	Fordham White Hairdresser

92   **Retail Services**

Agency:	Jung von Matt/Limmat, Zürich	Agency:	Zapping, Madrid
Creative Director:	Urs Schrepfer	Creative Directors:	Uschi Henkes
Art Directors:	Martin Friedlin		Urs Frick
	Lukas Frei	Copywriter:	Virginia Mosquera
Photographer:	Roger Schneider	Art Director:	Gabriel Hueso
Client:	Settebello Restaurant	Client:	El Sibarita
			Catering Service

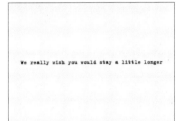

We really wish you would stay a little longer

fakta
It only takes 5 minutes

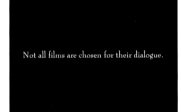

Not all films are chosen for their dialogue.

 EROTIKA
The best porn movies around.

www.sexerotika.com

Agency:	Uncle/Grey, Århus	**Agency:**	Haibun, Milan
Creative Director:	Per Pedersen	**Creative Directors:**	Guido Cornara
Copywriters:	Thomas Falkenberg		Agostino Toscana
	Ulrik Feldskov Juul	**Copywriter:**	Paola Morabito
Production:	Lassie Film,	**Art Directors:**	Fabio La Fauci
	Copenhagen		Agostino Toscana
Director:	Jan Gleie	**Production:**	Haibun
Producers:	Stig Weiss	**Director:**	Agostino Toscana
	Jan Pedersen	**Producer:**	Cesare Fracca
Client:	Fakta Supermarket,	**Client:**	Erotika Video Rental Store,
	"Boxing Kangaroo"		"Dialoguc"

A woman doing her shopping in a Fakta supermarket is astonished when a man hurtles into a pile of boxes, having been punched by somebody out of frame. Somebody…or something: a kangaroo wearing boxing gloves bounces onto the screen, and punches another customer. The boxing kangaroo is a misguided attempt by Fakta to make its customers stay longer by providing unusual entertainment. Fakta – it only takes five minutes to shop there.

The real action happens off screen in this commercial for an erotic video rental store. All we see is a technician holding up cue cards for the actors on the set of a porn movie. Obviously, what we read is meaningless without the…er…sound effects of two people having sex. The caption points out: "Not all films are chosen for their dialogue." Erotika – for the best porn movies around.

94 **Financial Services**

Agency:	DDB, Amsterdam	In a sleazy New York warehouse, an ambitious
Creative Director:	Martin Cornelissen	Mafioso named Vinnie hands over a bag of cash
Copywriter:	Sikko Gerkema	for a stolen horse – a European champion, the
Art Director:	Sanne Braam	vendor tells him. At the Belmont Park racetrack
Production:	De Schiettent	the next day, Vinnie's wonder horse is about to
Director:	Sven Super	make its debut. Vinnie's boss introduces him to
Producers:	Christel Hofstee	the Godfather, whispering in an aside: "You've
	Pascale van den Berge	made him very happy." The Mafiosi look on as
	Marloes van den Berg	the race begins. And they're off! Except Vinnie's
Client:	Centraal Beheer	horse, which prances about near the starting
	Insurance, "Horse"	gate. It's a champion all right – at dressage.
		Vinnie looks pained. Is he insured for this?

 Financial Services **95**

Agency:	Contrapunto, Madrid
Creative Director:	Antonio Montero
Copywriter:	Miki Exteberria
Art Director:	Rubèn Navio
Client:	Sanitas Family Plan
	Insurance

Ed Fagan
Collective claimant against banks

Ed Fagan
Collective claimant against banks

bank coop
The clean Swiss bank.

Manuel Noriega

Imelda Marcos

Mobutu Sese Seko

Sani Abacha

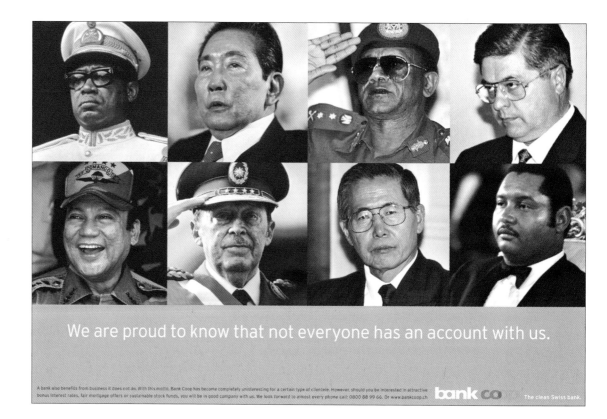
We are proud to know that not everyone has an account with us.

A bank also benefits from business it does not do. With this motto, Bank Coop has become completely uninteresting for a certain type of clientele. However, should you be interested in attractive bonus interest rates, fair mortgage offers or sustainable stock funds, you will be in good company with us. We look forward to almost every phone call: 0800 88 99 66. Or www.bankcoop.ch   bank coop   The clean Swiss bank.

96   Financial Services

Agency:	Ruf Lanz, Zürich
Creative Directors:	Danielle Lanz
	Markus Ruf
Copywriters:	Markus Ruf
	Thomas Schoeb
Art Director:	Danielle Lanz
Production:	Condor Communications
Director:	Martin A. Fueter
Producer:	David Haisch
Client:	Coop Swiss Bank,
	"Ed Fagan" &
	"Money Launderers"

The main character in this commercial is Ed Fagan, a lawyer well known in Switzerland for having successfully sued Swiss banks over their shady dealings, mainly involving Holocaust money. Fagan arrives at Zürich airport, where he is surrounded by journalists. One reporter asks him: "What do you think of Bank Coop?" Fagan hesitates, and then replies: "Never heard of them." The implication is clear: Bank Coop is the clean Swiss bank.

In a second commercial, the screen fills with clips of unsavoury political figures: Manuel Noriega, Imelda Marcos, Mobutu Sese Seko, Sani Abacha. The caption reads: "We are proud that not everybody has an account with us." Bank Coop is the clean Swiss bank.

Agency:	Ruf Lanz, Zürich
Creative Directors:	Danielle Lanz
	Markus Ruf
Copywriters:	Thomas Schoeb
	Markus Ruf
Art Director:	Danielle Lanz
Client:	Coop Swiss Bank

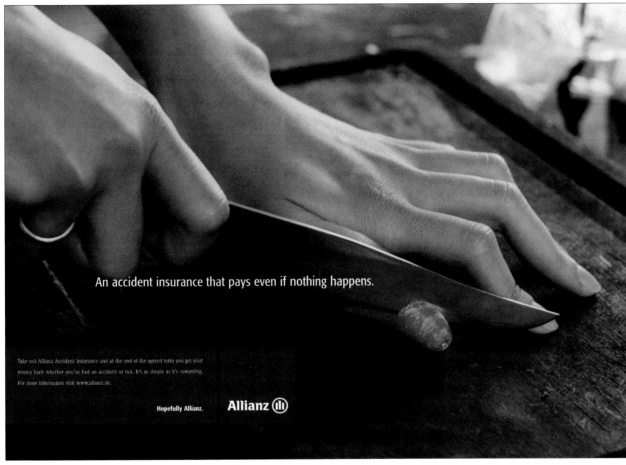

Agency:	Bates International Advertising, Barcelona
Creative Directors:	Roland Vanoni
	Arndt Dallmann
Copywriter:	Jörg Bredendieck
Art Director:	Mick Traen
Photographer:	Pedro Vikingo
Client:	Allianz Accident Insurance

98   Financial Services

Agency:	Louis XIV DDB, Paris	**Agency:**	Publicis Conseil, Paris
Creative Directors:	Bertrand Suchet	**Creative Directors:**	Antoine Barthuel
	Olivier Moine		Daniel Fohr
	Nicolas Chauvin	**Copywriter:**	Sébastien Aime
Copywriter:	Olivier Moine	**Art Director:**	Stephan Ferens
Art Director:	Nicolas Chauvin	**Production:**	Les Télécréateurs
Production:	Wanda	**Director:**	Noam Murro
Director:	Philippe Stoelzl	**Producers:**	Arno Moira
Client:	CNP Insurance, "There		Patricia Lucas
	Will Always Be Life"	**Client:**	AGF Insurance,
			"We All Do That"

Photographs take us on a trip through time. A woman emerges from a photo lab with a family snapshot. As the domestic scene comes to life, a framed picture on a shelf transports us to the 1960s. A couple hold an album cover featuring post-war school-children. Now we're at school, where a boy has a picture of fishermen in a storm. We enter the scene, and are propelled into a photo on a fisherman's locket, of his parents. Finally, an ancient camera – now an exhibit in the lab – brings us back to the present. CNP Insurance – life will always be life.

Imagine if people were like ostriches – burying their heads in the sand whenever anything went wrong. The spot provides a few illustrations, with a lorry driver trying to avoid dealing with a spilled load, a man burying his head in the boardroom table, and various other people unable to cope with ageing, births, pregnancy, accidents, arguments and stress. But with AGF Insurance, you can face life.

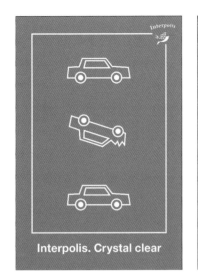

Interpolis. Crystal clear

Interpolis. Crystal clear

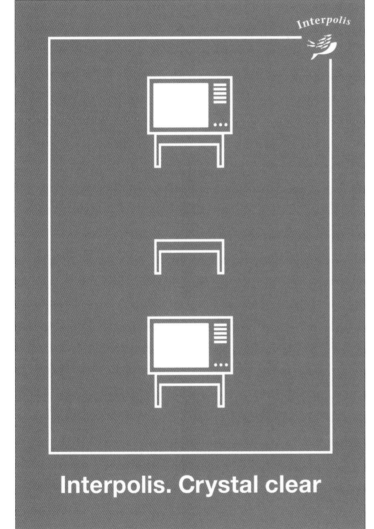

Interpolis. Crystal clear

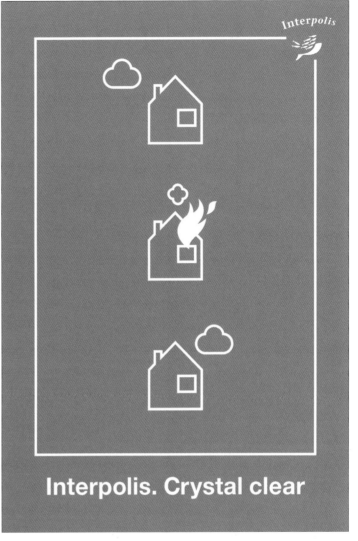

Interpolis. Crystal clear

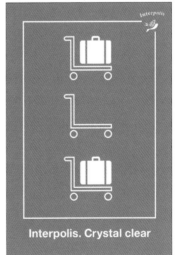

Interpolis. Crystal clear

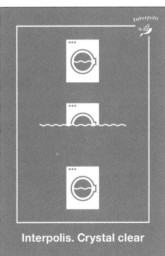

Interpolis. Crystal clear

Agency: FHV BBDO, Amstelveen
Creative Directors: Sander Bakker
David Snellenberg
Illustrator: Richard van der Laken
Client: Interpolis Insurance

Not happy with your salary?

Just wait until you retire.

Agency:	Lowe Brindfors, Stockholm		Agency:	Publicis, Zürich
Creative Director:	Johan Nilsson		Creative Directors:	Uwe Schlupp
Copywriter:	Björn Hjalmar			Jean Etienne Aebi
Art Director:	Carl Dalin		Copywriter:	Tom Zurcher
Client:	Foreningssparbanken		Art Director:	Dominik Oberwiler
	Retirement Plans		Client:	Swiss Mobiliar Insurance

Financial Services   **101**

Agency:	Futura DDB, Ljubljana
Creative Director:	Vital Verlilč
Copywriters:	Bojan Jablanovec
	Zoran Gabrijan
Production:	Propeler
Director:	Kristoffer Dios
Client:	Triglav Insurance, "Trailer"

A clumsy family arrive at an ancient city in their mobile home. In a marketplace, they attempt to park the bulky vehicle. The wife gets out to direct her husband into the narrow space with hand signals. But as she waves away a fruit vendor, the husband misinterprets her instructions and backs into a priceless statue, decapitating it. Embarrassed, his wife gets back into the passenger seat and they drive away from the scene of the crime. But there is more trouble to come…Are these people insured?

Agency:	Storåkers McCann, Stockholm
Copywriters:	Mia Cederberg
	Edwin von Werder
Art Directors:	Klaudia Carp
	Enis Püpülek
Production:	Stink, Stockholm
Director:	Jesper Hiro
Producers:	Anna Adamson
	Christer Kilde
	Fabian Mannheimer
Client:	Mastercard, "The Big Catch"

"Outback survival weekend: $500." A voiceover lists the cost of a man's holiday, while the images on the screen reflect his experiences. "Titanium fishing rod: $120." The rod dips dramatically – it looks like a big catch. "Carbon steel hunting knife: $40." The fish has been landed and lies gasping at the man's feet – but he seems unwilling to kill it. Encouraged by his friends, he tenderly picks it up and releases it back into the river. "Daring to show your feelings – priceless." There are some things money can't buy. For everything else, there's MasterCard.

Look, up there!

Hey, isn't that eh...

Come here. Yeah, it's...

Ah no... where?

Where's the camera?
- Come on guys. Please.

No really.

When's it going on air?

Just call us.

Centraal beheer

The insurance company
in Apeldoorn. (055) 579 8000

Need help for your banking on the net?

via DEXIA Bank

---

102 **Financial Services**

Agency:	DDB, Amsterdam	A man is cleaning the guttering of his house
Creative Director:	Martin Cornelissen	when the ladder slips from under his feet,
Copywriter:	Bas Korsten	leaving him dangling precariously by his
Art Director:	Michael Jansen	fingertips. A couple of joggers hear his cries
Production:	Czar.nl	for help, and run to the rescue. But they
Director:	Rogier van der Ploeg	recognise him as the Dutch presenter of
Producers:	Jan Koopmans	Candid Camera, and assume they are the
	Marloes van den Berg	victims of a televised gag. One of them
Client:	Centraal Beheer	snorts: "Grab the ladder! Nice try!" They jog
	Insurance,	off, leaving the stricken TV presenter
	"Candid Camera"	hanging from the creaking gutter…

Agency:	Duval Guillaume,	An elderly man types the words www.dexia.be
	Brussels	into his old portable typewriter. Then he sits
Creative Director:	Jens Mortier	back and waits. Need help with banking on
Copywriter:	Peter Ampe	the net? Perhaps you'd better call Dexia
Art Director:	Katrien Bottez	Netbanking for advice.
Producer:	Andreas Hasle	
Client:	Dexia Netbanking,	
	"Typewriter"	

Agency:	Duval Guillaume, Brussels	Agency:	Duval Guillaume, Brussels
Creative Director:	Jens Mortier	Creative Director:	Jens Mortier
Copywriter:	Peter Ampe	Copywriter:	Peter Ampe
Art Director:	Katrien Bottez	Art Director:	Katrien Bottez
Photographer:	Peter De Mulder	Photographer:	Frank Uyttenhove
Client:	Dexia Bank Retirement Plan	Client:	Dexia Banking

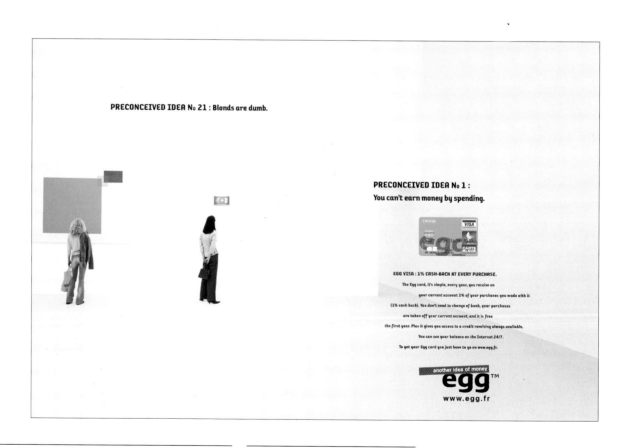

Agency:	BDDP & Fils, Paris	"Preconceived idea no. 45: sex sells." The	**Agency:**	BDDP & Fils, Paris
Creative Director:	Olivier Altmann	caption is followed by the unlikely image	**Creative Director:**	Olivier Altmann
Copywriter:	Thierry Albert	of a skinny naked man selling fruit by the	**Copywriter:**	Thierry Albert
Art Director:	Damien Bellon	roadside. But motorists speed past,	**Art Director:**	Damien Bellon
Production:	Ze prod	unnerved by his unappealing appearance.	**Photographer:**	Nick Meek
Director:	Marvu Coeman	"Preconceived idea no. 1: you can't earn	**Client:**	Egg Banking Services
Producer:	Christine Bouffort	money while spending." Wrong. As the		
Client:	Egg Banking Services, "The Seller"	narrator tells us, the new Egg debit card gives you one per cent cash back with every purchase.		

Agency:	Hasan & Partners, Helsinki	**Agency:**	Philipp und Keuntje, Hamburg
Creative Director:	Timo Everi	**Creative Directors:**	Hartwig Keuntje
Copywriter:	Antti Einiö		Diether Kerner
Art Director:	Juha Larsson	**Copywriter:**	Olivier Gill
Photographer:	Erwin Olaf	**Art Director:**	Jan Ehlbeck
Client:	If Insurance, Online Services	**Photographer:**	Bernd Westphal
		Client:	Jan Kneiding Financial Services

Agency:	Leo Burnett, Prague	Mourners begin a slow and sombre funeral procession in a church graveyard. Suddenly, another procession appears – moving much more quickly. In fact, it's speeding around the churchyard with indecent haste, and the accompanying musicians are practically tripping over themselves to keep up. There is something grimly amusing about the sight. The coffin bearers skid around a corner and practically hurl the coffin into the grave. "Enjoy your speed," says the caption of this road safety commercial, "to the end."
Creative Director:	Basil Mina	
Copywriter:	Martin Charvat	
Art Director:	Martin Pasecky	
Production:	Stillking Films	
Director:	Jakub Kohak	
Producer:	Premysl Grepl	
Client:	UAMK Road Safety "Funeral"	

THANK YOU FOR HELPING ME KEEP THE DREAM ALIVE

I control Cuba with a cold disregard for human rights. Lessons I learned in Eastern Europe. You obviously have not learned from those lessons. You don't seem to object. Recently, I cracked down on 75 dissidents. Just 2 weeks after being taken into custody, they were imprisoned for up to 28 years. Not a word from you. Less than a week later I executed by firing squad three men who were part of a group that commandeered a ferry in an effort to reach the freedom of the American coast. Still no word from you. As we speak, I hold another 52 people on death row. You remain silent. Your silence can mean only one thing. Approval. Venceremos! The dream lives on.

FIGHT HIM. VISIT WWW.AMNESTY.CZ

THANKS FOR YOUR SUPPORT

For the past 20 years I have ruled Zimbabwe with a blatant disregard for Human Rights. Not once did you object. You never spoke up. You never let me know you disapproved. So I take it for granted that you approve. When I arrested and tortured Gabriel Shumba, you were silent. Even though Shumba told the world he was repeatedly subjected to electric shocks from electrodes placed on his tongue, feet and genitals. Equally, when Tonderai Machiridza, a member of the opposition, was beaten to death by my Police, we never heard a peep from you. My thugs have made Zimbabwe one of 10 most dangerous countries for a journalist, thanks in part to the silent approval of good people such as yourself. Your indifference is truly gratifying. With your continuing silent support we can look forward to many more years of terror.

FIGHT HIM. VISIT WWW.AMNESTY.CZ

THANK YOU FOR YOUR SILENCE

Since 1977 we've killed more than 870 people in the United States. You've never expressed your outrage, indignation or disgust. In fact, as we speak, over 3520 souls are waiting their turn on death row. And we fully expect your silent approval. The United States leads a coalition of only 5 nations (including Iran, Nigeria, Saudi Arabia and the Democratic Republic of the Congo) who execute child offenders. Since 1990, we have executed 19 child offenders, compared to 14 such executions reported in the rest of the world combined. It gets better. We 're currently using electro-shock equipment [including stun belts, shackle boards, and stun guns] in our prisons. Hey, we're even exporting this stuff! And you haven't uttered a word. So I want to take this opportunity to offer my heart felt thanks. Your silence is music to my ears.

FIGHT HIM. VISIT WWW.AMNESTY.CZ

Agency: Leo Burnett, Prague
Creative Director: Basil Mina
Copywriter: Vera Cesenkova
Art Director: Jiri Langpaul
Client: Amnesty International

Last year, in Portugal, one fifth of the people
who died in traffic accidents were not inside of a car.
Respect traffic signs. Respect life.

Associação de Cidadãos Auto-Mobilizados

A SAFETY BELT SAVES YOUR LIFE. THINK IT OVER.

PROVINCE OF BRESCIA
DEPARTMENT OF PUBLIC WORKS

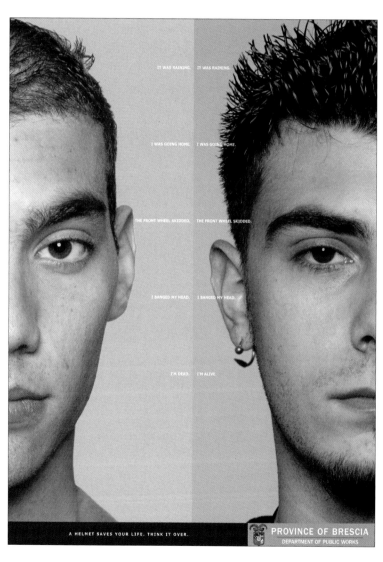

A HELMET SAVES YOUR LIFE. THINK IT OVER.

PROVINCE OF BRESCIA
DEPARTMENT OF PUBLIC WORKS

Agency:	FCB Portugal, Lisbon	Agency:	DDB, Milan
Creative Director:	Luis Silva Dias	Creative Director:	Enrico Bonomini
Copywriter:	Vasco Condessa	Copywriter:	Enrico Bonomini
Art Director:	João Roque	Art Director:	Marco Turconi
Photographer:	Francisco Prata	Photographer:	Stefano Gilera
Client:	Associação Auto Mobilizados, Road Safety	Client:	Provincia di Brescia, Road Safety

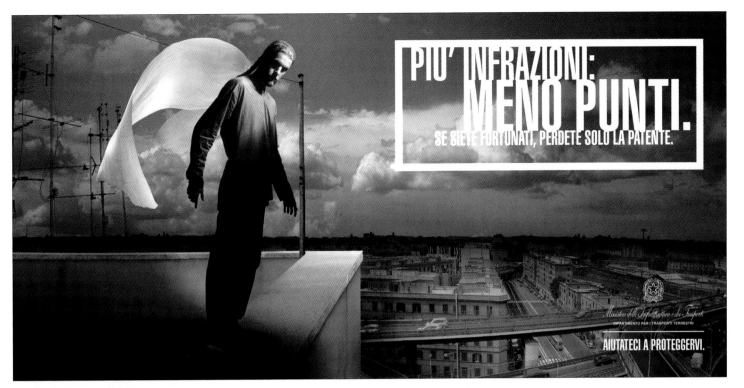

Agency:	Grey Worldwide, Rome	The more violations the less points. If you're lucky you'll only lose your licence.
Creative Directors:	Antonio Maccario Stefano De Filippi	
Copywriter:	Antonio Maccario	You've only got one life. Keep two hands on the steering wheel.
Art Director:	Stefano De Filippi	
Photographer:	Valerio De Bernadinis	If you go too fast your angel is going to lose you.
Client:	Department of Transportation, Road Safety	No helmet, no miracles.
		Zero alcohol and you'll be driving for a hundred years.

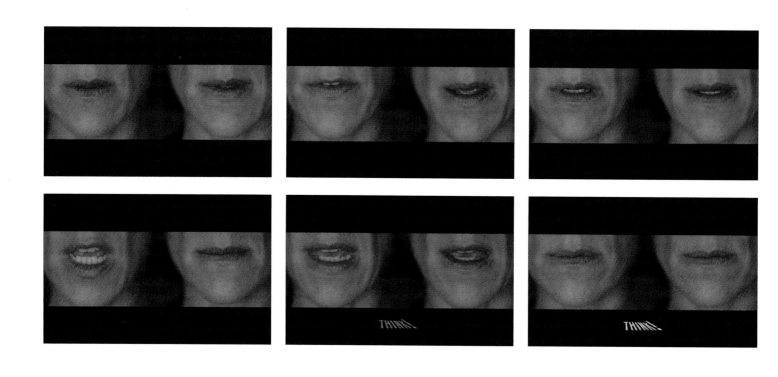

110   **Public Interest**

Agency:	Abbott Mead Vickers BBDO, London
Creative Directors:	Nick Worthington
	Paul Brazier
Copywriter:	Nick Worthington
Art Director:	Paul Brazier
Production:	Paul Weiland
	Film Company
Director:	Susan Roberson
Producers:	Mary Francis
	Yvonne Chalkley
Client:	DFT Road Safety, "Two Things at Once"

This simple but effective spot shows two mouths talking. The confusing thing is that they are saying different things at the same time. By paying very close attention, we can hear that one is saying: "You're four times more likely to have a road accident when you're on a mobile phone." Appropriately, the other is commenting: "It's hard to concentrate on two things at the same time." Think! Switch off your mobile phone.

Agency:	BDDP & Fils, Paris
Creative Director:	Olivier Altmann
Copywriter:	Bruno Delhomme
Art Director:	Andréa Leupold
Production:	Big Production
Producers:	Christine Bouffort
	Géraldine Fau
Client:	ASFA Association, "Animals' Life"

We open with a shot of a busy highway. Incredibly, we see a fox flying above the road and landing safely on the other side. A deer, a rabbit and a couple of squirrels repeat the trick. When we enter the foliage by the roadside, we see various other animals queuing up to use a trampoline – the only way they can avoid getting squished by motorists. In the real world, the French highway protection service is creating pathways for animals under roads.

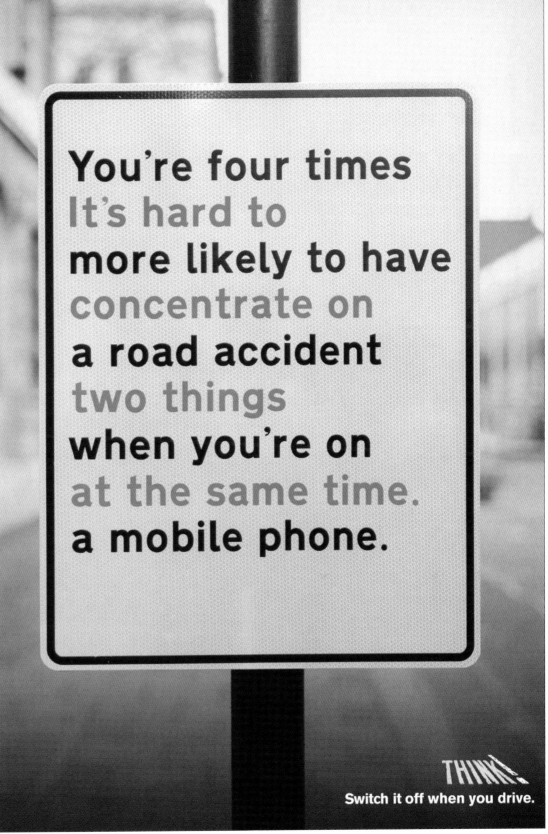

You're four times
It's hard to
more likely to have
concentrate on
a road accident
two things
when you're on
at the same time.
a mobile phone.

THINK!
Switch it off when you drive.

Agency: Abbott Mead Vickers BBDO, London
Creative Directors: Nick Worthington
Paul Brazier
Copywriter: Nick Worthington
Art Director: Paul Brazier
Photographer: Rik Pinkcombe
Illustrator: Mark Elwood
Client: DFT Road Safety, "Two Things at Once"

Agency:	Lowe, Amsterdam	Agency:	Euro RSCG Partners,
Creative Director:	Pieter van Velsen		Madrid
Copywriter:	Dylan de Backer	Creative Director:	Eva Cobo
Art Director:	Joris Kuijpers	Copywriter:	David Martin
Client:	Polderweg	Art Director:	Victor Martin
	Animal Shelter	Client:	WWF Adena

Public Interest **113**

Agency:	H2E Hoehne Habann Elser, Ludwigsberg
Creative Director:	Paul Holcmann
Copywriter:	Lorenz Ritter
Art Directors:	Florian Weber
	Goesta Diehl
	Holger Schaefers
	Birgit Hogrefe
Client:	Bundesverband Tierschutz, Animal Rights

WE WANT TO PROTECT ALL SPECIES, AND ONE IN PARTICULAR.
ENVIRONMENT, DIVERSITY, SOLIDARITY: PEOPLE AND COMMUNITIES. THE PROTAGONISTS OF THE FUTURE. | LEGAMBIENTE

Agency:	Publicis, Frankfurt
Creative Directors:	Michael Boebel
	Harald Schmitt
	Tom Tilliger
Copywriter:	Florian Beck
Art Director:	Florian Beck
Photographer:	Johannes G. Krzeslack
Client:	Animal Peace

Agency:	McCann-Erickson, Milan
Creative Directors:	Federica Ariagno
	Giorgio Natale
Copywriter:	Gianluca Villa
Art Director:	Federico Fanti
Photographer:	Luca Perazzoli
Client:	Legambiente,
	Environmental Protection

PICK
IT UP
before your
KIDS
DO

Clean up your dog's ▲

PICK
IT UP
before your
KIDS DO

Clean up your dog's ▲

Pick it up
before your
kids do

Clean up your dog's ▲

Agency:	Euro RSCG, Prague
Creative Director:	Eda Kauba
Copywriter:	Filip Kukla
Art Director:	Anna Barton
Photographer:	Peter Vajgl
Illustrator:	Ales Micka
Client:	Prague Municipal Council, Clean Streets Initiative

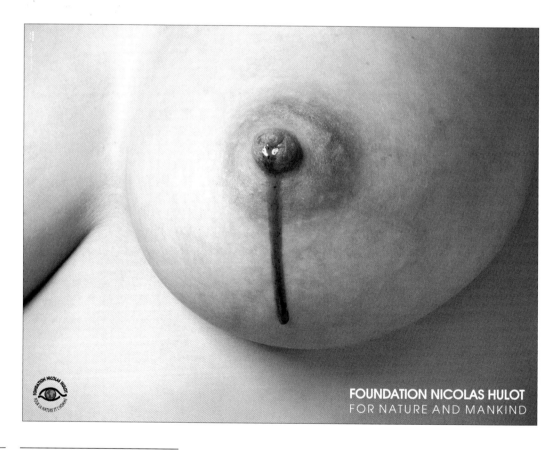

FOUNDATION NICOLAS HULOT
FOR NATURE AND MANKIND

Agency:	Zapping, Madrid
Creative Directors:	Uschi Henkes
	Urs Frick
Copywriter:	Mercedes Lucena
Art Director:	Gabriel Hueso
Client:	Amigos De La Tierra,
	Fuel Spill Catastrophe Aid

Agency:	CLM BBDO, Paris
Creative Director:	Anne de Maupeou
Copywriter:	Olivier Dermaux
Art Director:	Mathieu Vinciguerra
Photographer:	Arno Bani
Client:	The Nicolas Hulot
	Foundation

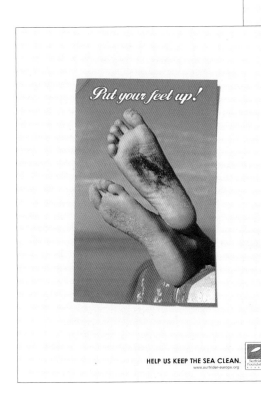

IF ONLY THE SEA COULD DEFEND ITSELF.

HELP US KEEP THE SEA CLEAN.

www.surfrider.org

Put your feet up!

HELP US KEEP THE SEA CLEAN.
www.surfrider-europe.org

Great view!

HELP US KEEP THE SEA CLEAN.
www.surfrider-europe.org

WE MISS YOU...

HELP US KEEP THE SEA CLEAN.
www.surfrider-europe.org

Agency:	Young & Rubicam, Paris
Creative Director:	Hervé Riffault
Copywriter:	Loïc Froger
Art Director:	Bernard Lebas
Production:	Première Heure
Director:	Emmanuel Bellegrade
Producers:	Jerôme Ruki
	Julie David-Mathio
Client:	Surfrider Association, "The Sandal"

A jogger runs along a deserted beach. Spotting an abandoned sandal just above the tide line, he picks it up with an expression of disgust and throws it into the sea. A second later, the shoe flies back and smacks him on the side of the head. It is followed by a hail of junk – a TV, a car tyre, a shopping trolley, tin cans, and nameless other bits of wreckage. The terrified man has to dodge them to avoid being hit. If only the sea could defend itself…

Agency:	Young & Rubicam, Paris
Creative Director:	Hervé Riffault
Copywriter:	Loïc Froger
Art Director:	Bernard Lebas
Photographer:	Bernard Sebastien
Client:	Surfrider Association

Agency:	Ogilvy & Mather, Brussels		**Agency:**	Leo Burnett, Prague
Creative Director:	Phil Van Duynen		**Creative Director:**	Basil Mina
Copywriter:	Veronique Hermans		**Copywriter:**	Michael Yee
Art Director:	Phil Van Duynen		**Art Director:**	Michael Martin
Photographer:	Christophe Gilbert		**Photographer:**	Michael Martin
Client:	CNAPD, National Coordination for Peace and Democracy		**Client:**	Amnesty International

LADDH
Ligue Algérienne
pour la Défense
des Droits de l'Homme

CAMPAIGN FOR ALGERIAN HUMAN RIGHTS. WWW.FIDH.ORG

Agency: Saatchi & Saatchi, Paris
Creative Director: Benoît Schmider
Copywriter: Alban Penicaut
Art Director: Stéphane Lecoq
Photographer: Catherine Louis
Client: LADDH, Algerian League
for the Defense of
Human Rights

IN THE CONGO, IT HAS BEEN SEPTEMBER 11 EVERY DAY FOR THE PAST 4 YEARS.

In 4 years, 3.5 million people have been killed in the Congo. Add it up. That comes to between 2000 and 3000 victims per day. We must fight to bring the authors of these massacres in Eastern Congo to justice. And for the death penalty and the use of child soldiers to be abolished.

Amnesty International
www.amnesty.be

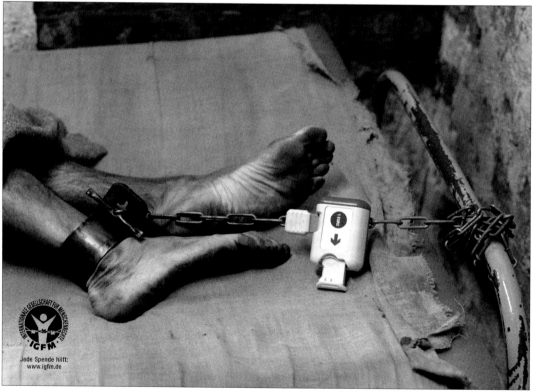

Agency:	Air, Brussels
Creative Director:	Eric Hollander
Copywriter:	Benoît Menetret
Art Director:	Didier Vanden Brande
Client:	Amnesty International

Agency:	Grabarz & Partner, Hamburg
Creative Directors:	Ralf Heuel
	Dirk Siebenhaar
Copywriter:	Simon Lotze
Art Director:	Margret Jansen
Photographer:	Andreas Fromm
Client:	IGFM, International Society for Human Rights

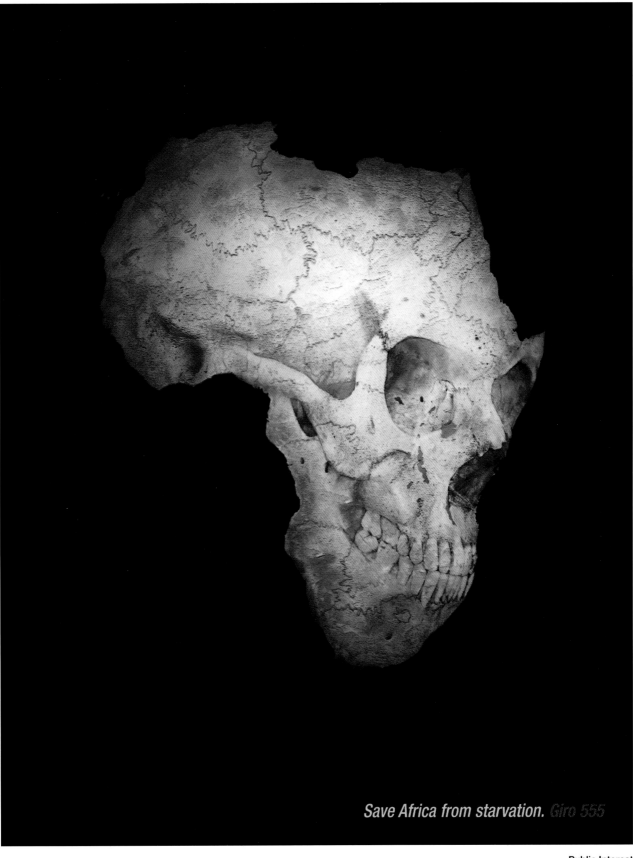

Save Africa from starvation. Giro 555

Agency:	Amsterdam Advertising,
	Amsterdam
Creative Directors:	Darre Van Dijk
	Piebe Piebenga
Copywriter:	Piebe Piebenga
Art Director:	Darre Van Dijk
Photographer:	Arno Bosma
Illustrator:	Fulco Smit Roeters
Client:	Giro 555
	Fundraising for Africa

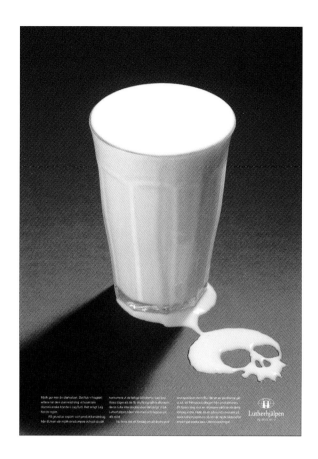

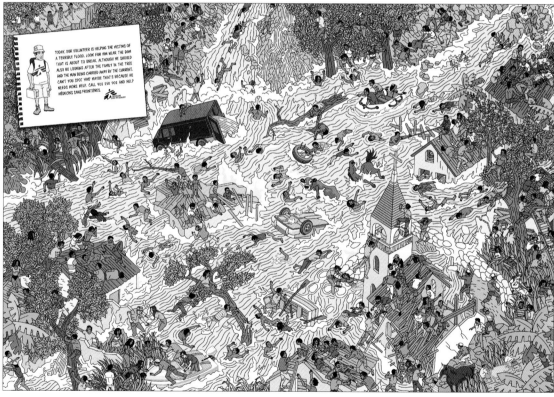

Agency:	Lydeking, Stockholm	The ad attacks EU milk subsidies that	Agency:	McCann-Erickson,
Creative Director:	Magnus Svensson	result in milk being dumped in third-		Madrid
Copywriters:	Niklas Synning	world countries to the detriment of local	Creative Director:	Nicolás Hollander
	Stefan Gustafsson	producers.	Copywriter:	David Moure
Art Directors:	Johan Adelstål		Art Director:	Victor Aguilar
	Sophie Månsson		Illustrator:	Alvaro Ortega
Client:	Lutheran Church Aid		Client:	Medicos Sin Fronteras

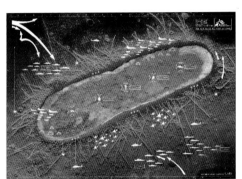

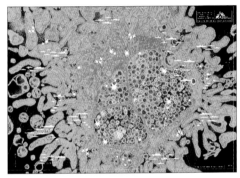

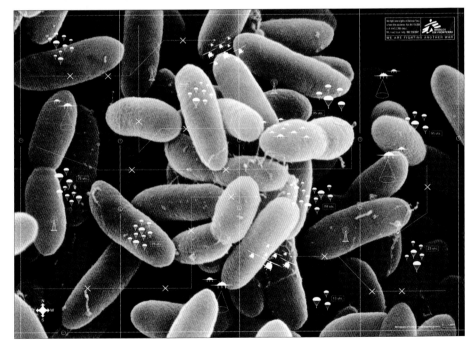

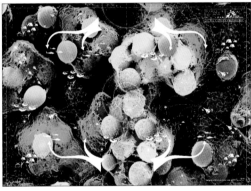

Agency: McCann-Erickson, Madrid
Creative Director: Nicolás Hollander
Copywriter: Isabel López
Art Director: Vanessa Sanz
Client: Medicos Sin Fronteras

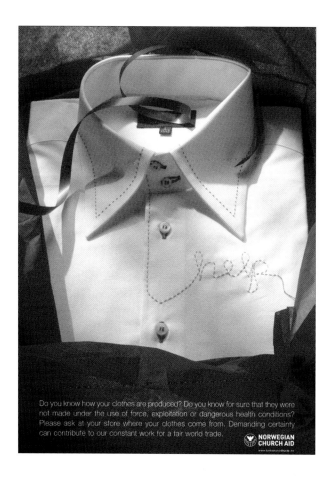

Do you know how your clothes are produced? Do you know for sure that they were not made under the use of force, exploitation or dangerous health conditions? Please ask at your store where your clothes come from. Demanding certainty can contribute to our constant work for a fair world trade.

NORWEGIAN CHURCH AID

www.kirkensnodhjelp.no

GO TIDY YOUR ROOM!

AND THE KIDS' ROOM AND OUR ROOM AND THE FRONT ROOM AND THE REST OF THE HOUSE AND THEN DO THE WASHING UP MOP THE FLOOR CLEAN THE TOILETS AND THEN COME SIT ON MY KNEE I PROMISE I'LL BE GENTLE.

Every year more than **30.000 children** are taken from their homes in Benin and sold into domestic slavery abroad.

In total 1.2 million children are bought and sold every year. And every year, Unicef, together with committed local authorities, tries to stop this buying and selling. On our website there is a petition. This petition will put pressure on the Belgian government to put pressure on the governments of the countries affected. Because to get them to act, we need you to act. Please sign the petition at www.unicef.be

STOP CHILD TRAFFIC

unicef

SIT STILL!

NO NOT LIKE THAT, MORE SLUMPED. SADDER. MAKE THEM FEEL SORRY FOR YOU. KEEP YOUR EYES DOWN. AND THAT MONEY ARM UP. AND YOU LIMP PROPERLY THIS TIME OR I'LL DO YOUR LEG FOR REAL.

Every year, **3.000 Albanian kids** are sold into begging in other countries.

In total 1.2 million children are bought and sold every year. And every year, Unicef, together with committed local authorities, tries to stop this buying and selling. On our website there is a petition. This petition will put pressure on the Belgian government to put pressure on the governments of the countries affected. Because to get them to act, we need you to act. Please sign the petition at www.unicef.be

STOP CHILD TRAFFIC

unicef

---

124   **Public Interest**

Agency:	JBR McCann, Oslo	Agency:	Publicis, Brussels
Copywriter:	Carina Laurhammer	Creative Director:	Marco Calant
Art Director:	Kjetill Nybø	Copywriter:	Jean-Marc Wachsmann
Photographer:	Roger Fredricks	Art Director:	Jean-Marc Wachsmann
Client:	Norwegian	Photographer:	Bernard Foubert
	Church Aid Fundraising	Client:	UNICEF Campaign Against
			Child Trafficking

Agency: J. Walter Thompson, Istanbul
Creative Director: Deniz Barlas
Copywriter: Gurkan Canakci
Production: Baba Film
Director: Selim Demirdelen
Producers: Arda Erkman
Deniz Tokcan
Client: 183 Child Helpline, "Fairy Tale"

In Istanbul, a small boy finds a telephone box token on the street. He pockets it as if it is something extremely precious. In the next scene, as he collects his dog and his blanket, we see that he is living on the streets. He takes the dog to a telephone box, inserts the coin and dials a special number – the fairy tale line. Soothed by the story, he attempts to sleep. Don't deceive homeless children with temporary gifts of money, food, or even compassion. Call the Child Help Line, and find out what you can really do.

Agency: J. Walter Thompson, Lisbon
Creative Director: João Espirito Santo
Copywriter: Gabriela Hunnicut
Art Director: Jorge Barrote
Photographer: Francisco Prata
Client: APAV, Portuguese Association For Women's Rights

Stop trafficking.

WOMAN TO WOMAN

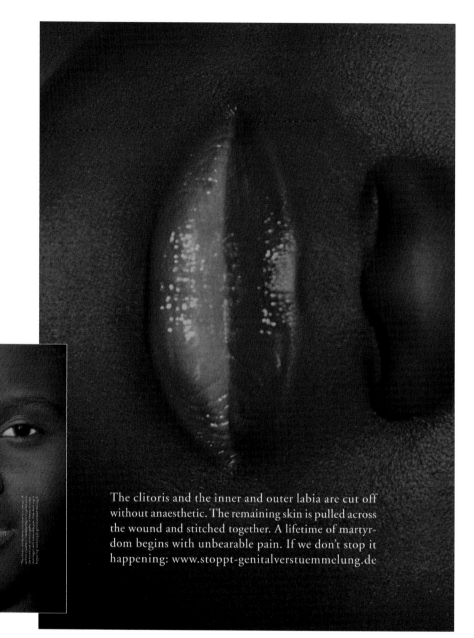

The clitoris and the inner and outer labia are cut off without anaesthetic. The remaining skin is pulled across the wound and stitched together. A lifetime of martyrdom begins with unbearable pain. If we don't stop it happening: www.stoppt-genitalverstuemmelung.de

Agency:	Paradiset DDB, Stockholm	Agency:	.start, Munich
Copywriters:	Christer Klinth	Creative Directors:	Peter Hirrlinger
	Camilla Hilarius		Andreas Klemp
Art Directors:	Niklas Bergström		Stefan Hempel
	Kjell Doktorow	Copywriter:	Doris Haider
Photographer:	Lasse Kärkkäinen	Art Director:	Stephanie Rauch
Illustrator:	Mussi Rosander	Photographer:	Chris Scott
Client:	Woman to Woman	Client:	Terres Des Femmes

Public Interest 127

Agency:	Storåkers McCann, Stockholm	
Copywriter:	Martin Marklund	
Art Director:	Enis Pupulek	
Production:	Mekano Film	
Director:	Jesper Ericstam	
Producers:	Stefan Falk	
	Leila Falkenberg	
	Petra Lindfors	
Client:	Eurofakta, "The Bill" & "The Market Place"	

A group of Swedish girls are in a French café. One of them asks for the bill. Then she tells the long-suffering waiter: "We want to pay separately." The waiter looks pained as they debate their shares. "I want to pay for one pommes frites and the salmon…" "And I want to pay for a beer and two sausages…" "And I'll pay for the water, but not the Fanta." "Don't worry – I'll pay for the Fanta…" They give him a stack of credit cards. Even if the Swedes join the common currency, some things will never change.

Two Swedish tourists are in a N. African market, looking at a carpet. "Five thousand!" mutters the man, shaking his head doubtfully. "Try to bargain with him," suggests his wife. The man says to the rug seller: "Four thousand nine hundred." The vendor can hardly believe his ears. What a sucker! "No problem – it's yours." If the Swedes join the common currency, some things will never change.

Passive Exposure to Tobacco Smoke in Children". BMJ 1994

Profs. Cook & Strachan, Thorax 1999, 54

NHS

Protect children,
Don't make them breathe cigarette smoke.

0800 169 0 169
www.givingupsmoking.co.uk

SMOKING KILLS
500 NON-SMOKERS
EACH YEAR.

Agency:	Abbott Mead Vickers BBDO, London	**Agency:**	Mac Film, Stockholm
Creative Director:	Peter Souter	**Creative Directors:**	Michael Rosengren
Copywriter:	Richard Foster		Annika Westerhult
Art Director:	John Horton		Christofer Vibenius
Production:	Therapy Films	**Copywriter:**	Niklas Nilsson
Director:	Malcolm Venville	**Production:**	Mac Film, Stockholm
Producers:	Daniel Todd	**Client:**	Rökfritt Anti-Smoking,
	Ruth Hannett		"Lucky Stroke"
Client:	DOH Anti-Smoking,		
	"Smoking Kids"		

We see several little children doing what kids do – playing with train sets, drawing, watching TV…And then we see that smoke is coming out of their mouths and nostrils. The juxtaposition with their innocent faces is shocking. The voiceover explains: "If you smoke around children, they smoke too. Every year, thousands of children have to go to hospital because of breathing other people's cigarette smoke."

A workman has just finished laying a carpet, so he decides to have a well-earned cigarette. But where did he leave the pack? His gaze falls on a lump in the carpet. His cigarettes! To save time and embarrassment, he quickly stamps the bulge down. The lady of the house appears to congratulate him on his work – and to return his ciggies. "I found them on the kitchen table." The man looks confused, until a little girl enters the room. "Mummy, have you seen my hamster?" Smoking kills 500 non-smokers a year.

IF YOU SMOKE WHEN YOU'RE PREGNANT SO DOES YOUR BABY.

If you want to stop, we will listen and can help.
Freephone: 0800 587 4865

Sunderland **NHS**
Teaching Primary Care Trust

Agency:	Different, Newcastle upon Tyne
Creative Directors:	Mark Martin
	Chris Rickaby
Copywriter:	Peter Ampe
Art Directors:	Ian Millen
	Stewart Allan
	Carlo Reale
Photographer:	Chris Auld
Client:	NHS Sunderland

DON'T GO TO SLEEP WITH A CIGARETTE.
Fires started by cigarettes kill more people than any other kind of fire.

TAKE YOUR CHILD OUT OF THE SUN.
OR SOMEONE ELSE WILL.

TAKE YOUR CHILD OUT OF THE SUN.
OR SOMEONE ELSE WILL.

130   **Public Interest**

Agency:	Arc, London		**Agency:**	Heimat, Berlin
Creative Directors:	Graham Mills		**Creative Directors:**	Guido Heffels
	Jack Nolan			Jürgen Vossen
Copywriter:	Martin Duckworth		**Copywriter:**	Andreas Manthey
Art Director:	David Bradbury		**Art Director:**	Marc Wientzek
Photographers:	Colin Prior		**Photographer:**	Wolfgang Stahr
	Chris Frazer-Smith		**Illustrator:**	Ole Bahrmann
Client:	Derbyshire		**Client:**	Deutsche Krebshilfe,
	Fire Service			Skin Cancer Prevention

Agency:	Ogilvy Denmark, Copenhagen
Creative Director:	Mads Ohrt
Copywriter:	Mads Ohrt
Art Director:	Mads Ohrt
Photographer:	Frederic Lindstrom
Client:	Danish Cancer Society

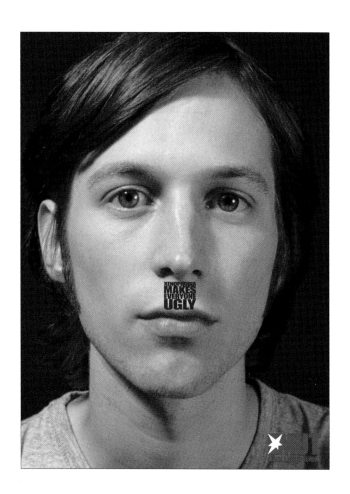

Agency:	Leagas Delaney, Hamburg	Agency:	J. Walter Thompson,
Creative Directors:	Stefan Zschaler		Lisbon
	Hermann Waterkamp	Creative Director:	João Espírito Santo
Copywriters:	Jana Liebig	Copywriter:	Rui Soares
	Mo Whiteman	Art Director:	Pedro Magalhaes
Art Director:	Mo Whiteman	Photographers:	Rui Soares
Photographer:	Olaf Blecker		Pedro Magalhães
Client:	Stern, Civil Courage	Client:	Salvation Army

For many people there is no hope in the street. **S.O.S. RACISME**

For many people there is no freedom in the street. **S.O.S. RACISME**

For many people there is no progress in the street. **S.O.S. RACISME**

Agency:	Tandem DDB, Madrid
Creative Director:	Mario Gascon
Copywriter:	David Perez
Art Director:	Bernat Sanroma
Photographer:	Nacho Juarez
Client:	SOS Racisme Catalunya

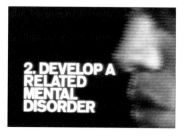

Agency:	TBWA\London	"How to rip off the British public," is the ironic	Agency:	TBWA\Germany, Berlin
Creative Director:	Trevor Beattie	caption at the beginning of this depiction of the	Creative Directors:	Kurt-Georg Dieckert

Agency: TBWA\London
Creative Director: Trevor Beattie
Copywriter: James Sinclair
Art Director: Ed Morris
Production: Method Films
Director: Richard Anthony
Producers: Patrick Duguid
Diane Croll
Client: The Big Issue
Foundation, "Rip Off"

"How to rip off the British public," is the ironic caption at the beginning of this depiction of the events that lead to homelessness. To an angry rock soundtrack, the grainy images show the main character following the commercial's "suggestions": 1. Get yourself abused as a child; 2. Develop a related mental disorder; 3. Allow it to destroy your marriage; 4. Lose your job; 5. Escape through addiction; 6. Start sleeping rough. Finally we see the young man huddled in a doorway, as a passing stranger drops a coin into his paper cup. The homeless aren't rip-off merchants.

Agency: TBWA\Germany, Berlin
Creative Directors: Kurt-Georg Dieckert
Stefan Schmidt
Copywriters: Athanassios Stellatos
Helge Bloeck
Art Director: Gritt Pfefferkorn
Photographer: Andreas Bitesnich
Client: Behinderten
Sportverband Berlin,
Handicapped Sports

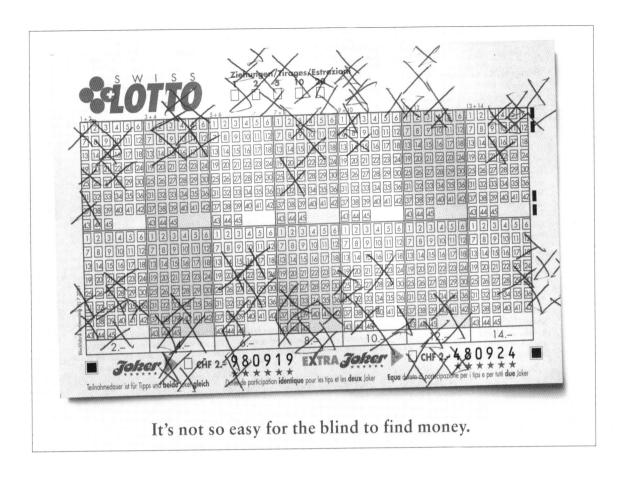

It's not so easy for the blind to find money.

Can you read in the dark?

Exceptional children can.

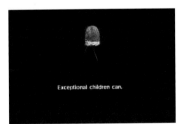

konto bariéry
Disabled Children's Fund of Slovakia
10073-216020/4900

Public Interest   **135**

Agency:	Ruf Lanz, Zürich		**Agency:**	Wiktor Leo Burnett, Bratislava
Creative Directors:	Danielle Lanz		**Creative Directors:**	Raffo Tatarko
	Markus Ruf			Peter Kacenka
Copywriter:	Markus Ruf		**Copywriters:**	Igor Brossmann
Art Director:	Danielle Lanz			Marika Majorova
Photographers:	Stefan Minder		**Art Director:**	Patricia Schafferova
	Felix Schregenberger		**Production:**	Monarch
Client:	Muehlehalde		**Director:**	Dominik Miskovsky
	Home for the Blind		**Producers:**	Peter Princ
				Olga Detaryova
				Tomas Ruckay
			Client:	Konto Bariéry Fund.

This beautifully shot black and white film takes us on a train journey through the countryside, in the company of a little girl who appears to be staring out of the window. When the train enters a tunnel, she opens her book. "Can you read in the dark?" the caption says. "Exceptional children can." As the train emerges from the tunnel, we see that the little girl is reading Braille. Not everything is as it appears.

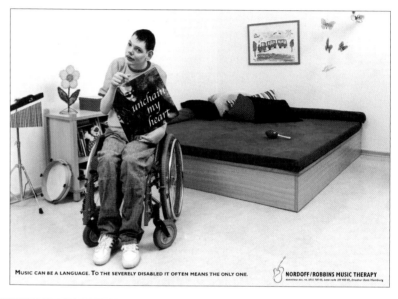

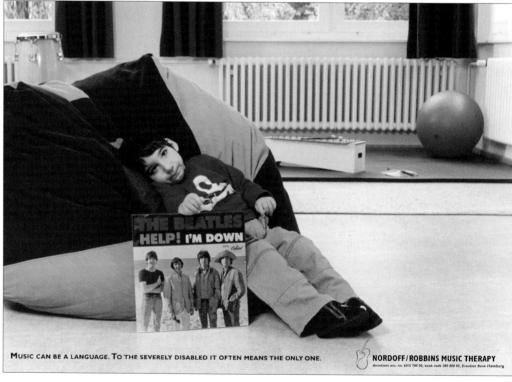

Agency: Kolle Rebbe, Hamburg
Creative Directors: Patricia Wetzel
Judith Stoletzky
Copywriter: Judith Stoletzky
Art Directors: Franziska Raether
Henriette Bokemeyer
Photographer: Timm Brockfeld
Client: Bundesvereinigung
Lebenshilfe, Association
for Support of the Mentally
Handicapped.

Agency: Heimat, Berlin
Creative Directors: Guido Heffels
Jürgen Vossen
Copywriter: Ole Vinck
Art Director: Caren Seelenbinder
Photographer: William Howard
Illustrator: Anna Kiefer
Client: Nordoff/Robbins
Music Therapy

Public Interest 137

Agency:	Leo Burnett, Warsaw	A driver is savagely cut up by another
Creative Director:	Darek Zatorski	motorist, and is forced to slam on his
Copywriter:	Darek Szablak	brakes. His passenger – who was putting
Art Director:	Lukasz Ufnalewski	on her make-up – ends up with lipstick all
Photographer:	Lukasz Kosmicki	over her face, but it could have been more
Production:	ITI Film Studio	serious. When the couple spot the road-hog
Director:	Darek Zatorski	parking a few seconds later, the man stops
Producers:	Joanna Brodzinska	to confront the reckless driver. But when he
	Janusz Wlodarski	sees that the other man is in a wheelchair,
Client:	Integracja,	he changes his mind, muttering an apology.
	Disability Awareness,	"Why do you treat us differently?" asks the
	"Pirate"	caption. 2003 was the year of the disabled.

Agency:	Leo Burnett, Warsaw	"And the neighbours?" enquires a man
Creative Director:	Darek Zatorski	looking around an apartment with a
Copywriter:	Darek Szablak	property agent. She tells him that they are
Art Director:	Lukasz Ufnalewski	deaf and dumb. "You know how they are –
Production:	Film Republic	nice and quiet!" Cut to the man trying to
Director:	Michal Bulik	sleep in his new bedroom, but being kept
Producer:	Kartarzyna Gorska	awake by his neighbours noisily making
Client:	Integracja,	love. On the other side of the wall we see
	Disability Awareness,	the energetic couple, now communicating
	"Neighbours"	affectionately in sign language after their
		exertions. Why should disabled people be
		any different?

ARE YOU DEAD?
DID YOU DIE IN A HOUSE FIRE?

If so we´d love to hear from you!

♦ what s it like being burnt to death?

♦ does it hurt?

♦ did you smell like chicken?

♦ the afterlife, where s good?

♦ still got your whatever happens, happens attitude´

♦ do you know elvis?

♦ do you regret not spending £5 on a smoke alarm?

helpline: 0800 169 0320

A mil ion
peo le hav
hear ng
proble s.

ⓢ hrf.

H rd of
hear ng?
Y u're not
alon .

ⓢ hrf.

Agency:	The Union Advertising Agency, Edinburgh	**Agency:**	Ruth, Stockholm
Creative Directors:	Simon Scott Andrew Lindsay	**Creative Director:**	Fredrik Claesson
Copywriter:	Adam Smith	**Copywriter:**	Tosse Sund
Art Director:	Mark Williams	**Art Director:**	Fredrik Claesson
Client:	Lothian & Borders Fire Brigade	**Client:**	The Swedish Association of Hard of Hearing People

ISRAEL PALESTINE
ישראל פלשתין 2003

PEACE

Public Interest   **139**

Agency:	Lemel Cohen, Tel Aviv
Creative Director:	Yossi Lemel
Copywriter:	Yossi Lemel
Art Director:	Yossi Lemel
Photographer:	Yisrael Cohen
Client:	Israel Palestine Political Criticism

Agency:	McCann-Erickson, Frankfurt	Agency:	Lowe Brindfors, Stockholm
Creative Director:	Walter Roux	Creative Director:	Johan Nilsson
Copywriter:	Thomas Auerswald	Copywriter:	Monica Hultén
Art Director:	Uli Happel	Art Director:	Joakim Blondell
Photographer:	Markus Hinzen	Photographer:	Philip Karlberg
Client:	Aidshilfe Frankfurt, Gay Counselling Center	Client:	Friends Against Bullying

DON'T WAIT TO BE DEPRIVED OF NEWS
TO STAND UP AND FIGHT FOR IT.

reporters
without borders
www.rsf.org

If you don't pay - others pay more

tv-fee.fi

Agency:	Saatchi & Saatchi, Paris	Filmed with a hidden camera, this film serves to catch people's reactions when their newspapers are suddenly snatched from their hands. The endline: "Don't wait to be deprived of news to stand up and fight for it".	
Creative Director:	Benoît Schmider		
Copywriter:	Guillaume Blanc		
Art Director:	Florian Roussel		
Production:	Les Dissidents		
Directors:	Benoît Lemoine		
	Pascal Vasselin		
Production:	Pascal Dupont		
Producer:	Martine Joly		
Client:	Reporters Without Borders, "No Press Today"		

Agency:	Dynamo, Helsinki
Creative Director:	Benoît Schmider
Copywriter:	Guillaume Blanc
Art Director:	Florian Roussel
Production:	Otto Film
Director:	Joakim & Toft
Producer:	Ari Laitinen
Client:	The Finnish Television Licence Fee Administration, "Restaurant"

In an expensive restaurant, a man drains his coffee cup as he is presented with the bill. Getting up, he deposits the bill on a neighbouring couple's table. Then he leaves. Astonished, the couple look at the bill – which is obviously huge. If you don't pay, others pay more. So pay your TV licence.

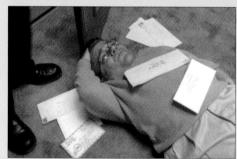

Agency:	Forsman & Bodenfors, Gothenburg	A man enters his apartment to find a tall stranger lying on his hall table. "Who are you?" "I'm Bill." "But I thought I got rid of you last month!" Everyone hates it when they receive a big bill. In contrast, a neighbour finds a midget Bill lying on his doormat. He treats the newcomer courteously: "Hi Bill – nice sweater!" In the second execution, another lanky Bill is lying with his foot stuck in a man's mail box. For smaller bills, try Tele2 Telecommunications.
Copywriters:	Oscar Askelöf	
	Martin Ringqvist	
Art Director:	Silla Öberg	
Production:	Hungry Man	
Director:	John O'Hagen	
Producers:	Carrie Hart	
	Charlotte Most	
Client:	Tele2 Telecommunications, "Mailslot" & "Mailbox"	

2315 m altitude
267 cowpats
4 alpine houses
1 network

10,358 individual snowflakes
526 sleeping marmots
7 freezing bikers
1 network

28 km of footpaths
12 campfires
3 hours of rain
1 network

Orange is the only mobile phone network that lets you phone from the Albula pass*.
Hardly a surprise, considering how we work incessantly on making our network
better for you – even in the remotest corners of Switzerland. Like to find out more?
Then call 0800 804 804 or go to www.orange.ch

* as of 3.06 p.m. on 10 October 2002

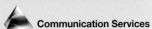

The future's bright. The future's Orange.

▲ **Communication Services** **143**

Agency:	Lowe, Zürich
Creative Director:	Keith Loell
Copywriter:	Martin Stulz
Art Director:	Simon Staub
Photographers:	Noe Flum
	Christian Grund
Client:	Orange
	Telecommunications

144 **Communication Services**

Agency:	Forsman & Bodenfors, Gothenburg		**Agency:**	Lowe, Zürich
Copywriter:	Martin Ringqvist		**Creative Director:**	Keith Loell
Art Director:	Kim Cramer		**Copywriter:**	Nicole Glaus
Photographer:	Berno Hjälmrud		**Art Director:**	Fernando Perez
Client:	Comviq Telecommunications, Cashcards		**Photographer:**	Max Schmid
			Client:	Orange Telecommunications

BILL 6' 8"

BILL 3' 7"

BIG BILLS SUCK.

SMALL BILLS DON'T.

networks of thoughts
networks of ambitions
networks of power
one network connects them all

networks through countries
networks through companies
networks through lives
one network connects them all

networks carrying goods
networks carrying ideas
networks carrying profits
one network connects them all

networks shaping cities
networks shaping events
networks shaping deals
one network connects them all

Agency:	Forsman & Bodenfors, Gothenburg	
Copywriters:	Oscar Askelöf	
	Martin Ringqvist	
Art Director:	Silla Öberg	
Production:	Hungry Man	
Director:	Johan O'Hagen	
Producers:	Carrie Hart	
	Charlotte Most	
Client:	Tele2 Telecommunications, "Demo"	

Two men called Bill stand side by side. One is six feet eight inches tall. The other is a diminutive three foot seven. The taller man is making a strange sucking noise with his pursed lips. The other is silent. That's because big bills suck. Small bills don't.

Agency:	Lowe, Zürich
Creative Director:	Keith Loell
Copywriter:	Martin Stulz
Art Director:	Simon Staub
Photographers:	Noe Flum
	Christian Grund
Client:	Orange Telecommunications

146   **Communication Services**

Agency: Forsman & Bodenfors, Gothenburg
Copywriter: Martin Ringqvist
Art Director: Kim Cramer
Production: Camp David
Director: Christoffer Von Reis
Producers: Johan Persson
Charlotte Most
Markus Bergkvist
Client: Comviq Telecommunications, "Hiccups" & "Japanese Tourists"

An anonymous man in a raincoat continually shocks those around him by letting out blood-curdling yells. In an office lobby, on the bus and in a restaurant, he makes people jump and frightens babies. Finally we see him on the phone to his wife, who has hiccups. "Did it work then?" he asks. "No – we'll have to try again." In a second version, some Japanese tourists get the screaming treatment. But on the other end of the line, his wife still has hiccups…With Comviq you get a lot more talk for your money.

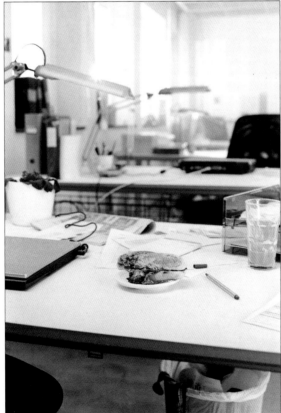

Agency: Abby Norm, Stockholm
Creative Director: Stefan Aaröe
Copywriter: Håkan Nyberg
Photographer: Daniel Norrby
Client: Dialect Mobile Phones

148   **Communication Services**

Agency: New Deal DDB, Oslo
Copywriter: Torbjørn Kvien Madsen
Art Director: Rune Markhus
Production: Big Deal DDB
               4½
Director: Marius Holst
Producers: Per-Henry Knudsen
               Håkon Øverås
Client: Telenor ADSL,
               "Restaurant"

In a restaurant, a man orders lunch. The waiter has only taken a few paces when the man calls him back again. "Yes, I ordered some food. I don't mean to bother you, but I see that many others have been served already. I was wondering when I will get mine." The waiter looks utterly baffled. After you've experienced Telenor's high speed internet access with ADSL, everything else seems slow.

Agency: New Deal DDB, Oslo
Copywriter: Stig Bjølbakk
Art Director: Henrik Sander
Production: 4½
Director: Marius Holst
Producers: Turid Øversveen
               Per-Henry Knudsen
Client: Telenor Housephones,
               "Theatre"

Two friends spot each other across a crowded theatre. Oblivious of those around them, they begin an extremely personal conversation. "Britt! I haven't seen you for ages." "We've been living in Spain. After Arnstein's bankruptcy we had to lay low for a while." They discuss the merits of their respective partners – who are right next to them. "I've got myself a lover… Just until I find something better." "Arnstein's so grumpy after his prostate problems – I can't stand him touching me." Mobiles are useful, but some things are better said on a private line.

Agency:	Saatchi & Saatchi, Vienna	**Agency:**	CLM BBDO, Paris
Creative Director:	Ingeborg Frauendorfer	**Creative Directors:**	Vincent Behaeghel
Copywriter:	Christoph Reicher		Anne De Maupeou
Art Director:	Alexander Kowatschitsch		Bernard Naville
Client:	Mobilkom Austria, A1 MMS Service	**Copywriter:**	Fred Lutgé
		Art Director:	Dimitri Guerassimov
		Production:	Irène
		Director:	Christophe Navarre
		Producers:	Guillaume de Bary
			Pierre Marcus
			France Monnet
		Client:	Wanadoo Internet Provider, "Respect"

Press photos on the front page of national newspaper, Der Standard were transferred to an ad inside the newspaper to demonstrate picture transfers via MMS on mobile phones. (See also page 308).

What is it about this young boy that earns him such respect? An elderly woman gives up her seat on the Metro for him. Policemen bow. Everywhere he goes, people stand to attention, salute, or kiss his hand. Finally, we see the words on his red t-shirt: "I am bl@ck warrior_67." To those who play games on the internet, his high scores have made him a legend.

Agency:	New Deal DDB, Oslo	The office party is over. A cleaner slowly
Copywriter:	Egil Alv Andreassen	sweeps up the confetti and clears away the
Art Director:	Tone Garmann	empty bottles and paper cups. Then he
Production:	Big Deal DDB	finds a smart black jacket draped over a
	Kraftwerk Production	chair. Looking at the label inside, he sees a
Director:	Steinar Borge	name and begins searching for the owner in
Producers:	Per-Henry Knudsen	the residential phone book. But even with
	Guri N. Hilland	the Ditt Distrikt phone book he's unlikely to
Client:	Findexa, Ditt Distrikt Local	find Hugo Boss.
	Directory, "Hugo Boss"	

Agency:	Bates, Oslo	An anxious football supporter from Norway
Creative Director:	Thorbjørn Naug	is desperately trying to find his mates at an
Copywriters:	Pål Sparre-Enger	international match. But his mobile phone
	Carl Baekken	doesn't work in the stadium. His friends are
	Eva Sannum	concerned – partly because of the letters
Art Directors:	Thorbjørn Naug	painted on their bare chests. When they
	Lars Holt	stand up to cheer, the letters spell out NO
	Jørgen Lauritzen	WAY. Their mate – the letter R – is still
Production:	Motion Blur	missing! Finally, Y goes off to find him. As
Director:	Harald Zwart	luck would have it, he suddenly appears and
Client:	Telenor Mobile Internet	joins the line – which now spells NO WAR.
	Provider, "No Way"	Get better mobile coverage, with Telenor.

Hi-Fi SOUND   SAGEM

Agency:	Lowe Digitel, Zagreb
Executive CD:	Dario Vince
Creative Director:	Krešimir Purgar
Copywriter:	Teo Tarbarić
Production:	Felina Films, Ljubljana
Director:	Peter Bratuša
Producers:	Tomaž Žontar
	Tvrtko Kurbaša
Client:	HT Mobile,
	MMS Info Service

Cheerleaders are going through their paces when a mobile phone bleeps. One of them breaks off her routine to look at the message. She bursts into tears – as do her companions when they see the phone's screen. Soon they are all in hysterics, hugging each other and shuddering. Even male members of the crowd begin to weep. Finally we see the news item on the phone: George Clooney has just got married. Receive news bulletins on your phone, with HT Mobile.

Agency:	Publicis Conseil, Paris
Creative Directors:	Antoine Barthuel
	Daniel Fohr
Copywriter:	Mario Eymieux
Art Director:	Patrice Letarnec
Photographer:	Les Cyclopes
Client:	Sagem Mobile Phones

Agency:	.start, Munich
Creative Director:	Andreas Klemp
Copywriters:	Doris Haider
	Kristina Popp
Art Directors:	Stephanie Rauch
	Eva Schaefer
Client:	Yahoo!
	Internet Provider

This advertising free area is presented by Yahoo! In order to guarantee you the same peacefulness in your emailbox, there is a new spam filter on www.yahoo.de

Agency:	Duval Guillaume, Brussels
Creative Director:	Jens Mortier
Copywriter:	Paul Servaes
Art Director:	Alain Janssens
Photographer:	Kurt Stallaert
Client:	Belgacom ADSL

Agency:	Chemistry, Dublin	**Agency:**	Shalmor Avnon
Creative Director:	Mike Garner		Amichay/Y&R,
Copywriter:	Ted Barry		Tel Aviv
Art Directors:	Dave Croft	**Creative Directors:**	Gideon Amichay
	Richard Chaney		Tzur Golan
Production:	Russel Avis	**Copywriter:**	Amit Gal
Director:	Damien O'Donnell	**Art Director:**	Oren Vermus
Producers:	Anne Marie Curran	**Production:**	Paradiso
	Alex Simpson	**Director:**	Ohav Flantz
Client:	Meteor MMS Service	**Producers:**	Ariel Pridan
			Shira Robas
		Client:	Orange, "Football"

A man writes the word "Lunch?" on a sheet of paper, before approaching a cage of cuddly but terrified hamsters. He tucks the note into a hamster's tiny paws, and then hurls the creature out of the office window. In the street below, a girl fields the rodent with a baseball glove. She reads the note, writes a reply, and then fires the furry courier back using a slingshot. Unfortunately, the animal hits the wrong window – a closed one. There are easier ways of staying in touch. Try Meteor's unlimited free texts.

A removal man skilfully catches an antique vase tossed to him by a mischievous colleague. Suddenly the removal team embark on a fast-moving game of American football, with the vase as the ball. The fragile object survives all the moves they can make, until finally the removal man leaps into the truck – where he marks a touchdown by throwing the "ball" to the floor. It smashes into a million pieces. Some people were born to play. Happily, Orange phones now include games.

Agency:	Leo Burnett, Warsaw	On a snowy country road, a motorcyclist is intrigued by the large piles of fresh snow that lie at regular intervals along the road. A little while later, he finds himself stuck behind a Volkswagen Beetle. Suddenly, a huge pile of snow falls onto him from the trees above. As the Beetle pulls away, we see that it has a tower of Ikea boxes strapped to its roof rack, which keep dislodging snow from the branches of overhanging trees. The Ikea winter sale is now on.
Creative Director:	Darek Zatorski	
Copywriter:	Teresa Biernacka	
Art Director:	Joanna Krasucka	
Production:	Moland Film Company, Oslo	
Directors:	Nic Osborne Sune Maroni	
Producers:	Mone Mikkelsen Janusz Wlodarski	
Client:	Ikea, "Let it Snow"	

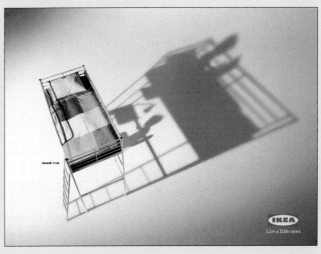

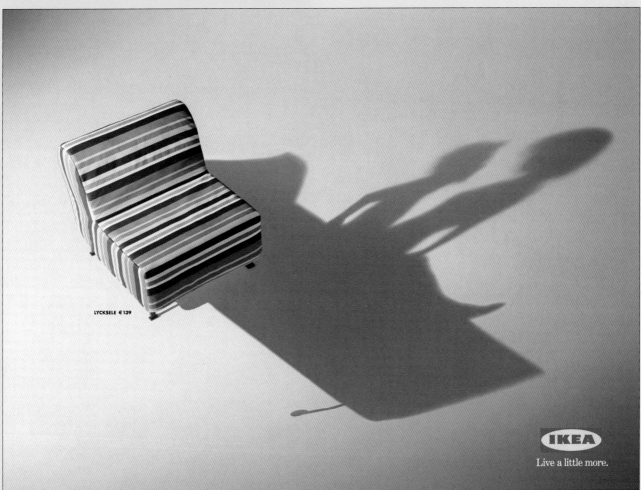

Agency: Hasan & Partners, Helsinki
Copywriter: Timothy Petersen
Art Director: Esko Moilanen
Photographer: Jaap Vliegenthart
Client: Ikea

156   **Homes, Furnishings & Appliances**

Agency:	Abby Norm, Stockholm		
Creative Director:	Emil Frid		
Copywriter:	Catarina Drugge		
Production:	Tre Vänner		
Client:	Mio Furniture Stores, "Mio News"		

Disturbed by a sudden clap of thunder outside, a man reading in his living room accidentally spills a cup of coffee over his armchair. He curses and stands up to examine the stain. "Don't worry about it," says his partner – and chucks her own coffee over the chair for good measure. A second later, she kicks over the floor lamp. Bored of your old furniture? Check out the new stuff at Mio.

Agency:	Grey Worldwide, Stockholm
Creative Director:	Lennart Lusth
Copywriter:	Robert Almén
Art Director:	Lennart Lusth
Production:	Mekano Film
Director:	Johan Skog
Producers:	Stefan Falk
	Anders Walter
Client:	Electrolux
	Ultra Silencer
	Vacuum Cleaner

Is there a poltergeist in this apparently ordinary household? A man is woken by a toy car racing down the hallway under its own power. In the next room, his sleeping little girl drops her teddy bear, which also slides across the floor. The man sits bolt upright, perplexed. Half asleep, the little girl leaves her bed and walks down the hallway to the living room, where her teddy is attached to the vacuum cleaner. She turns the cleaner off, and rescues teddy. The Electrolux Ultra Silencer quiet vacuum cleaner – don't forget to turn it off.

Agency:	D'Adda, Lorenzini, Vigorelli, BBDO, Milan
Creative Directors:	Giovanni Porro Stefano Campora
Copywriter:	Stefano Campora
Art Director:	Giovanni Porro
Photographer:	Pier Paolo Ferrari
Client:	Cassina Furnishings

DESIGNED TO BE USED. R̃ Rörstrand
Exclusive Swedish china

Agency:	Forsman & Bodenfors, Gothenburg		Agency:	Clemmow Hornby Inge, London
Copywriter:	Björn Engström		Creative Director:	Charles Inge
Art Director:	Anders Eklind		Copywriter:	Tony Barry
Photographer:	Pelle Bergström		Art Director:	Tony Barry
Client:	Rörstrand, Exclusive Swedish China		Producer:	David Wilsher
			Client:	British Gas

Agency:	Publicis, Frankfurt	**Agency:**	LG&F, Brussels
Creative Director:	Ljubomir Stoimenoff	**Creative Director:**	Christophe Ghewy
Copywriter:	Christoph Tratberger	**Copywriter:**	Paul Servaes
Art Director:	Daniel Wudtke	**Art Director:**	Benoit Hilson
Client:	Tefal Cookwear	**Photographer:**	Christophe Gilbert
		Client:	Beka

Agency:	Grey Worldwide, Milan	Here you can see a door, a piece of
Creative Director:	Antonio Maccario	furniture or any other part of your life.
Copywriter:	Paolo Airaghi	
Art Director:	Michele Salati	
Photographer:	Riccardo Bagnoli	
Client:	Vinci Arredamenti	
	Handmade Furniture	

Agency:	Welcome to Orange County,
	Soller - Mallorca
Photographer:	Philippe Merie
Client:	Ikea

Agency:	Ajans Ultra, Istanbul
Creative Director:	Hakki Misirlioglu
Copywriter:	Erdem Sinan Ates
Art Director:	Cem Sultan Sehirli
Photographer:	Tamer Yilmaz
Client:	Step Hali Floor Coverings

162 **Household Maintenance**

Agency:	Saatchi & Saatchi, Paris	A man's shirt gets stuck in the closing doors
Creative Director:	Benoît Schmider	of a train. A woman in a gym wrenches off her
Copywriter:	Jean-François Fournon	sweat-drenched singlet. The caption says:
Art Director:	Benoît Raynert	"They constantly get mistreated." Is this an ad
Production:	Stink, London	about stress? "They suffer in silence." A girl
Director:	James Brown	watches TV, her sweater pulled over her
Producers:	Daniel Bergmann	knees. A discouraged football fan buries his
	Christine Muller	head in his shirt. And a small boy's mother
	Catia Di Giambattista	tugs him towards her by his collar. "They are
Client:	Ariel Style Laundry Detergent,	pulled at from all sides." A girl's sweater snags
	"Everyday Life of Clothes"	on a door handle. "Who cares about clothes
		and how they get stretched?" Ariel Style
		detergent cares.

BLACK SHIRTS WILL ALWAYS BE BLACK SHIRTS.

BLACK DRESSES WILL ALWAYS BE BLACK DRESSES.

BLACK PANTS WILL ALWAYS BE BLACK PANTS.

 Household Maintenance **163**

Agency:	Lowe, Lisbon
Creative Director:	João Pires
Copywriter:	Nuno Gaspar
Art Director:	João Pires
Photographer:	Francisco Prata
Client:	Skip Black Velvet Laundry Detergent

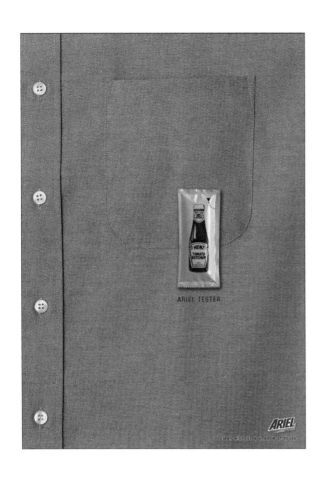

164   **Household Maintenance**

Agency:	Saatchi & Saatchi, Warsaw		**Agency:**	McCann-Erickson, Madrid
Creative Director:	Jacek Szulecki		**Creative Director:**	Nicolás Hollander
Copywriter:	Jakub Korolczuk		**Copywriter:**	Monica Moro
Art Director:	Ryszard Sroka		**Art Director:**	Raquel Martinez
Photographer:	Jacek Piekarzewski		**Client:**	Bruguer Paints
Client:	Ariel Laundry Detergent			

Agency:	Euro RSCG Partners, Barcelona
Creative Directors:	Alex Ripollés
	Jose Mª Batalla
Copywriter:	Alex Ripollés
Art Director:	Josep Marin
Photographer:	Joan Garrigosa
Client:	Flor Fabric Softner

Keeps things in one piece.

Presto
Hand Washing Powder
No more stains.

Presto
Hand Washing Powder
No more stains.

Agency:	Olympic DDB, Bucharest	Agency:	J. Walter Thompson, Lisbon
Creative Director:	Bradut Florescu	Creative Director:	João Espírito Santo
Copywriter:	Tudor Chirila	Copywriter:	Rui Soares
Art Director:	Alexandru Micu	Art Director:	Pedro Magalhães
Photographer:	Alexandru Micu	Photographer:	Francisco Prata
Client:	Power Duck Tape	Client:	Presto Hand Washing Powder

Agency:	Mediamix, Maribor	Agency:	TBWA\Brussels
Creative Director:	Toni Tomasek	Creative Director:	Jan Macken
Copywriter:	Toni Tomasek	Copywriter:	Vincent Daenen
Art Directors:	Nenad Cizl	Art Director:	Muriel Verbist
	Vlado Trifkovic	Photographer:	Frank Uyttenhove
Photographer:	Andrej Cvetnic	Client:	Sadolin
Client:	Vileda PurActive		Wood Treatment
	Dish Sponge		

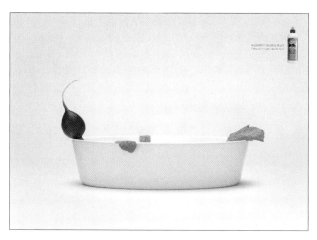

Agency:	Young & Rubicam, Copenhagen		**Agency:**	Team/Young & Rubicam, Dubai
Creative Director:	Peder Schack		**Creative Director:**	Sam Ahmed
Copywriter:	Peder Schack		**Copywriter:**	Shahir Ahmed
Art Director:	Peder Schack		**Art Director:**	Syam Manohar
Client:	Electrolux 2000 Watts, Vacuum Cleaner		**Photographer:**	Suresh Subramanium
			Client:	Madeleine Vegetal Wash

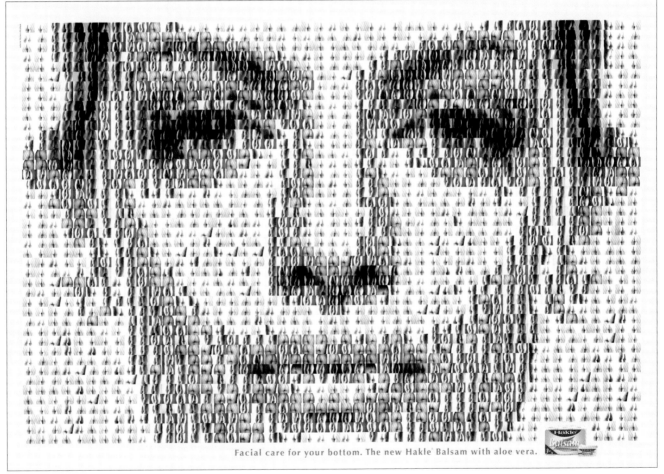

Facial care for your bottom. The new Hakle Balsam with aloe vera.

Agency:	Leo Burnett, Warsaw	Agency:	Advico Young & Rubicam, Zürich
Creative Director:	Darek Zatorski		
Copywriter:	Maciek Porebski	Creative Director:	Hansjoerg Zuercher
Art Director:	Martin Winther	Copywriter:	Hansjoerg Zuercher
Client:	Vizir Laundry Detergent	Art Director:	Roland Scotoni
		Photographer:	Julien Vonier
		Client:	Hakle Balsam Toilet Paper

Nobody can resist
in front of a FinePix.

FUJIFILM

Agency:	Marini Dotti e Associati, Milan	When a tourist prepares to photograph a cathedral with his Fuji FinePix camera, two men run into frame. Stockings over their heads and a bag of money clearly identify them as bank robbers. Nonetheless, they strike a number of amusing poses for the camera. Then they run off. Next, two cops appear on the scene. They also stop to pose for the lens. Later, the cops compare the snaps with the robbers – in a jail cell. Nobody can resist in front of a FinePix.
Creative Director:	Lorenzo Marini	
Copywriter:	Elisa Maino	
Art Director:	Mauro Maniscalco	
Production:	Harrold Motion Picture	
Director:	Jamie Lane	
Producer:	Valter Buccino	
Client:	Fujifilm Digital Cameras, "Escape"	

Agency:	TBWA\Paris
Creative Director:	Erik Vervroegen
Copywriter:	Eric Helias
Art Director:	Jorge Carreño
Photographer:	Dimitri Daniloff
Client:	Sony PlayStation 2

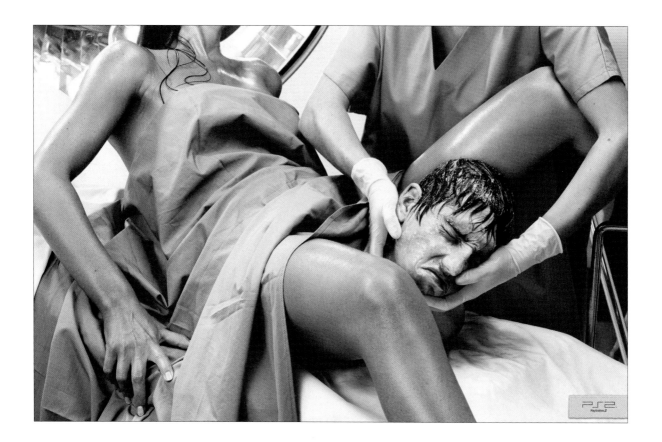

Agency:	TBWA\Paris	Agency:	TBWA\Paris
Creative Director:	Erik Vervroegen	Creative Director:	Erik Vervroegen
Copywriter:	Eric Helias	Copywriter:	Eric Helias
Art Director:	Jorge Carreño	Art Director:	Jorge Carreño
Photographer:	Dimitri Daniloff	Photographer:	Marc Gouby
Client:	Sony PlayStation 2	Client:	Sony PlayStation 2

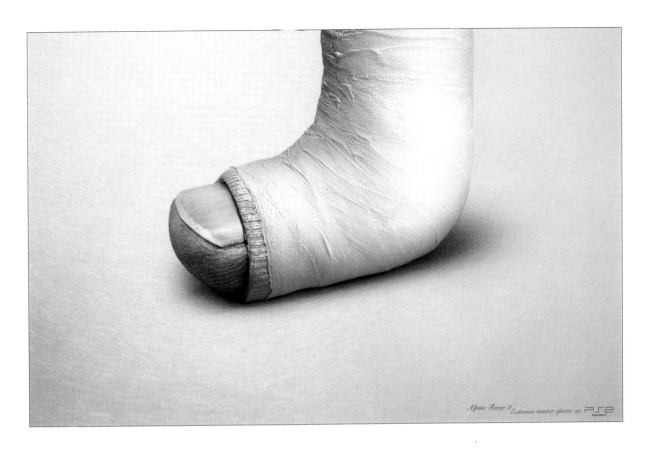

Agency:	TBWA\Paris	
Creative Director:	Erik Vervroegen	
Copywriter:	Eric Helias	
Art Director:	Jorge Carreño	
Photographer:	Olivier Reindorf	
Client:	Sony PlayStation	
	Alpine Racer 3	

Agency:	TBWA\Paris
Creative Director:	Erik Vervroegen
Copywriter:	Eric Helias
Art Director:	Jorge Carreño
Photographer:	Eric Matheron
Client:	Sony PlayStation 2

In Sports Illustrated's annual swimsuit edition, featuring a collection of scantilly-clad top models, Playstation offers something even more real; "Marguerita Gérard: swimsuit from her sister, glasses by Social Security."

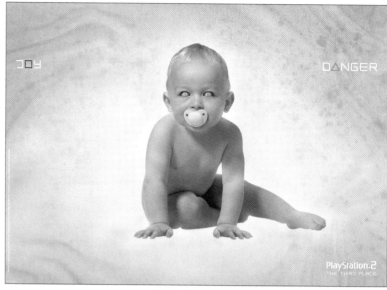

174   **Audiovisual Equipment & Accessories**

Agency:	TBWA\Germany, Berlin
Creative Directors:	Kurt-Georg Dieckert
	Stefan Schmidt
Copywriter:	Stefan Schmidt
Art Directors:	Kurt-Georg Dieckert
	Christine Taylor
Photographer:	Alexander Gnaedinger
Client:	Sony PlayStation 2

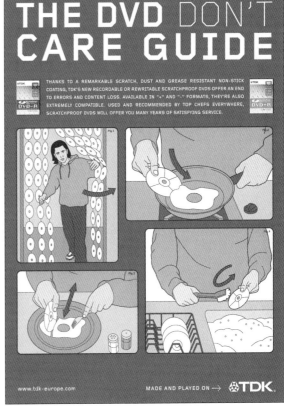

Audiovisual Equipment & Accessories   **175**

Agency: ADK Europe, Amsterdam
Creative Director: Dan Mawdesley
Copywriter: Dan Mawdesley
Art Directors: Fleur Westerbeek
Mark Dickens
Dan Mawdesley
Illustrator: Dannes Wegman
Client: TDK Scratchproof DVDs

Agency:	Forsman & Bodenfors, Gothenburg
Copywriter:	Jonas Enghage
Art Director:	Kim Cramer
Production:	Anders Skog Films
Director:	Anders Skog
Producers:	Sonia Maggioni
	Charlotte Most
Client:	Libero Diapers, "Time for a Wee"

During a long trip into the countryside, a father stops the car so the family can get out and pee. It's pouring with rain, but clearly they can't wait another second before relieving themselves. From the dry cosiness of the car, a baby watches them with a smile on his face. The family return to the car, soaking wet. As they drive on, the baby looks pleased with himself. Libero diapers keep him dry.

New
Remington
bikini
trim, &
shape

▲ **Toiletries & Health Care**   **177**

Agency:	Grey, London
Creative Director:	David Alberts
Copywriter:	Jimmy Blom
Art Director:	Jonathan Marlow
Photographer:	Alan Clarke
Client:	Remington Bikini
	Trim & Shape

178　**Toiletries & Health Care**

Agency:	Shalmor Avnon Amichay/Y&R, Tel Aviv
Creative Directors:	Gideon Amichay Yoram Levi
Copywriter:	Matan Orian
Art Director:	Tal Riven
Production:	Gefen Productions
Director:	Yoram Ever Hadani
Producers:	Eyal Gefen Lilach Gur Arieye
Client:	Kalgaron Cold Medicine, "New Mother"

A father addresses his son. "It's time for you to meet someone." But the son is in no mood for the same old conversation, as he's got a bad cold. Then his father calls Sally into the room – and she's a real stunner. The son thinks dad has fixed him up, until his father says: "Meet your new mother!" Those two are together?! When it's hard to swallow, try Kalgaron tablets and spray. "And another thing," dad adds. "Soon you'll have a little baby brother!" When it's REALLY hard to swallow, try Kalgaron Forte extra strength.

Agency:	G7, Warsaw
Creative Directors:	Przemek Bogdanowicz Maciek Kowalczuk
Copywriters:	Magda Komorek Maciek Kowalczuk
Art Director:	Bartek Ignaciuk
Production:	Film Republic
Director:	Chuk Chuk
Client:	Alldays Sanitary Towels, "Arcade"

An arcade running alongside an old building is a good excuse for a loving couple to play a little game – with the girl hiding behind each pillar. But what her partner can't see – but the camera allows the viewer to share – is that she is using the stolen seconds of privacy to adjust her jeans. Something is clearly giving her discomfort. The final frame suggests that she try comfortable, discreet Alldays sanitary towels.

NUROFEN | PAIN BARRIER

[keep it off]

Agency:	McCann-Erickson, London	Agency:	FCB Portugal, Lisbon
Creative Director:	Luke White	Creative Director:	Luis Silva Dias
Copywriter:	Marc Bennett	Copywriter:	Cláudio Lima
Art Director:	Marc Bennett	Art Director:	Tico Moraes
Photographer:	Daniel Holdsworth	Photographer:	Francisco Prata
Client:	Nurofen Painkiller	Client:	Off Insect Spray

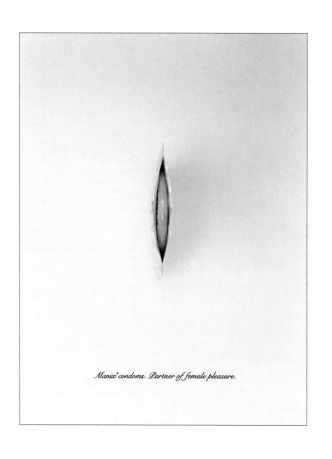

Manix condoms. Partner of female pleasure.

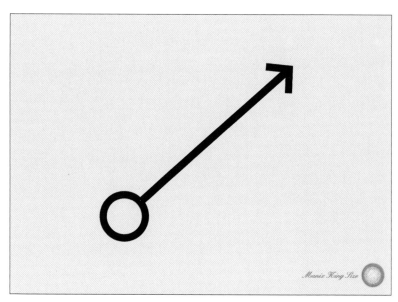

Manix King Size

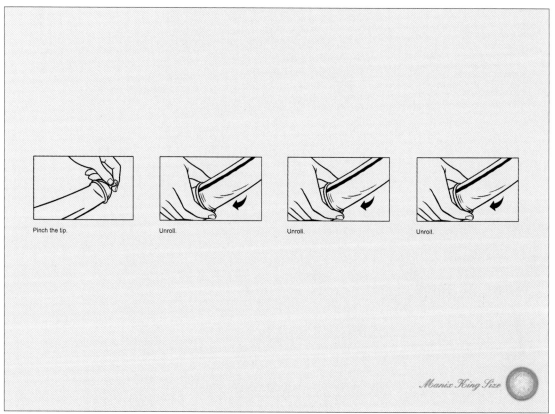

Pinch the tip.

Unroll.

Unroll.

Unroll.

Manix King Size

180 **Toiletries & Health Care**

Agency:	BDDP & Fils, Paris	**Agency:**	BDDP & Fils, Paris
Creative Director:	Olivier Altmann	**Creative Director:**	Olivier Altmann
Copywriter:	Thierry Albert	**Copywriter:**	Vincent Pedrocchi
Art Director:	Damien Bellon	**Art Director:**	Xavier Beauregard
Photographer:	Léon Steel	**Client:**	Manix King Size
Client:	Manix Condoms		Condoms

Agency:	McCann-Erickson, Prague	**Agency:**	BDDP & Fils, Paris
Creative Director:	Philip Pec	**Creative Director:**	Olivier Altmann
Copywriters:	Alis Fiala	**Copywriter:**	Thierry Albert
	Philip Pec	**Art Director:**	Damien Bellon
Art Director:	Leos Carda	**Photographer:**	Vincent Dixon
Photographer:	Marek Novotny	**Client:**	Manix Endurance
Client:	Durex Condoms		Condoms

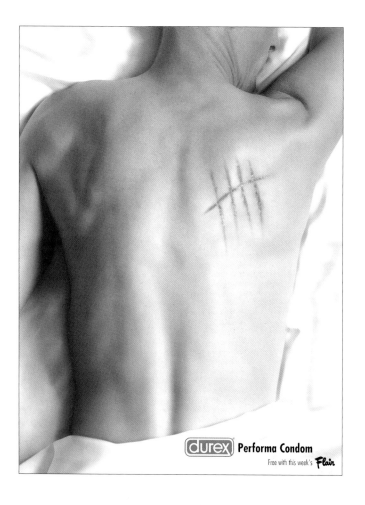

durex Performa Condom
Free with this week's *Flair*

durex chocolate flavoured condoms
Free with this week's **HUMO**

durex chocolate flavoured condoms
Free with this week's **HUMO**

182   **Toiletries & Health Care**

Agency:	Duval Guillaume, Brussels		**Agency:**	Duval Guillaume, Brussels
Creative Director:	Jens Mortier		**Creative Director:**	Jens Mortier
Copywriter:	Peter Ampe		**Copywriter:**	Peter Ampe
Art Director:	Katrien Bottez		**Art Director:**	Katrien Bottez
Photographer:	Koen Demuynck		**Illustrator:**	Mark Borgions
Client:	Durex Performa Condoms, Flair Promotion		**Client:**	Durex Chocolate Flavoured Condoms, Humo Promotion

Agency: King, Stockholm
Client: Easy Condoms

As soon as a black spot appears, use Clearasil.

AT LAST, YOU CAN SLEEP AS YOU LIKE.

BRAND NEW LIBRESSE GOODNIGHT WITH FLEXSYSTEM.
Moulds to your body to prevent leakage.

AT LAST, YOU CAN SLEEP AS YOU LIKE.

BRAND NEW LIBRESSE GOODNIGHT WITH FLEXSYSTEM.
Moulds to your body to prevent leakage.

184   **Toiletries & Health Care**

Agency:	Grey, Brussels
Creative Director:	Jean-Charles della Faille
Copywriter:	Sophie Colens
Art Director:	Damien Walckiers
Client:	Clearasil

Agency:	Forsman & Bodenfors, Gothenburg
Copywriters:	Oscar Askelöf
	Emma Zetterholm
Art Directors:	Johan Eghammer
	Lotta Ågerup
Photographer:	Gösta Reiland
Client:	Libresse Goodnight Sanitary Towels

Agency:	Forsman & Bodenfors, Gothenburg	Outside a petrol station, a cool young man fills up his moped. As he goes inside to pay, he passes a pretty girl, who checks him out appreciatively. Pausing beside his moped, she uncaps the petrol tank, shoves a Libresse sanitary towel inside, and puts the cap back on. A couple of miles down the road, the moped splutters to a halt – out of gas. The girl pulls up in her car to give the boy a lift. Bodyform Invisible sanitary towels are highly absorbent.	**Agency:**	Euro RSCG, Stockholm
Copywriters:	Emma Zetterholm Oscar Askelöf		**Creative Director:**	Fredrik Dahlberg
			Copywriter:	Fredrik Dahlberg
Art Directors:	Johan Eghammer Silla Öberg		**Art Director:**	Mathias Wikström
			Photographer:	Toby Maudsley
Production:	Renck/Åkerlund Film		**Client:**	Matador Razors
Director:	Johan Renck			
Producers:	Martina Stöhr Charlotte Most Markus Bergkvist			
Client:	Libresse Bodyform, "Petrol Station"			

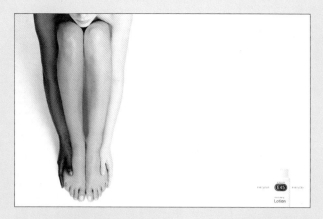

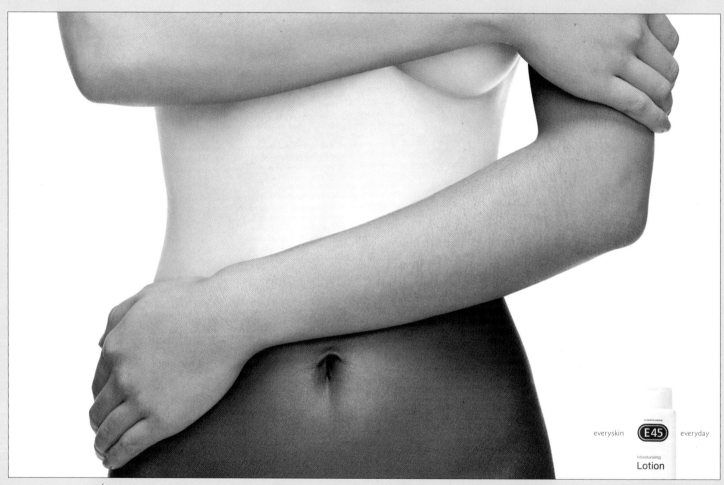

Beauty Products

Agency:	Magic Hat, London
Creative Director:	Marc Bennett
Copywriters:	Damon Hutson-Flynn
	Rob Brown
Art Directors:	Rob Brown
	Damon Hutson-Flynn
Photographer:	John Akehurst
Client:	E45 Body Lotion

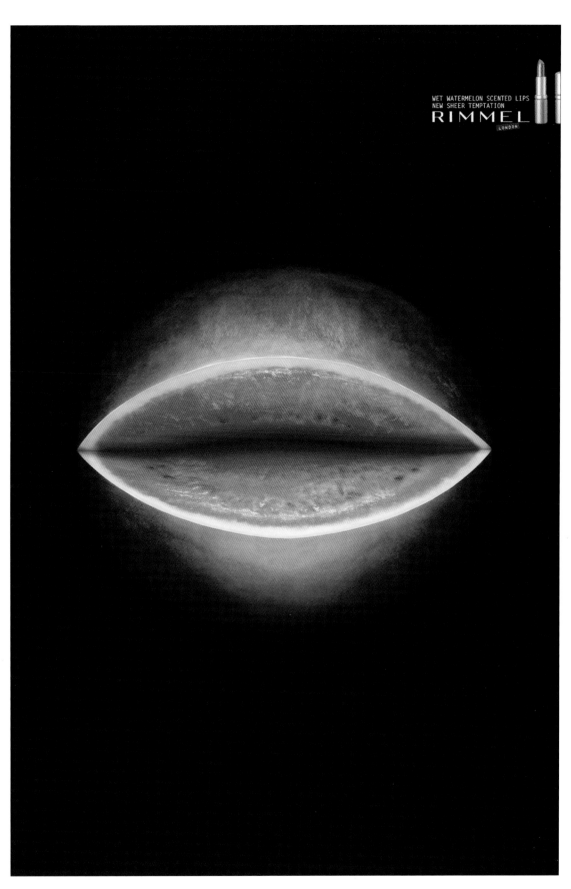

Agency: J. Walter Thompson,
                    Barcelona
Creative Director: Àlex Martínez
Copywriter: Jesús Galiana
Art Director: Carles Puig
Photographer: Miquel Fernández
Client: Rimmel Lipsticks

188 **Beauty Products**

Agency:	J. Walter Thompson, London	Agency:	Pristop, Ljubljana
Creative Director:	Charity Charity	Creative Director:	Mija Gačnik
Copywriter:	Sara Stoneham	Copywriter:	Aljoša Bagola
Art Director:	Lex Quinn	Art Director:	Ivona Šutila
Photographer:	Paul White	Photographer:	Aljoša Rebolj
Client:	Veet Bikini Kit, Depilatory Cream	Client:	Mercator Hair Colouring

Hydrating shampoo with plant milk.

Agency:	Publicis Conseil, Paris
Creative Directors:	Antoine Barthuel
	Daniel Fohr
	Béatrice Dallies-Labourdette
Copywriter:	Alain Saulnier
Art Director:	Jérôme Pelletier
Photographer:	Stéphane Coutelle
Client:	Garnier Ultra Doux Shampoo

Agency:	McCann-Erickson, Vienna
Creative Director:	Bernd Misske
Art Director:	Bernhard Sassmann
Photographer:	Heinz Henninger
Client:	L'Oréal Solar Expertise Sun Lotion

A photo of the official L'Oréal model, Laetitia Casta was featured on the front cover of the Austrian magazine "Woman". A mirror image was used on the back cover using a local look-alike model to promote L'Oréal Solar Expertise sun lotion.

Many serious diseases can be
treated effectively today.

Unfortunately some can not.

We're working hard on it.
And the progress we make encourages us.

The women and men doing research in
Switzerland's pharmaceutical companies.

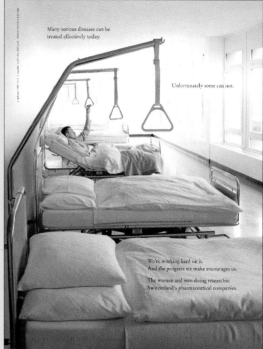

Many serious diseases can be
treated effectively today.

Unfortunately some can not.

We're working hard on it.
And the progress we make encourages us.

The women and men doing research in
Switzerland's pharmaceutical companies.

190   **Prescription Products & Services**

Agency:	Advico Young & Rubicam, Zürich
Creative Director:	Daniel Comte
Copywriter:	Wolfgang Krug
Art Director:	Valentina Herrmann
Photographer:	Odile Hain
Client:	Interpharma Research

Agency:	Junction 11, Weybridge	Agency:	Junction 11, Weybridge
Creative Directors:	Richard Rayment	Creative Directors:	Richard Rayment
	John Timney		John Timney
Copywriter:	Richard Rayment	Copywriter:	Richard Rayment
Art Director:	John Timney	Art Director:	John Timney
Photographer:	Bob Wing	Photographer:	Bob Wing
Client:	Ivax Corporate	Client:	GlaxoSmithKilne,
			ReQuip Treatment for
			Parkinson's Disease

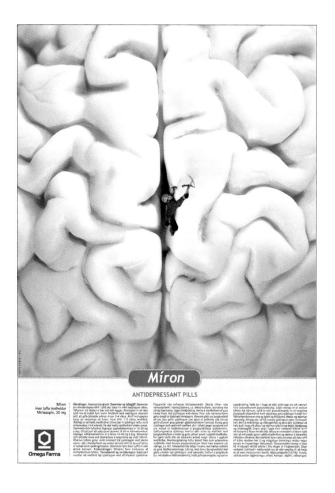

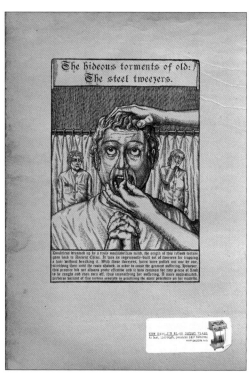

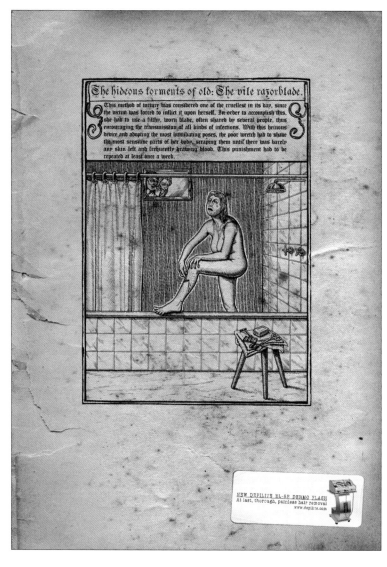

Agency: The White House,
                     Reykjavik
Creative Directors: Sverrir Bjornsson
                     Stefan Einarsson
Copywriter: Stefan Einarsson
Art Director: Stefan Einarsson
Photographer: Arnaldur Halldorsson
Client: Miron Antidepressant

Agency: Zapping, Madrid
Creative Directors: Uschi Henkes
                     Manolo Moreno Marquez
                     Urs Frick
Copywriter: Mercedes Lucena
Art Director: Victor Gomez
Client: Lat Dermo Flash Epilation
                     System

Have you ever heard someone's heart sing?

There are some feelings
words alone just can't explain.
But when they happen,
there's no mistaking them.
By changing the way
people feel about their asthma,
Seretide may change
the way they feel about life.

Seretide
salmeterol/fluticasone propionate

Control patients can feel

Strepfen
cures acute sore throat

Agency:	Torre Lazur McCann, London	Agency:	McCann-Erickson, Warsaw
Creative Director:	Don Nicolson	Creative Director:	Damir Brajdic
Copywriter:	Matthew Macland	Copywriter:	Iwona Kluszczyńska
Art Director:	Craig Chester	Art Director:	Wojtek Dagiel
Photographer:	Peter Seaward	Photographer:	Jacek Wolowski
Client:	Seretide Asthma Treatment	Client:	Strepfen Sore Throat Remedy

HONDA
The Power of Dreams

Agency:	Wieden + Kennedy, London	A cog rolling along a sloped plank gently bumps into a larger cog. This small movement triggers off a chain reaction. Various automobile parts work in harmony, like falling dominoes. Each movement trips a successive action. Finally, as the last mechanism falls into place, the new Honda Accord rolls smoothly off a ramp. Isn't it nice when things just work?
Creative Directors:	Tony Davidson	
	Kim Papworth	
Copywriter:	Ben Walker	
Art Director:	Matt Gooden	
Production:	Partizan, London & Paris	
Director:	Antoine Bardou-Jacquet	
Producers:	James Tompkinson	
	Rob Steiner	
Client:	Honda Accord, "Cog"	

Agency:	TBWA\Paris
Creative Director:	Erik Vervroegen
Copywriter:	Manoelle van der Vaeren
Art Director:	Sebastien Vacherot
Photographers:	Eastcott Momatiuk
	Art Wolfe
	Pete Atkinson
	Martin Harvey
	Nigel Dennis
	Brian Hawkes
Client:	Nissan 4x4 Range

Small but tough. Polo.

Agency:	Tandem DDB, Madrid		
Creative Director:	Jose Mª Roca De Vinyals		
Copywriters:	Oscar Vidal		
	Pepe Colomer		
Art Directors:	Quito Leal		
	Josep Mª Basora		
Production:	Lee Films International, Madrid		
	Missing Sparky, Barcelona		
Director:	Pep Bosch		
Producers:	Angel Recio		
	Julia Carrasco		
	Vicky Moñino		
Client:	VW Polo Match, "Thanks"		

A hapless lorry driver with a cargo of new VW Polos is forced to slam on his breaks when a dog ambles into the middle of a deserted highway. A red VW breaks free of its moorings, sails over the driver's cab, and begins trundling down the road. By chance, it comes to rest in front of a pair of hitch-hikers. Miraculously, the keys are in the ignition. "Thanks," says one of the hikers, raising his eyes to heaven. They get in the car and drive away.

Agency:	DDB, London
Creative Directors:	Jeremy Craigen
	Euan Paterson
Copywriters:	Dylan Harrison
	Fergal Ballance
	Simon Veksner
Art Directors:	Dylan Harrison
	Fergal Ballance
	Nick Allsop
Photographer:	Paul Murphy
Client:	Volkswagen Polo

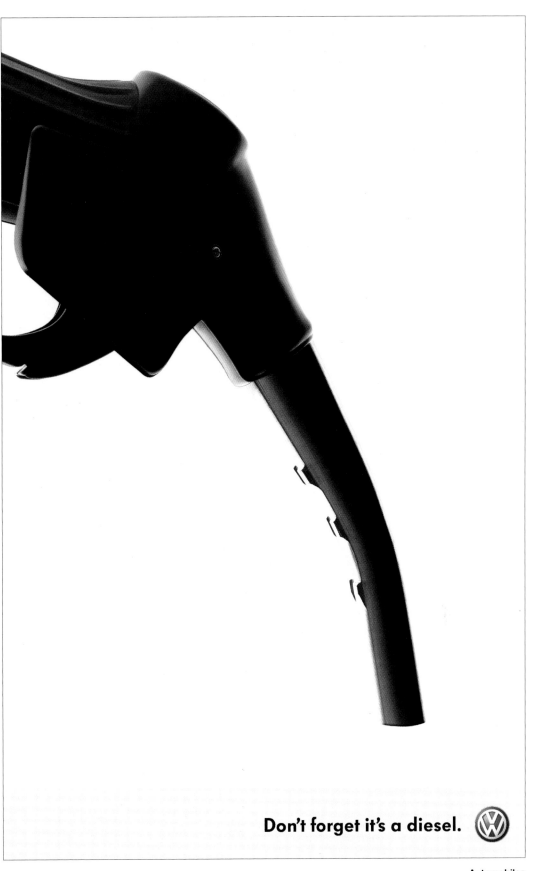

Don't forget it's a diesel.

Agency:	DDB, London
Creative Directors:	Jeremy Craigen
	Euan Paterson
Copywriter:	Adam Tucker
Art Director:	Justin Tindall
Photographer:	Jason Tozer
Client:	Volkswagen Diesels

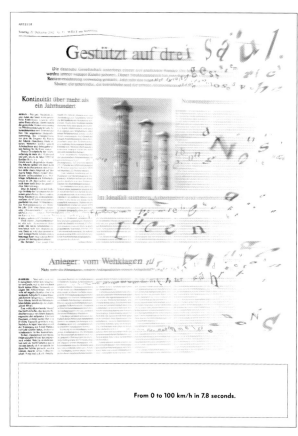

From 0 to 100 km/h in 7.8 seconds.

580 mm wading depth.

45° hill-climbing ability.

The Touareg

198   **Automobiles**

Agency:	Grabarz & Partner, Hamburg
Creative Directors:	Ralf Nolting
	Patricia Pätzold
	Rallf Heuel
Copywriters:	Martien Delfgaauw
	Thies Schuster
Art Director:	Derik Meinköhn
Photographer:	Nico Weymann
Client:	Volkswagen Touareg

The Rabbit is back.

The Rabbit is back.

Agency:	DDB, Brussels
Creative Director:	Dominique van Doormaal
Copywriters:	Grégory Titeca
	Mohammed Oudaha
	Sandrine Felot
Art Directors:	Grégory Titeca
	Mohammed Oudaha
	Emmanuel Colin
Photographer:	Christophe Gilbert
Client:	Volkswagen Golf Rabbit

Tough. The Polo

New Beetle Cabriolet

Agency:	DDB Germany, Berlin	Agency:	DDB, Amsterdam
Creative Director:	Amir Kassaei	Creative Directors:	Michael Jansen
Copywriter:	Lina Jachmann		Bas Korsten
Art Director:	Wiebke Bethke	Copywriter:	Bas Korsten
Photographer:	Holger Wied	Art Directors:	Michael Jansen
Client:	Volkswagen Polo		Matthijs van Wensveen
		Photographer:	Paul Ruigrok
		Client:	Volkswagen,
			New Beetle Cabriolet

Agency: Medina Turgul DDB,
Istanbul
Copywriter: Kerem Özkut
Art Director: Ferit Yantur
Client: Volkswagen,
New Beetle Cabriolet

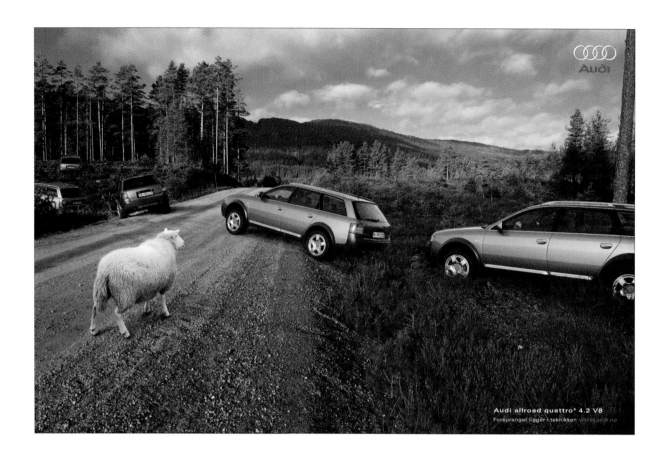

202 **Automobiles**

Agency:	Bates, Oslo		Agency:	Bates, Oslo
Creative Director:	Thorbjørn Naug		Creative Director:	Thorbjørn Naug
Copywriter:	Øystein Halvorsen		Copywriter:	Øystein Halvorsen
Art Directors:	Thorbjørn Naug		Art Director:	Thorbjørn Naug
	Lars Holt		Client:	Audi RS6
Photographer:	Glen Røkeberg			
Client:	Audi Allroad Quattro			

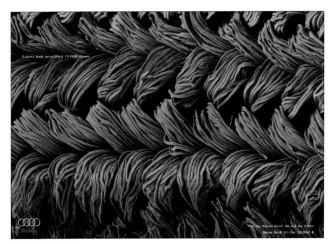

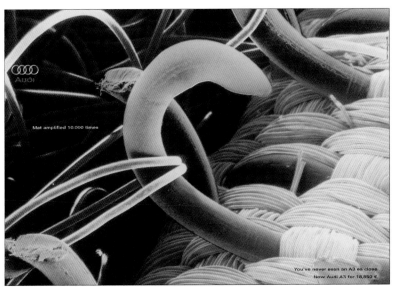

Agency:	Tandem DDB, Madrid
Creative Directors:	Danny Ilario
	Alberto Astorga
Copywriter:	Alejandro Arriagada
Art Director:	Xavi Sole
Client:	Audi A3

Agency:	Saatchi & Saatchi, Frankfurt
Creative Directors:	Benjamin Lommel
	Harald Wittig
	Carsten Heintzsch
Copywriters:	Wolfgang Schaupp
	Eva Kinkel-Clever
Art Directors:	Birol Bayraktar
	Kirsten Hohls
Photographer:	Jan Steinhilber
Client:	Audi, Brand Features

www.mercedes-benz.se   Any excuse to keep looking. The new E-Class Estate.   Mercedes-Benz

Agency:	Lowe People, Stockholm	**Agency:**	Springer & Jacoby, Paris
Creative Director:	Björn Ståhl	**Creative Director:**	Frank Rey
Copywriter:	Björn Ståhl	**Copywriter:**	Josselin Pacreau
Art Director:	Wayne Hanson	**Art Directors:**	Christian Vouhé
Client:	Mercedes-Benz		Benjamin Adida
	E-Class Estate	**Photographer:**	Gulliver Theis
		Client:	Mercedes-Benz
			CLK-Class
			Coupé 55 AMG

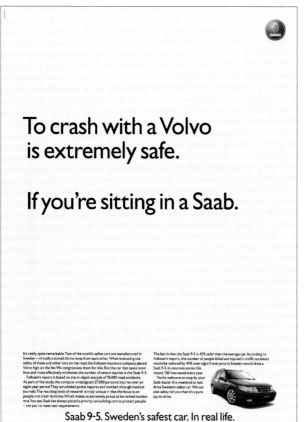

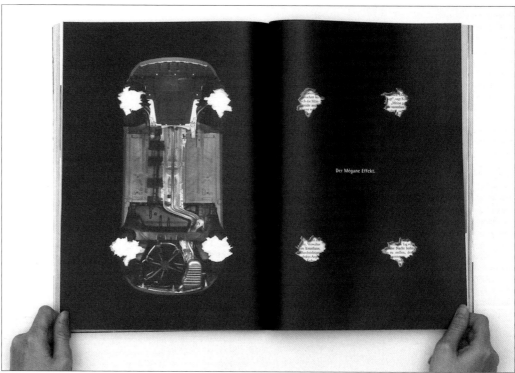

Agency:	Lowe Brindfors, Stockholm	Agency:	Publicis, Frankfurt	The four-page insert illustrates the Renault
Creative Director:	Magnus Wretblad	Creative Directors:	Michael Boebel	Mégane's dynamic yet safe road holding in
Copywriter:	Kalle Widgren		Dirk Bugdahn	a simple but vivid way. The centre pages
Art Director:	Magnus Wretblad		Hadi Geiser	are lightly glued together at four points –
Photographer:	Pål Allan	Copywriter:	Benito Babuscio	exactly where the car's four wheels are
Client:	Saab 9-5	Art Directors:	Alexander Gockel	shown. At first the reader is irritated, then
			Dirk Bugdahn	gets the message: the Mégane literally
		Photographer:	Peter Duettmann	sticks to the road.
		Client:	Renault Mégane	

Automobiles 207

208 Automobiles

Agency:	Gitam/BBDO, Ramat-Gan	Various hitchhikers aren't having much luck as they stand by roadsides holding up optimistic thumbs and bits of card indicating their destinations: Rome, Amsterdam, Paris…Meanwhile, a more discriminating female hitchhiker holds up a sign saying: "Volvo." It's not where you're going – it's how you get there.	
Creative Directors:	Yigal Shamir		
	Amir Hasfari		
Copywriter:	Ofer Golan		
Art Director:	Orna Nemirovsky		
Production:	Maurizio Santarelli, Rome		
Director:	Gigi Piola		
Producers:	Osnat Trabelsi		
	Shirli Zaltsman		
	Maya Meiri		
	Yvonna Krugliak		
Client:	Volvo Cars, "Hitchhiker Girl"		

Agency:	Fallon, London	In the Skoda factory, a young man begins fixing Skoda badges to the bonnets of cars. But when sleek luxury automobiles appear on the production line, he stops work – convinced that they are destined to receive a different logo. Alarms bells begin to ring, and the production line is halted. The young man is scolded by his colleagues. Then the production line goes into reverse, so he can put Skoda badges on the new Skoda Superbs. It's a Skoda too – honest.	
Creative Directors:	Richard Flintham		
	Andy McCloud		
Art Director:	Martin Krejzlik		
Production:	Stink, London		
	Jo! Schmid, Berlin		
Director:	Martin Schmid		
Producers:	Robert Herman		
	Michael Schmid		
	Kirsty Burns		
Client:	Skoda Superb, "Badges"		

The new Porsche Boxster, irresistible.

Agency: DDB, Brussels
Creative Director: Dominique van Doormaal
Copywriters: Gregory Titeca
  Mohamed Oudaha
Art Directors: Gregory Titeca
  Mohamed Oudaha
Photographer: Pierre Pironet
Client: Porsche Boxster

Agency:	Saatchi & Saatchi, London
Creative Director:	Tony Granger
Copywriter:	Hugh Todd
Art Director:	Adam Scholes
Production:	Outsider
Director:	Matthijs van Heijningen
Producers:	Anna Hashmi
	Emma Scott
Client:	Toyota Corolla, "Key Party"

At a wife-swapping party, men put their car keys in a glass bowl on the coffee table, and women get to pick their partners by lucky dip. One beautiful woman picks a set of keys and disappears upstairs with a paunchy middle-aged man. Then a rather large and unattractive woman begins rummaging in the bowl. The men look nervous, until she pulls out a key. Then they all stand up at once. The Toyota Corolla is a car to be proud of.

Agency:	Saatchi & Saatchi, London
Creative Director:	Tony Granger
Copywriter:	Mike Campbell
Art Director:	Colin Jones
Production:	Outsider
Director:	Matthijs van Heijningen
Producers:	Anna Hashmi
	Emma Scott
Client:	Toyota Corolla, "Party Dress"

A father and his little girl in her pink fairy outfit are sprayed with muddy water by a passing motorist. Further down the street, they notice a parked Toyota Corolla with a splash of mud on its wing. A man approaches, and the father demands: "Is this your car?" Although the stranger quickly puts two and two together, he can't bring himself to deny it. "Yes," he says. The father floors him with single punch. The little girl follows up with a kick. The Toyota Corolla is a car to be proud of.

Agency:	LG&F, Brussels	Agency:	Saatchi & Saatchi, Warsaw
Creative Director:	Christophe Ghewy	Creative Director:	Jacek Szulecki
Copywriters:	Joeri Van Den Broeck	Copywriter:	Dariusz Olech
	Tim Driesen	Art Director:	Agnieszka Niska-Wójcik
Art Directors:	Tim Driesen	Photographer:	Jacek Wolowski
	Joeri Van Den Broeck	Client:	Toyota Land Cruiser
Photographer:	Marc Muench		
Client:	Toyota Land Cruiser		

212   **Automobiles**

Agency:	SWE, Schumacher Wessman & Enander, Stockholm	**Agencies:**	BETC Euro RSCG & Euro RSCG Worldwide, Paris
Creative Director:	Björn Schumacher	**Creative Director:**	Rémi Babinet
Copywriter:	Hedvig Hagwall-Bruckner	**Copywriters:**	Rémi Noël
Art Director:	Andreas Hellström		Yoann Ameline
Production:	Forsberg & Co	**Art Director:**	Eric Holden
Director:	Patrik Forsberg	**Production:**	Wanda
Producer:	Bitte Söderlind	**Producers:**	Fabrice Brovelli
Client:	Toyota Avensis, "Knee Airbag"		Simon Chater Robinson
			Carole Casolari
		Director:	Philippe André
		Client:	Peugeot 206, "Metamorphosis"

His torso swathed in padding, a mechanic urges his colleague to hit him. "Are you sure?" "Come on – hit me!" A caption tells us that all car manufacturers have got much better at safety. The man's colleague grabs a crowbar and swings it at his knees, way below the padding. He falls to the ground in excruciating pain. A second caption adds: "But almost all of them have forgotten about your knees." The Toyota Avensis is the first car in Europe with a knee airbag as standard

A sad little abandoned car tries to attract the attention of passers by. Whenever someone comes into view, its radio springs to life, with a crooner singing, "Love me…please love me…." But everyone ignores the battered automobile. Finally, with a huge effort, the desperate car puffs itself up into the shape of a Peugeot 206. A man lingers for a second, taking a closer look – but then walks away. Exhausted, the car collapses back into its boxy former shape. Not every car is lucky enough to be a 206.

xDrive. All-wheel drive, the BMW way.

Feel like a kid again.

New BMW
3 Series
Coupé diesel

www.bmw.fr

Agency:	D'Adda, Lorenzini, Vigorelli, BBDO, Milan	**Agency:**	BDDP & Fils, Paris
Creative Director:	Gianpietro Vigorelli	**Creative Director:**	Olivier Altmann
Copywriters:	Vicky Gitto	**Copywriter:**	Thierry Albert
	Stefano Rosselli	**Art Director:**	Damien Bellon
Art Directors:	Vicky Gitto	**Photographer:**	Andy Glass
	Stefano Rosselli	**Client:**	BMW S3 Coupé Diesel
Photographer:	Pier Paolo Ferrari		
Client:	BMW S3 xDrive		

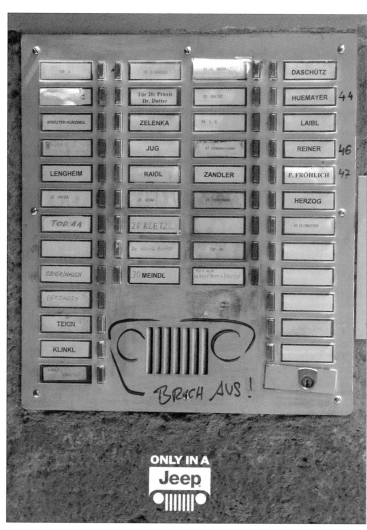

Agency:	BBDO/Pentamark, Copenhagen	
Creative Directors:	Jesper Hansen	
	Jonas Hanson	
Copywriters:	Jesper Hansen	
	Masse Bergkvist	
Art Director:	Jonas Hanson	
Photographer:	Per Anderson Jorgensen	
Client:	Jeep Cherokee	

Agency:	BBDO, Vienna	Break free !
Creative Director:	Markus Enzi	
Copywriter:	Alexander Hofmann	
Art Director:	Emanuela Sarac	
Photographer:	Emanuela Sarac	
Illustrator:	Christian Brezina	
Client:	Jeep	

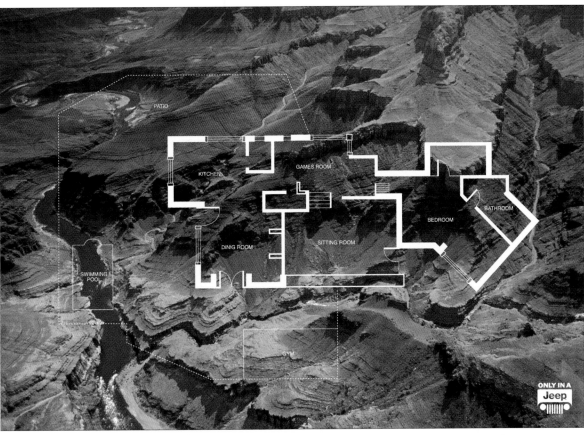

Agency:	Matter & Partner, Zürich	Agency:	Contrapunto, Madrid
Creative Directors:	Daniel Matter	Creative Directors:	Antonio Montero
	Philipp Skrabal		Carlos Sanz De Andino
Copywriter:	Michael Kathe		Carlos Jorge
Art Director:	Sabine Ries	Copywriters:	Félix del Valle
Photographers:	Julien Vonier		Miguel Madariaga
	Matthieu Simonet	Art Director:	Santiago Winer
Client:	Jeep Grand Cherokee	Illustrator:	Santiago Winer
		Client:	Jeep

216 **Automobiles**

Agency:	TBWA\España, Barcelona		Agency:	RKCR/Y&R, London
Creative Directors:	Xavier Munill		Copywriter:	Mike Boles
	Chris Garbutt		Art Director:	Jerry Hollens
	Joan Teixidó		Production:	MJZ
Copywriters:	Xavier Munill			(Morton Jankel Zander)
	Miquel Sales		Director:	Fredrik Bond
	Marçal Guash		Producers:	Lena Postmyr
Art Directors:	Tomás Descals			Debbie Turner
	Alex Martin			Amanda Goodship
Photographer:	Jaume Diana		Client:	Land Rover, "Gator"
Client:	Nissan 4x4 Range			

Pedestrians flee as a full-sized alligator stomps down a city street, jaws snapping and tail lashing at café tables. But one man confronts the massive reptile, making strange clicking and squeaking noises that seem to calm it. He then clamps its jaws shut with his bare hands, and wrestles it into an open manhole cover. It slithers back into the sewer. Where the hell did he learn how to do that? Brushing himself down, our hero climbs into his rugged all-terrain Land Rover Freelander. Been anywhere interesting lately?

THE ADVENTURE IS CALLING YOU.

Automobiles 217

Agency:	Young & Rubicam, Paris		Agency:	Young & Rubicam, Brussels
Creative Director:	Hervé Riffault		Creative Director:	Eric Vanden Broeck
Copywriter:	Jean-François Sacco		Copywriter:	Vincent De Roose
Art Director:	Gilles Fichteberg		Art Director:	Emmanuel Duriau
Photographer:	Andy Glass		Photographer:	Pascal Habousha
Client:	Land Rover		Client:	Land Rover

Agency:	CLM BBDO, Paris	"Mmm-hmm, mmm-hmm." At a petrol
Creative Directors:	Vincent Behaeghel	station, the cashier mumbles into a mobile
	Bernard Naville	phone, apparently listening intently to the
Copywriters:	Axel Orliac	person on the other end. Taking some
	Laurent Dravet	money from a customer, he rolls his eyes
Art Directors:	Axel Orliac	apologetically. Yet still he utters wordless
	Laurent Dravet	murmurs of agreement. Suddenly, another
Production:	Quad	customer emerges from the toilet, takes
Director:	Remy Belvaux	back his mobile, and gives the cashier a
Producers:	Camille Lipmann	thumbs-up gesture of thanks. Then the
	Pierre Marcus	customer takes up the refrain. "Mmm-hmm,
Client:	Total Petrol Stations,	mmm-hmm…" They're a helpful bunch at
	"The Telephone"	Total petrol stations.

Don't make your car nervous.
Take it to an authorized service stationon

Don't frighten your car.
Take it to an authorized service station

Don't stress out your car.
Take it to an authorized service station

 Automotive & Accessories **219**

Agency:	Leo Burnett, Warsaw
Creative Director:	Darek Zatorski
Copywriters:	Lukasz Witkiewicz
	Tomek Zielinski
Art Director:	Leszek Ziniewicz
Photographer:	Sebastian Hanel
Client:	Fiat Service Stations

We're teaching our cars to see, because mum can't be everywhere.

As a mother, knowing your child is alone on the streets can be a nightmare. Because, like it or not, you can't always be there to protect them. That's why we're working on a Pedestrian Recognition System for our cars. This technology will help drivers to avoid accidents by warning them if there are people on the road ahead. And may well become every mother's dream. At DaimlerChrysler Research we're developing these intelligent technologies today. For the automobile of tomorrow.

To obtain more detailed information on the 'Vision of Accident-free Driving' visit www.daimlerchrysler.com.

DAIMLERCHRYSLER
Answers for questions to come.

Agency:	Springer & Jacoby, London	Agency:	Springer & Jacoby, London
Creative Director:	Robin Weeks	Creative Director:	Robin Weeks
Copywriters:	Ben Carson	Copywriters:	Ben Carson
	Thomas Chudalla		Thomas Chudalla
Art Directors:	Elliot Harris	Art Directors:	Elliot Harris
	Tony Hector		Tony Hector
Production:	Pagan Films	Photographer:	F.A. Cesar
Director:	Vaughan Arnell	Client:	DaimlerChrysler Corporate
Producers:	Adam Sawyer		
	Claire Sparksman		
Client:	DaimlerChrysler Corporate "Mothers"		

As a little girl walks home from school, her supernatural mother seems to watch over her. The mother observes from a series of extraordinary vantage points: the top of a telephone box; a fountain; a lamppost; and various tall buildings. When a car zooms out of an alley, it automatically brakes to avoid hitting the girl. She arrives home safe and sound. In real life a mother's eyes can't be everywhere, so DaimlerChrysler is developing cars that can "see" pedestrians.

People don't always see accidents coming. But their cars will.

'Accidents will happen', as the saying goes. Especially when people lose concentration. In fact, inattentiveness is one of the most frequent causes of mishaps, both at home and on the road. Which is why we're developing cars that can actually recognise obstacles independently. The car will then alert the driver to a potential hazard and help to avoid it. DaimlerChrysler Research is already creating intelligent technologies like this today, for the automobile of tomorrow. Because one day we hope there will be a new saying: 'Accidents won't happen'.

To obtain more detailed information on the 'Vision of Accident-free Driving' visit www.daimlerchrysler.com.

DAIMLERCHRYSLER
Answers for questions to come.

Just what the environment needs from a car. Water.

If nature had one wish, what do you think it would be? A car that doesn't produce exhaust? We thought so too. That's why our hydrogen powered Fuel Cell vehicles only emit water. In fact, as they've proven in recent road tests, they may well be the alternative drive systems of the future. At DaimlerChrysler Research we're developing these intelligent technologies today. For the automobiles of tomorrow.

To find out more about 'Energy for the Future' visit www.daimlerchrysler.com.

DAIMLERCHRYSLER
Answers for questions to come.

Automotive & Accessories   **221**

Agency:	Springer & Jacoby, London
Creative Director:	Robin Weeks
Copywriter:	Ben Carson
Art Directors:	Azar Kazimir
	Elliot Harris
Photographers:	Alan McPhail
	F.A. Cesar
Client:	DaimlerChrysler Corporate

The new Ninja.

125 PS. 161 kg.

F¥CK ¥OU!

Kawasaki is back.

COPIES NEVER WORK AS WELL.

GENUINE PARTS   Keep it original.

THE LAND ROVER EXPERIENCE

222   **Automotive & Accessories**

Agency: AHA PuttnerBates,
                     Vösendorf
Creative Director: Alexandra Ehrlich
Copywriter: Ali Seemann
Art Director: Alexandra Ehrlich
Production: Roman Valent Film
Director: Roman Valent
Producer: Christof Benzer
Client: Kawasaki Ninja

A clapped-out tractor trundles along an
Austrian road at a snail's pace. Suddenly,
a green blur rips past, triggering a speed
camera. But the powerful Kawasaki
Ninja motorcycle is so fast that it doesn't
register on the camera – which accidentally
records only a picture of the tractor,
apparently travelling at a speed of 263
kilometres per hour.

Agency: Team/Young & Rubicam,
                     Dubai
Creative Director: Sam Ahmed
Copywriter: Gordon Ray
Art Director: Komal Bedi Sohal
Illustrator: Anil Palyekar
Client: Land Rover Parts

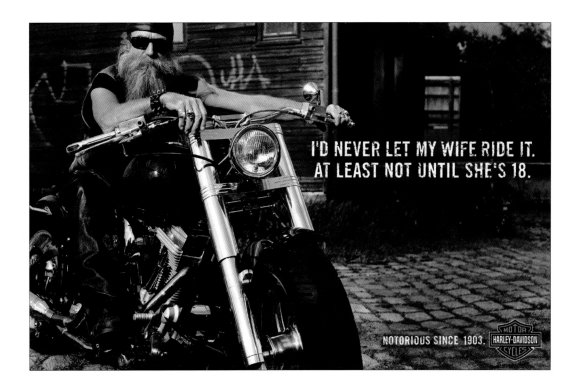

Agency: Aimaq Rapp Stolle, Berlin   Agency: BBDO, Berlin
Creative Director: Oliver Frank   Creative Director: Stefan Fredebeul
Copywriter: Oliver Frank   Art Director: Andreas Breunig
Art Director: Jens Orrillo   Client: Harley Davidson
Photographer: Uwe Böhm
Client: Harley Davidson

HIGH PERFORMANCE THROUGH THOUSANDS OF CURVES.

MICHELIN
En iyi performans sürekli olandır.

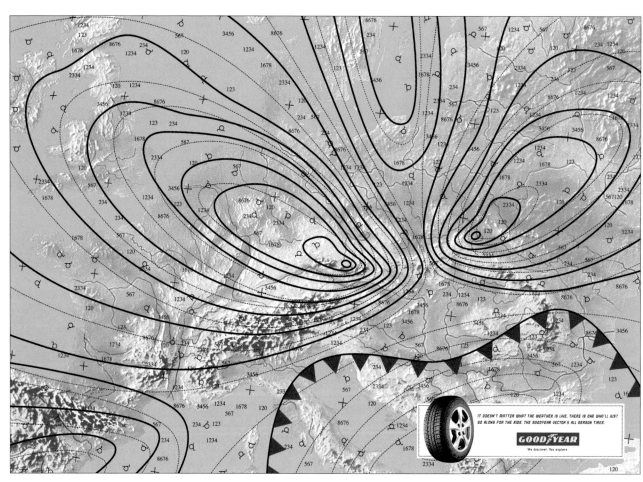

IT DOESN'T MATTER WHAT THE WEATHER IS LIKE. THERE IS ONE WHO'LL JUST
GO ALONG FOR THE RIDE. THE GOODYEAR VECTOR 5 ALL SEASON TIRES.

GOOD YEAR
We discover. You explore.

224 **Automotive & Accessories**

Agency:	TBWA\Istanbul	Agency:	Leagas Delaney,	
Creative Director:	Derya Tambay		Hamburg	
Copywriter:	Bulent Ilterberk	Creative Director:	Mo Whiteman	
Art Director:	Guven Haktanir	Copywriter:	Nils Busche	
Illustrator:	Erol Gunes	Art Director:	Kristina Erdmann	
Client:	Michelin Tyres	Client:	Goodyear Tyres	

Agency:	.start, Munich	Agency:	TBWA\Germany, Berlin	Whatever goes wrong it won't
Creative Directors:	Stefan Hempel	Creative Directors:	Wolfgang Bahle	be the Primastar.
	Peter Hirrlinger		Kai Roeffen	
	Andreas Klemp	Copywriter:	Donald Tursman	
Copywriter:	Doris Haider	Art Director:	Rainer Schmidt	
Art Director:	Stephanie Rauch	Photographer:	Andy Green	
Client:	Landuris Trucks	Illustrator:	Klaus Knuth	
		Client:	Nissan Primastar	

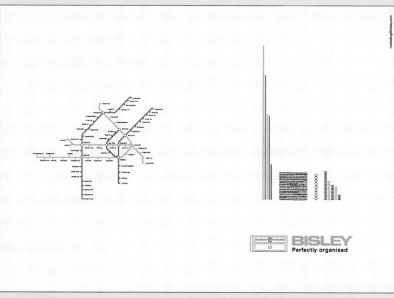

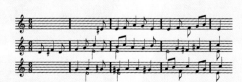

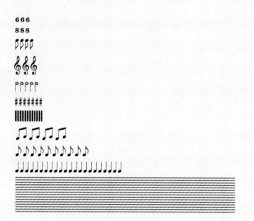

Agency:	Kolle Rebbe, Hamburg
Creative Directors:	Sebastian Hardieck
	Christoph Everke
Copywriter:	Klaus Huber
Art Director:	James cè Cruickshank
Illustrators:	James cè Cruickshank
	Andreas Krallmann
Client:	Bisley Office Furnishings

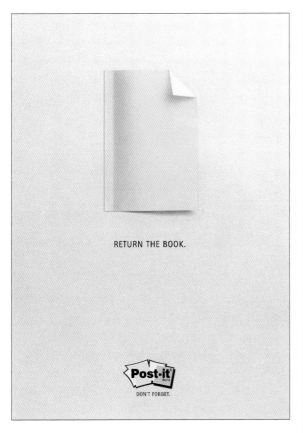

RETURN THE BOOK.

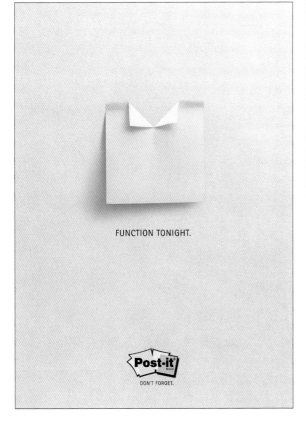

FUNCTION TONIGHT.

PICK UP THE LAUNDRY.

Agency:	Team/Young & Rubicam, Dubai
Creative Director:	Sam Ahmed
Copywriter:	Gordon Ray
Art Director:	Komal Bedi Sohal
Photographer:	Suresh Subramanium
Illustrator:	Rajeev Sangdhore
Client:	Post-it Notes

see what's next   EIZO high-end-monitors

Agency:	Euro RSCG MRT, Lisbon	A series of posters rolled up and down
Creative Director:	Jorge Teixeira	mimicking the action of a lift in order to
Copywriter:	Mário Nascimento	promote Thyssen elevators.
Art Director:	Paulo Ramalho	
Photographer:	Chico Aragão	
Client:	Thyssen Elevators	

Agency:	Butter, Düsseldorf
Creative Directors:	Frank Offermanns
	Frank Stauss
Copywriters:	Simone Butzbach
	Simone Schroeder
Art Directors:	Elisabeth Feldhaus
	Heinke Haberland
	Nadine Schlichte
	Katharina Voss
Photographer:	Mareike Foecking
Client:	Eizo Monitors

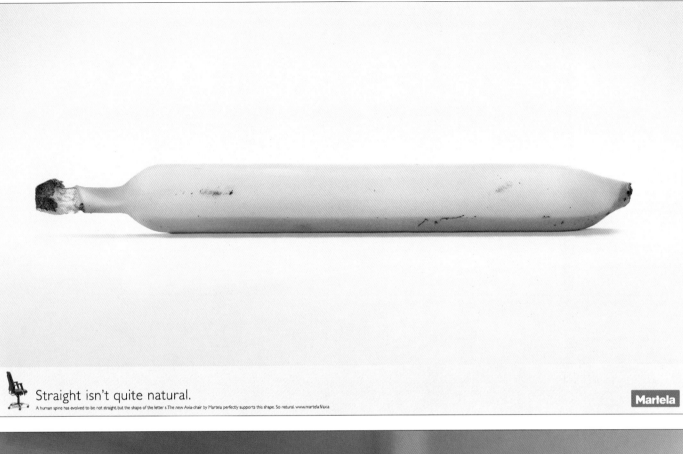

Straight isn't quite natural.
A human spine has evolved to be not straight, but the shape of the letter s. The new Axia-chair by Martela perfectly supports this shape. So natural. www.martela.fi/axia

Martela

Straight isn't quite natural.
A human spine has evolved to be not straight, but the shape of the letter s. The new Axia-chair by Martela perfectly supports this shape. So natural. www.martela.fi/axia

Martela

Agencies:	TBWA\PHS, Helsinki
	Tequila\PHS, Helsinki
Creative Directors:	Markku Ronkko
	Mika Wist
Copywriter:	Markku Ronkko
Art Director:	Mika Wist
Photographer:	Oskari Hellman
Client:	Martela Office Chairs

Imagine. You're sitting in a cinema, wa

no espano, no franzo aber you verstand. Habe you un

Holy merde!
You es une bloody
genio!

Le primero
multiculti
fuckin'grande

Eurolingo-hero!

Europe is damn exciting,
you better understand it!

inlingua
language schools

Agency:	Kolle Rebbe, Hamburg
Creative Directors:	Judith Stoletzky
	Patricia Wetzel
Copywriter:	Stefan Wübbe
Art Director:	Kay-Owe Tiedemann
Production:	Die Scheinfirma
Directors:	Christian Reimann
	Moritz Glaesle
Producers:	Henning Stamm
	Ana López
Client:	Inlingua Language School,
	"Eurolingo"

"Imagine, you're sitting in a cinema watching une commercial spot, when suddenly the texto begins to change in un foreign lingua. What la hell is that, you wonder?" This ad marks the debut of Eurolingo, a blend of nine foreign languages. Using easily recognisable words, it demonstrates that learning a foreign language is perhaps not as hard as it sounds. "You, who have permanente had school-problemos, rapido comprend esta lingua." Europe is damn exciting – you better under stand it. Inlingua Language School can help.

 **Business Services** 231

Agency:	LG&F, Brussels
Creative Director:	Christophe Ghewy
Copywriter:	Philip Vandenberghe
Art Director:	Iwein Vandevyver
Photographer:	Kris Van Beek
Client:	AXA Belgium Recruitment

SORRY
JOE PYTKA

EXCUSE US
TONY KAYE

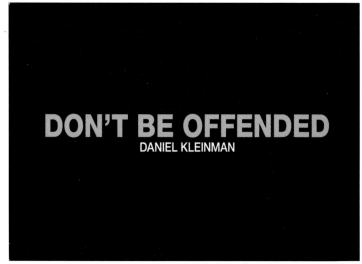

DON'T BE OFFENDED
DANIEL KLEINMAN

NO HARD FEELINGS
TRACKTOR

WE DIDN'T MEAN IT
FRANK BUDGEN

IT'S NOT PERSONAL
ALLEN COULTER

DON'T GET UPSET
PAUL GAY

IT'S JUST THAT...

RADIO ADVERTISING
WORKS.

DEAR VIEWERS, DUE TO THE RECESSION, WE COU...

WE COULD ONLY AFFORD TO RUN THE STORYBOARD.

...AR VIEWERS, DUE TO THE RECESSION, WE COULD ONLY AFFORD

PLEASE FORGIVE US.

NOW, MORE THAN EVER, IT'S BETTER

...OW, MORE THAN EVER, IT'S BETTER TO MAKE A RADIO CAMPAIGN...

RADIO ADVERTISING
WORKS.

---

232   **Business Services**

<table>
<tr><td>Agency:</td><td>Shalmor Avnon
Amichay/Y&R, Tel Aviv</td></tr>
<tr><td>Creative Directors:</td><td>Gideon Amichay
Asi Shavit</td></tr>
<tr><td>Copywriters:</td><td>Dudy Hevron
Yair Weiss</td></tr>
<tr><td>Production:</td><td>Ishay Hadas Productions</td></tr>
<tr><td>Director:</td><td>Gideon Amichay</td></tr>
<tr><td>Producers:</td><td>Ishay Hadas
Shira Robas</td></tr>
<tr><td>Client:</td><td>Israel Radio,
"Directors" & "Storyboard"</td></tr>
</table>

Who is apologising to all these famous commercials directors? "Sorry, Joe Pytka. Excuse us, Tony Kaye. No hard feelings, Traktor. We didn't mean it, Frank Budgen. Don't be offended, Daniel Kleinman..." and so on. The final line says it all: "It's just that radio advertising works." Those who don't believe it should ask Israel Radio.

Israel Radio is back again, this time teasing viewers by showing only the storyboard of an ad, "due to the recession". The caption explains: "Now, more than ever, it's better to make a radio campaign. Radio advertising works."

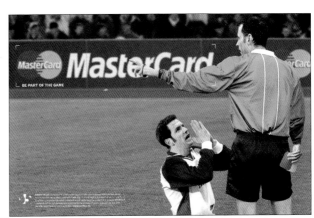

Agency:	Nordpol+ Hamburg Agentur für Kommunikation, Hamburg
Creative Director:	Lars Rühmann
Copywriter:	Ingmar Bartels
Art Directors:	Kristoffer Heilemann
	Mark Stehle
	Gunther Schreiber
	Bertrand Kirschenhofer
Client:	Sportfive Sportsmarketing

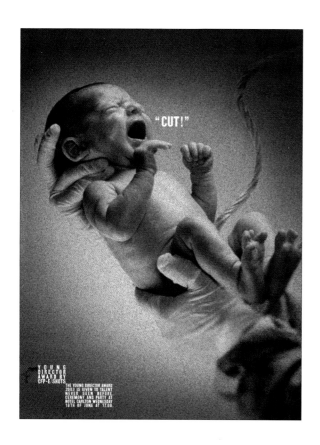

Agency:	TBWA\PHS, Helsinki		**Agency:**	Lowe, Dubai
Creative Directors:	Mira Leppanen		**Creative Director:**	Nirmal Diwadkar
	Zoubida Benkhellat		**Copywriter:**	Manoj Ammanath
Copywriter:	Mira Leppanen		**Art Director:**	Manish Sampat
Art Director:	Zoubida Benkhellat		**Photographer:**	Manish Sampat
Photographer:	Stephen Marks		**Client:**	MBR, Recruitment Site
Client:	CFPE & Shots,			
	Young Director Award			

Agency:	Chemistry, Dublin	Agency:	Leo Burnett & Target,
Creative Director:	Mike Garner		Bucharest
Copywriter:	Orla Doherty	Creative Director:	Bogdan Naumovici
Art Director:	Mike Garner	Copywriter:	Emilian Arsenoaiei
Illustrator:	Ray Fadden	Art Director:	Tudor Cuciuc
Client:	Recruit Ireland,	Client:	Golden Pages,
	Recruitment Site		Business Listings

DON'T LET SWISS ART & DESIGN DIE.
Vote NO to the elimination of the introductory course at
the Zurich Institute of Art and Design. Support the petition at: www.hgkz.ch.

236   **Business Services**

Agency:	J. Walter Thompson, Lisbon
Creative Director:	João Espírito Santo
Copywriter:	Rui Soares
Art Director:	Pedro Magalhães
Production:	Bambú, Lisbon
Director:	Henrique Serra
Producers:	Catarina Matos e Silva
	Jaime Graça
Client:	Potuguese Creative Club, "Pub"

In a dilapidated Portuguese bar, a group of elderly men are apparently about to start discussing football. "Santos – who do you think is gonna win this year?" asks the barman. "I think it's BBDO," states Santos. But his friends have other ideas. "You're crazy – for me it's Bates," says one, pausing in the middle of his game of dominos. "I'm not sure. TBWA or Euro," opines another. Everybody likes good advertising. The 5th Portuguese Creative Club Festival is coming soon…

Agency:	Publicis, Zürich
Creative Director:	Markus Gut
Copywriter:	Tom Zurcher
Art Directors:	Flavio Meroni
	Nadine Geissbuehler
Photographer:	Herzoggeissler
Client:	HGKZ, Zürich Institute for Design & Art

Agency:	DDB, Milan	**Agency:**	Grabarz & Partner, Hamburg
Creative Directors:	Giuseppe Mastromatteo	**Creative Directors:**	Ralf Heuel
	Stefano Tumiatti		Dirk Siebenhaar
Copywriter:	Stefano Tumiatti	**Copywriter:**	Sonja Wigbels
Art Director:	Giuseppe Mastromatteo	**Art Director:**	Ingo Otte
Photographer:	Fulvio Bonavia	**Photographer:**	Patrice Lange
Client:	New Partners,	**Client:**	Wieners & Wieners,
	Film Production Company		Proof-Reading Agency

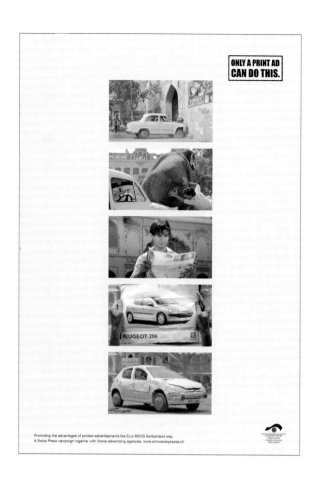

Business Services

Agency:	Euro RSCG, Zürich	Agency:	McCann-Erickson, Prague
Creative Directors:	Jürg Aemmer	Creative Director:	Philip Pec
	Frank Bodin	Copywriter:	Philip Pec
Art Director:	Miro Beck	Art Director:	Anna Mala
Client:	Swiss Press	Photographer:	Marek Kucera
	Association	Client:	Caledonian
			Language School

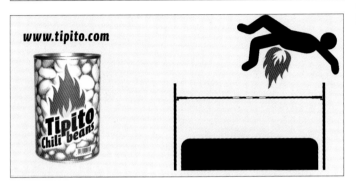

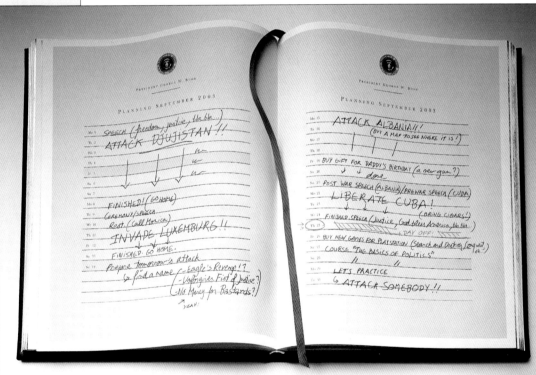

Agency:	Bob, Helsinki	The Tipito chili bean campain was created
Art Director:	Jon Granström	for an imaginary client to demonstrate the
Copywriter:	Timo Iivari	effectiveness of outdoor media. It led to the
Ilustrator:	Jaakko Veijola	creation of the chili bean olympics website,
Client:	JC Decaux,	showing recipies and a link to JC Decaux's
	Outdoor Media	site. The campain created a high level of

consumer interest and resulted in increased use of outdoor media.

Agency:	Publicis, Brussels	Each year this group of Belgian newspapers
Creative Director:	Marco Calant	organises the Full Page party where an award
Copywriter:	Catherine Quadens	is given for the best ad to appear in one of their
Art Director:	Jean-Marc Wachsmann	titles. In 2003 the party was planned in May,
Photographer:	Jean-François de Witte	but had to be postponed because of the war in
Client:	Full Page Press Group,	Iraq. The party was rescheduled for September
	Party Invitation	25th, a date that seemed to be risk-free according

to Bush's agenda.

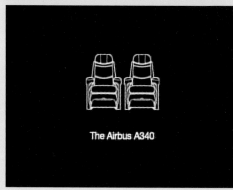

240 **Industrial & Agricultural Equipment**

Agency:	Euro RSCG C&O, Paris	Well known partnerships can be spoiled by the
Creative Directors:	Olivier Moulierac	addition of an unwelcome third party. Who likes the
	Jérôme Galinha	sound of Adam & Peter & Eve? Or Anthony & Ian &
Copywriter:	Chermine Assadian	Cleopatra? Or even Barbie & Steve & Ken? Because
Art Director:	Bruno Banaszuk	it understands that happy couples don't like to be
Production:	Cake Films	joined by an unknown stranger, the Airbus A340 has
Client:	Airbus A340, "Couples"	no middle seats in business class.

Developed from an age old recipe
Refined through generations
Purified and cooled
Then filled with lager

If you'd like packaging to reflect the quality of
your brand, nothing but glass will do.
For more information visit www.glasspac.com

GLΛSSPAC
BRANDS SHINE IN GLASS

Made with only natural ingredients
Blended to perfection
Roasted for 17 hours
Then filled with coffee.

GLΛSSPAC If you'd like packaging to reflect the quality of your brand, nothing
BRANDS SHINE IN GLASS but glass will do. For more information visit www.glasspac.com

Collected from a natural source.
Infused with minerals.
Purified twice.
Then filled with water.

GLΛSSPAC If you'd like packaging to reflect the purity of your brand, nothing but
BRANDS SHINE IN GLASS glass will do. To find out how it can work for you visit www.glasspac.com

 Industrial & Agricultural Equipment **241**

Agency:	Poulter Partners, Leeds
Creative Directors:	Paul Moran
	Graham Doran
Copywriters:	Andrea Panicca
	Claire Grainger
Art Director:	Paul Moran
Photographer:	Tim Morris
Client:	British Glass,
	Glasspac Packaging

Release the flavour!

A natural drive

242　**Industrial & Agricultural Equipment**

Agency:	BDDP & Fils, Paris	**Agency:**	Ehrenstråhle & Co. BBDO, Stockholm
Creative Director:	Olivier Altmann	**Creative Director:**	Per Ehrenstråhle
Copywriter:	Vincent Pedrocchi	**Copywriter:**	Per Ehrenstråhle
Art Director:	Xavier Beauregard	**Art Director:**	Petter Paulin
Photographer:	Vincent Dixon	**Photographer:**	Mikael Fjellström
Client:	Kubota Agricultural Materials	**Client:**	Alfa Laval Processing Equipment

www.silicone-resin-paints.co.uk

Agency:	Heimat, Berlin		**Agency:**	Wächter & Wächter
Creative Directors:	Guido Heffels			Worldwide Partners,
	Jürgen Vossen			Munich
Copywriter:	Thoams Winkler		**Creative Director:**	Ulrich Schmitz
Art Director:	Tim Schneider		**Copywriter:**	Wiltrude Neuber
Production:	Markenfilm, Wedel		**Art Directors:**	Bärbel Biwald
Director:	Peluca			Florian v. Kurnatowski
Producer:	Ruth Jansen		**Photographer:**	Corinna Holthusen
Client:	Hornbach,		**Client:**	Wacker Silicone
	"Old House"			Resin Paints

An elderly man lies gravely ill in bed, his life flashing before him. But wait – what was that business with the attic? Suddenly he bounds out of bed, walks to the shed, and fetches his tools. A few hours later, he has transformed the attic into a spare room. Satisfied, he gets back into bed, now able to die happy. Then he notices a stain on the ceiling. He sits up. There's always a job to be done. And Hornbach Home Improvement Stores can help.

In case of a hurricane
a badly fixed roof can cost you your life

Vous construisez, c'est pour longtemps. Or le risque que le toit de votre maison subisse des tempêtes
tropicales voire même un cyclone majeur reste très important. Et si vous ne respectez pas les Règles Antilles
tant pour le choix des matériaux que pour leur mise en œuvre, les conséquences pourraient être dramatiques.
Pour éviter cela, outre ses tôles garanties 10 ans, Biométal (usine du Robert et dans le réseau
partenaire) met à votre disposition les fixations ad-hoc ainsi que les conseils de professionnels pour que
votre toit soit monté dans les Règles de l'Art.

244 **Industrial & Agricultural Equipment**

Agency:	Cohiba, Lamentin - Martinique	Agency:	McCann, Malmö
Creative Director:	Alex Rolet	Creative Director:	Magnus Ingerstedt
Copywriter:	Alex Rolet	Copywriter:	Gunnar Petersson
Art Director:	Patrick Bertrand	Art Director:	Arne Wikström
Photographer:	Pascal Habousha	Photographer:	Carl Bengtsson
Client:	Biometal Corrugated Iron Roofs	Client:	Effekt

Agency:	LG&F, Brussels
Creative Director:	Christophe Ghewy
Copywriters:	Joeri Van Den Broeck
	Tim Driesen
Art Directors:	Joeri Van Den Broeck
	Tim Driesen
Photographer:	Frank Uyttenhove
Client:	Lamborghini Tractors

Agency:	Wieden + Kennedy, Amsterdam
Creative Director:	Paul Shearer
Copywriter:	Joe Ventura
Art Director:	Paul Shearer
Production:	Outsider, London
Director:	Dom & Nic
Producer:	Jasmine Kimera
Client:	Nike Europe, "Stream"

Spotting a stream of water running in the gutter outside his home, a curious jogger decides to follow it. His quest becomes an obsession as he pursues the stream down steps, through the city, and even down a manhole cover into the sewers. Emerging into a junkyard, he follows the stream into the woods, where it ends at a high waterfall. Pausing, he is accidentally knocked into the pool by an equally obsessed jogger – who in turn is pushed in by the national Kenyan running team. Enjoy the weather, with Nike sports gear.

▲ **Clothing & Fabrics** 247

Agency:	Storåkers McCann, Stockholm
Creative Director:	Martin Marklund
Copywriter:	Edwin von Werder
Art Directors:	Peter Eriksson
	Mattias Falk
Photographer:	Anti Wendel
Client:	Lee Jeans

ideal cityscape.
lover, of course.
I detest...

Supercool.
Before I met Zazie I was a fool.

She could not resist.

french connection
vive le fcuk!

248   Clothing & Fabrics

Agency:	TBWA\London
Creative Director:	Trevor Beattie
Copywriter:	Trevor Beattie
Art Director:	Bil Bungay
Production:	Paul Weiland Film Co.
Director:	Toby MacDonald
Producers:	Mary Francis
	Diane Croll
Client:	French Connection UK,
	"Vive le fcuk"

The hero of this tongue-in-chic homage to French New Wave cinema sees himself as an actor in the Belmondo mould (except when his mum rings, of course). Indeed, he dresses exactly like the main character from Godard's Breathless – and his girlfriend looks like she's stepped straight out of the film too. Together, they re-enact scenes of implacable Parisian coolness. Their dashing French Connection UK clothes undoubtedly help. "Vive le fcuk."

Agency:	TBWA\London
Creative Director:	Trevor Beattie
Copywriter:	Trevor Beattie
Art Director:	Bil Bungay
Client:	French Connection UK

THE NEW JERSEY

AND HOW TO WEAR IT

AVAILABLE NOW

Tested by extreme alpinists: the new Hooded Down Jacket made of white goose down with fitted hood against heat loss. To find out more, visit www.mammut.ch

STUFF FOR THE TOUGH.

Agency:	TBWA\Germany, Berlin	Agency:	Spillmann/Felser/
Creative Directors:	Kurt-Georg Dieckert		Leo Burnett, Zürich
	Stefan Schmidt	Creative Director:	Martin Spillmann
Copywriter:	Helge Bloeck	Copywriter:	Peter Brönnimann
Art Director:	Boris Schwiedrzik	Art Director:	Dana Wirz
Photographer:	Johann Sebastian Hanel	Client:	Mammut
Client:	Adidas Football Shirts		Outdoor Clothes

250   **Clothing & Fabrics**

Agency:	Abbott Mead Vickers BBDO, London
Creative Directors:	Nick Worthington
	Paul Brazier
Copywriter:	Nick Worthington
Art Director:	Paul Brazier
Production:	Harry Nash Films
Director:	Fredrik Bond
Producers:	Helen Williams
	Carol Powell
Client:	Wrangler Clothing, "Apartment" & "Cafe"

Dramatic scenes in a London apartment, as a young couple fight in slow motion. Don't worry – they're just pretending! Another man enters the room, carrying some shopping. Before he can react, the woman mimes the act of drawing back a bow and firing an arrow into his chest. He staggers into the hallway and "dies" in a splendid display of overacting. In the second spot, the same characters and their friends mime a slow-motion shootout in a greasy café. Wrangler clothing – because there's a bit of the West in all of us.

Agency:	The Union Advertising Agency, Edinburgh	Getting caught showing the lads our 'special' video.
Creative Directors:	Andrew Lindsay	
	Simon Scott	Calling her mother a malicious meddling
Copywriter:	Michael Hart	bitch. Twice.
Art Director:	Stephen Drummond	
Photographer:	Scott Mitchell	Urinating in her wardrobe. Drunk.
Client:	Jane Davidson	
	Lingerie	Laughing for a full 17 minutes when she mentioned marriage.

Seven dwarfs don't make a Prince.

252 **Clothing & Fabrics**

Agency:	TBWA\PHS, Helsinki		Agency:	Marini Dotti e Associati, Milan
Creative Directors:	Mira Leppanen			
	Zoubida Benkhellat		Creative Director:	Lorenzo Marini
Copywriter:	Mira Leppanen		Copywriter:	Elisa Maino
Art Director:	Zoubida Benkhellat		Art Director:	Lorenzo Marini
Illustrator:	Tommi Vallisto		Photographer:	Marco Lambiaghi
Client:	Nanso Clothing		Client:	Primizia Lingerie

enjoy the weather

- We won't tolerate this sort of behaviour in our carpark...

- Come on...Get a move on!
- I've just got this one sinner left.

- What are you doing...
You're not giving me a...

True professionals also use our workwear

- Exactly.

FRISTADS®

works everywhere

- That was lucky.

Agency:	Wieden + Kennedy, Amsterdam	A jogger is resting in a park when a man runs past her, splashing into a puddle and soaking her with muddy water. He holds up an apologetic hand, but she wants revenge. Catching up, she splashes into a puddle beside him. This sparks off a race that involves trying to get each other as wet as possible. Entering the city, they sprint towards a huge flood of water at a road junction. But just as they reach it, a coach hurtles past, soaking them both. Inside the coach are a host of football stars, including Sir Alex Ferguson and Rio Ferdinand. Enjoy the weather, with Nike.
Creative Director:	Paul Shearer	
Copywriters:	Paul Shearer	
	Carlo Cavallone	
Art Director:	Rachid Ahouyek	
Production:	Outsider, London	
Director:	Dom & Nic	
Producer:	Jasmine Kimera	
Client:	Nike "Puddles"	

Agency:	ANR.BBDO, Gothenberg	An over-zealous traffic warden is sticking fines on the windscreens of illegally parked cars. His colleague is irritated: "Get a move on!" "I've only got one sinner left," the perfectionist replies. He slaps a ticket on their own vehicle. His colleague is astonished: "What are you doing?" "Don't argue – you've been parked there for five minutes!" Getting into the car, the driver examines the fine. "Phew! You've only fined me half the amount. We're not really supposed to stop here at all." True professionals also use Fristads workwear.
Copywriter:	Hakan Larsson	
Art Director:	Hans-Erik Andreasson	
Production:	Efti	
Director:	Felix Herngren	
Producer:	Cornelia Opitz	
Client:	Fristads Workwear, "Traffic Warden"	

Agency:	Lowe & Partners, Madrid	Agency:	.start, Munich
Creative Director:	Luis López De Ochoa	Creative Directors:	Judith Homoki
Copywriter:	Idoia González		Lars Wohlnick
Art Director:	Rubén Señor	Copywriter:	Birgit Schuster
Photographer:	Santiago Esteban	Art Director:	Birgit Schuster
Client:	Mothercare	Photographer:	Kerstin Jacobsen
		Client:	Blush Dessous
			Lingerie Store

Great fashion always comes back.

SECOND HAND
DESIGNER FASHION
in bocca al lupo, Vienna

Clothing & Fabrics   **255**

Agency:	Demner, Merlicek & Bergmann, Vienna
Creative Director:	Joachim Glawion
Copywriters:	Florian Ludwig
	Claus Gigler
Art Director:	Francesco Bestagno
Photographer:	Staudinger & Franke
Client:	In Bocca Al Lupo, Second-Hand Designer Fashion

Agency:	Dimensión, San Sebastien
Creative Director:	Guillermo Viglione
Copywriters:	Guillermo Viglione
	Javier Vincente
	Mikel Aguado
Art Directors:	Iñigo Beldarrain
	Mikel Uribetxeberria
Production:	La Gloria, Barcelona
Director:	Mikel Alcarria
Client:	Linea Athletic Club Sportswear, "Streaker"

There's nothing too out of the ordinary about this televised soccer match. A player takes a dive to provoke a penalty and the commentators are as predictable as ever ("Very harsh decision – I think the referee's lost control there"). The only difference is that everyone is naked. The game is interrupted when a professional "streaker" appears, fully clad in new Athletic Club sportswear. As the commentators chuckle at his impudence, naked policemen escort him off the pitch.

Agency:	Wieden + Kennedy, Amsterdam	A basketball match is interrupted when
Creative Directors:	Carlos Bayala	the musician in the commentators' box
	Paul Shearer	stops playing his cheesy keyboard riff.
Copywriter:	Carlo Cavallone	This is the cue for a game of musical
Art Director:	Alvaro Satomayor	chairs on a grand scale, in which even
Production:	Traktor, Santa Monica, CA	the players are obliged to find a seat.
Director:	Ulf Johansson	The game ends up in a face-off between
Producers:	Philippa Smith	a young spectator – who has made the
	Tieneke Pavesic	mistake of going to the snack bar – and
	Annabelle Meyer	a player. Together they race towards the
Client:	Nike Europe,	last available seat, which the spectator
	"Musical Chairs"	grabs with only a millisecond to spare.

HITS THIS HARD USUALLY INVOLVE CRASH TEST DUMMIES.

adidas
FOREVER SPORT

IF YOU DON'T GO IN HARD
IT'S NOT A TACKLE, IT'S AN INSULT.

adidas
FOREVER SPORT

HE'S THE SPEED. YOU'RE THE BUMP.

adidas
FOREVER SPORT

THIS CYCLONE HAS TWO EYES.

adidas
FOREVER SPORT

Agency:	180 Amsterdam,
Executive CD:	Peter McHugh
Creative Director:	Andy Fackrell
Copywriters:	Peter McHugh
	Giles Montgomery
	Brad Roseberry
Art Director:	Stuart Brown
Client:	Adidas Rugby
	World Cup 2003

Agency:	Wieden + Kennedy, Amsterdam	
Creative Director:	Paul Shearer	
Copywriter:	Tim Wolfe	
Art Director:	Frank Hahn	
Production:	HSI Productions, Culver City, CA	
Directors:	Paul Hunter	
	John Taft	
Producers:	Kerstin Emhoff	
	Tony Stearns	
Client:	Nike, "Frisbee", "Football" & "Hoops"	

This series of Nike commercials introduces an animated "stickman" whose tricks are far from child's play. In each of the three spots, the stickman demonstrates that he is cooler, faster and smarter than the world's greatest freestyle frisbee, football and basketball players. At the end of his duel with the basketball dudes, he has even gained a female admirer: "That's right stickman! Do it, baby!"

Footwear & Personal Accessories

Footwear & Personal Accessories   **259**

Agency:	Wieden + Kennedy, Portland	A football game is interrupted by a naked "streaker". Naked, that is, except for his Nike Shox running shoes. These enable him to outrun the police and take a couple of kicks at the ball. Even the commentator is impressed by his speed: "And he's off – like a bull with gas."
Creative Director:	Hal Curtis	
Copywriter:	Jonathan Cude	
Art Director:	Matt Stein	
Production:	Gorgeous Enterprises, London	
Director:	Frank Budgen	
Producers:	Paul Rothwell Jennifer Smieja	
Client:	Nike Shox, "Streaker"	

Agency:	Wieden + Kennedy, Portland	On the New York subway, a girl in Nike Shox running shoes sits opposite a man eating a pretzel. The sight inspires her, and as the doors open she rockets out of the carriage and into the street. Hurtling through the city, she slaps some coins on a pretzel vendor's stand and grabs one of the snacks. Then she runs into Bleecker Street station and rejoins the subway train – getting back her old seat. The man who was sitting opposite her at the earlier station looks surprised, especially when she offers him a tissue to wipe mustard off his lip.
Creative Directors:	Hal Curtis Mike Byrne	
Copywriter:	Jonathan Cude	
Art Director:	Matt Stein	
Production:	Gorgeous Enterprises, London	
Director:	Tom Carty	
Producers:	Mary Ann Marino Thomas Harvey	
Client:	Nike Shox, "Pretzel"	

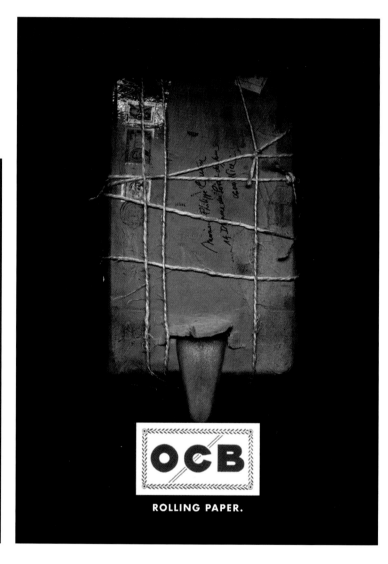

260   **Footwear & Personal Accessories**

Agency:	Bob, Helsinki	**Agency:**	Publicis Conseil, Paris
Copywriters:	Kari Eilola	**Creative Directors:**	Antoine Barthuel
	Timo Silvennoinen		Daniel Fohr
Art Director:	Anu Igoni	**Copywriter:**	Mario Eymieux
Photographer:	Marjo Tokkari	**Art Director:**	Patrice Letarnec
Client:	Seppälä	**Photographer:**	Franck Goldbronn
	Fashion Retailer	**Client:**	OCB Rolling Papers

Agency:	D'Adda, Lorenzini, Vigorelli BBDO, Milan
Creative Director:	Gianpietro Vigorelli
Copywriter:	Vicky Gitto
Art Directors:	Gianpietro Vigorelli
	Vincenzo Gasbarro
Photographer:	Carina Taira
Client:	Francesco Biasia
	Sacks & Bags

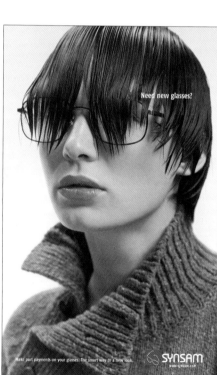

Agency:	Devarrieuxvillaret, Paris		**Agency:**	Marrakech, Stockholm
Copywriter:	Pierre-Dominique Burgaud		**Creative Director:**	Petrus Dahlin
Art Director:	Stéphane Richard		**Copywriter:**	Daniel Holmgren
Photographer:	Pascal Richon		**Art Director:**	Patrik Dunard
Client:	Miki Eyewear		**Photographer:**	Jörgen Brennicke
			Client:	Synsam Eyewear

Agency:	BETC Euro RSCG, Paris	Agency:	Aimaq Rapp Stolle, Berlin
Creative Director:	Rémi Babinet	Creative Director:	André Aimaq
Copywriter:	Eric Niesseron	Copywriter:	Olivier Frank
Art Director:	Safia Bouyahia	Art Director:	Tim Belser
Photographers:	Mert Alas	Photographer:	Heribert Schindler
	Marcus Piggott	Client:	Nike Zoom LJ
Client:	Louis Vuitton		Sport Shoes

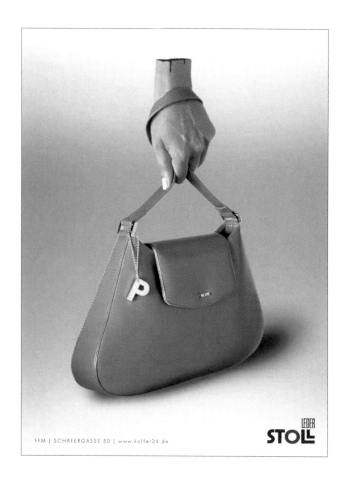

Footwear & Personal Accessories

Agency:	McCann-Erickson, Frankfurt	**Agency:**	HSCG, Amsterdam
Creative Director:	Erich Reuter	**Creative Director:**	Cas Sluiter
Copywriter:	Eva Schrempf	**Copywriter:**	Dick Schaafsma
Art Director:	Sonja Scheffczyk	**Art Director:**	Cas Sluiter
Photographer:	Jean-Pascal Günther	**Photographer:**	Peter Casell
Client:	Leder Stoll,	**Client:**	Ziengs Shoe Stores
	Leather Goods & Luggage		

The Dutch expression "Ik sta op..." means both "I am standing on..." and "I insist upon..."

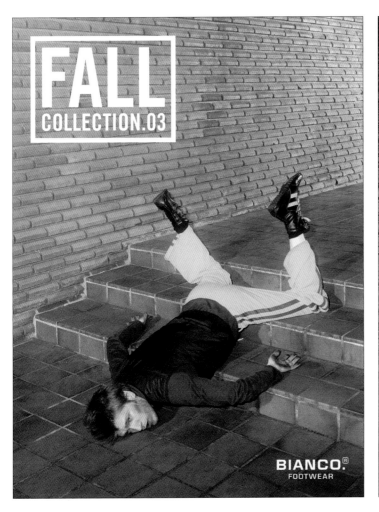

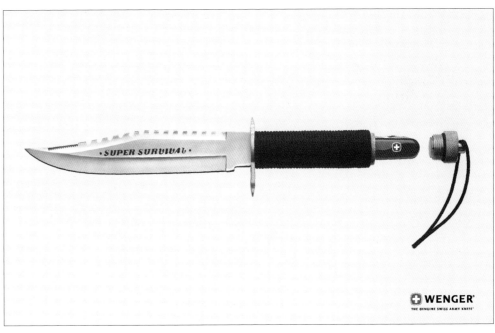

Agency:	&Co, Copenhagen	Agency:	LDV/Red Cell, Antwerp
Creative Directors:	Thomas Hoffmann	**Creative Directors:**	Werner Van Reck
	Robert Cerkez		Peter Aerts
Copywriter:	Kristel Krøier	**Copywriter:**	Carsten Van Berkel
Art Director:	Thomas Hoffmann	**Art Director:**	Fabian Sapthu
Photographer:	Casper Sejersen	**Photographer:**	Greg Smolders
Client:	Bianco Footwear	**Client:**	Wenger
			Swiss Army Knife

Read a bestseller every day.

The Daily Telegraph
Britain's best-selling daily broadsheet

telegraph.co.uk

Agency:	Clemmow Hornby Inge, London	We're at a birthday party, and a man is unwrapping a present. He reacts as if
Creative Director:	Charles Inge	it's a book by his favourite author: "I've
Copywriter:	Brian Turner	read all the others, but not this one!"
Art Director:	Micky Tudor	His friend says: "If you liked the others,
Production:	Outsider	you'll love this." In fact the present is a
Director:	David Lodge	copy of The Daily Telegraph, Britain's
Producers:	Garfield Kempton	best selling broadsheet newspaper.
	Anthony Falco	Read a bestseller, every day.
Client:	The Daily Telegraph, "Present"	

These three people can't stop.
These three people are exhausted.
These three people are running for three different reasons.

Behind every news story, there's a journalist.

TVE NEWS SERVICE.
Special correspondents all over the world.
More than 1,100 professionals.
17 reporters.
15 territorial centres.
2 production centres.
YOUR NEWS COMES FIRST.

These two people are exhausted.
These two people are not from here.
These two people have been at the same thing for days.
These two people aren't giving up.

Behind every news story, there's a journalist.

These three people haven't slept all night.
These three people are in a contaminated area.
These three people share the same fear.
These three people learned to stay right here.

Behind every news story, there's a journalist.

These five people share the same emotion.
These five people feel the same pain.
These five people share the same circumstance.
These five people are one.

Behind every news story, there's a journalist.

These two people don't share the same here.
These two people don't share the same tendencies.
These two people don't share the same madness.
These two people have the same freedom of expression.

Behind every news story, there's a journalist.

Media 267

Agency: FCB/Tapsa, Madrid
Creative Directors: Julian Zuazo
Aureli Arque
Iñaki Bendito
Copywriter: Tomas Ostiglia
Photographers: Luc Delahaye
James Nachtwey
Carlos Spottorno
David Higgs
Leonard Freed
Client: TVE News

Read a bestseller every day.

The Daily Telegraph
Britain's best-selling daily broadsheet

telegraph.co.uk

BEHIND EVERY STORY

BEHIND EVERY STORY
THERE'S A JOURNALIST

Agency:	Clemmow Hornby Inge, London	Liverpool soccer hero and TV sports commentator Alan Hansen is signing copies of his latest work at a bookstore. "I really liked it," says a fan, "couldn't put it down". It turns out that Hansen is signing copies of his column in The Daily Telegraph newspaper. Read a bestseller, every day.
Creative Director:	Charles Inge	
Copywriter:	Brian Turner	
Art Director:	Micky Tudor	
Production:	Outsider	
Director:	David Lodge	
Producers:	Garfield Kempton	
	Anthony Falco	
Client:	The Daily Telegraph, "Signing"	

Agency:	FCB/Tapsa, Madrid	In real news footage of a war zone, a man with a rifle zigzags desperately down a street, under heavy fire from a sniper. The voiceover says: "These two people are in hell. These two people are fighting for different causes. These two people are flirting with death. These two people may die." There is only one person on screen – the other is filming the scene. "Behind every story, there's a journalist."
Creative Directors:	Julian Zuazo	
	Aureli Arque	
	Iñaki Bendito	
Copywriter:	Tomas Ostiglia	
Producers:	Jesus Becedas	
	Francis Hernandez	
	Sergio Sanchez	
Client:	TVE News "Warrior"	

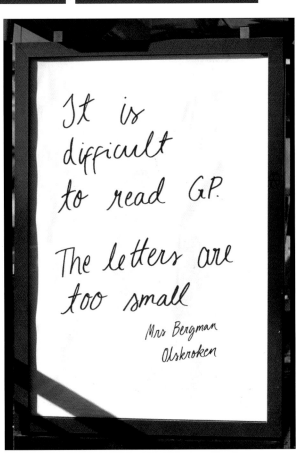

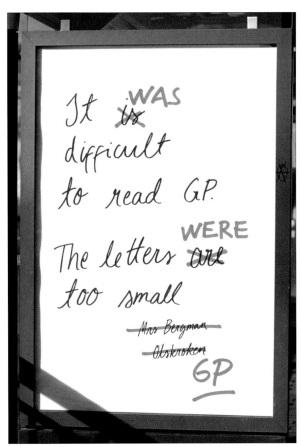

Agency:	Forsman & Bodenfors, Gothenburg	Days before the release of the redesigned Göteborgs-Posten, handwritten posters containing views about the newspaper were displayed all over the city. During the night before the release of the new style GP, all posters were changed.
Copywriters:	Martin Ringqvist Björn Engström	
Art Directors:	Staffan Forsman Staffan Håkanson	
Photographer:	Lennart Sjoberg	
Client:	Göteborgs-Posten Newspaper	

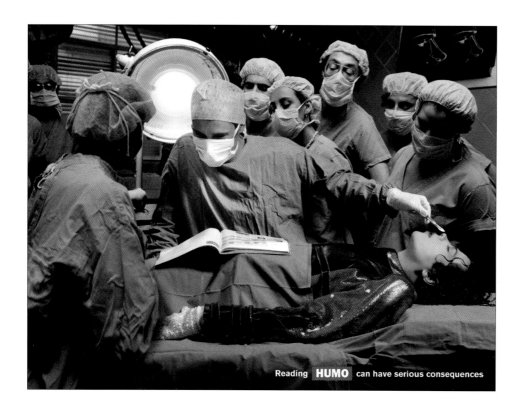

Reading **HUMO** can have serious consequences

UNDER CONSTRUCTION

Michael Jackson's Face | Sun 29th Sept 9pm

see five

Agency:	Duval Guillaume, Brussels	Agency:	TBWA\London
Creative Director:	Jens Mortier	Creative Director:	Trevor Beattie
Copywriter:	Peter Ampe	Copywriter:	Trevor Beattie
Art Director:	Katrien Bottez	Art Director:	Bil Bungay
Photographer:	Koen Demuynck	Client:	Five TV Channel, Michael Jackson Documentary
Client:	Humo Magazine		

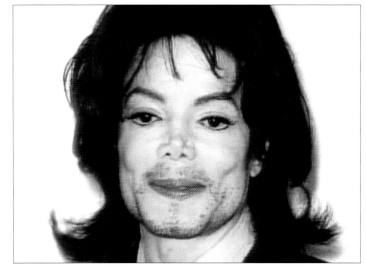

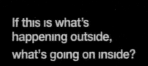

If this is what's
happening outside,
what's going on inside?

Michael Jackson's Face
Sun 29th Sept 9pm

see five

If this is what's happening outside, what's going on inside?

Michael Jackson's Face | Sun 29th Sept 9pm | **see five**

Agency:	TBWA\London
Creative Director:	Trevor Beattie
Copywriter:	Trevor Beattie
Art Director:	Bil Bungay
Production:	Buggg Films
Directors:	Stephen Ward
	Bil Bungay
Producers:	Trevor Beattie
	Lucy Wood
Client:	Five TV Channel,
	"Morphing Michael"

In a technically brilliant but chilling short film, we see Michael Jackson's face morph seamlessly over the years from that of an innocent child into the mask of the controversial figure he is today. The spot is a trailer for a TV documentary about the singer.

Agency:	TBWA\London
Creative Director:	Trevor Beattie
Copywriter:	Trevor Beattie
Art Director:	Bil Bungay
Client:	Five TV Channel,
	Michael Jackson
	Documentary

GERMANY'S HOTTEST TV CHANNEL.

www.beate-uhse.tv

GABRIEL GARCÍA MÁRQUEZ

Seventy years of solitude

OSCAR MONDADORI

30% off on all Mondadori books from March 8 to April 19.

MONDADORI

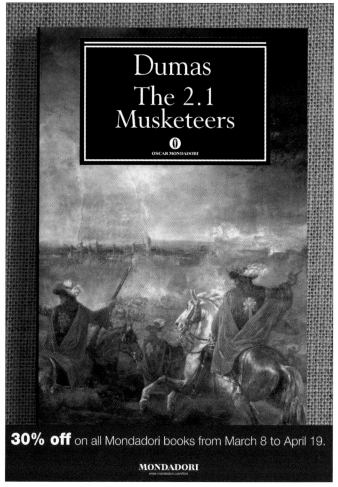

Dumas
The 2.1
Musketeers

OSCAR MONDADORI

30% off on all Mondadori books from March 8 to April 19.

MONDADORI

272   **Media**

Agency:	.start, Munich	Agency:	Saatchi & Saatchi, Italy
Creative Directors:	Judith Homoki	Creative Directors:	AgostinoToscana
	Lars Wohlnick		Guido Cornara
Copywriter:	Arndt Poguntke	Copywriter:	Giuseppe Mazza
Art Director:	Doreen Krause	Art Director:	Alessandro Stenco
Client:	Beate-Uhse	Photographer:	Enzo Monzino
	Erotic TV Channel	Client:	Mondadori Books

Agency:	TBWA\ El Alj & Partners, Casablanca	Reading abuse can cause personality disorders.
Creative Director:	Mehdi El Alj	
Copywriter:	Mehdi El Alj	
Art Director:	Sandrine Guinot	
Photographer:	Yougo Spiroski	
Client:	Version Homme Magazine	

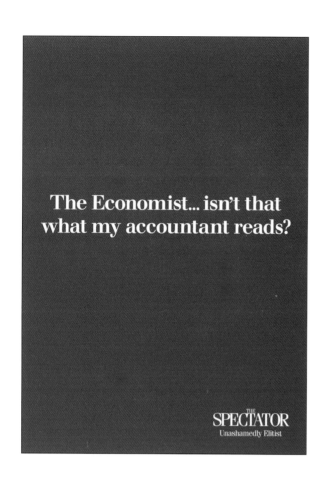

Agency:	Clemmow Hornby Inge, London	Agency:	Guye Benker Werbeagentur, Zürich
Creative Director:	Charles Inge	Creative Director:	André Benker
Copywriter:	Charles Inge	Copywriter:	Daniel Müller
Art Director:	Charles Inge	Art Director:	Barbara Strahm
Client:	The Spectator Magazine	Client:	Tages-Anzeiger

Does anyone ever ask for your opinion?
No, not you, that guy behind you.

What exactly is
the benefit of the doubt?

Ten signs you need to read The Economist.

10. Your last raise was in pounds, shillings and pence.

9. You thought the Hang Seng was a Chinese restaurant.

8. Your brilliantly balanced investment portfolio: lottery tickets and scratchcards.

7. The best thing that your head-hunter could offer you was something in pizza delivery.

6. You still think erudite is a kind of glue.

5. When your boss asked for your views on bonds, you told him Sean Connery was still your favourite.

4. When you asked for a company car they gave you a Hillman Avenger.

3. "Burkina Faso? Best centre half Real Madrid ever had."

2. You can't seem to find your name on the new phone list.

1. Anne Robinson feels sorry for you.

Agency:	Abbott Mead Vickers BBDO, London
Creative Directors:	Paul Belford
	Nigel Roberts
	Tim Riley
Copywriters:	Nigel Roberts
	Ben Kay
	Tim Riley
Art Directors:	Paul Belford
	Cam Blackley
Client:	The Economist Magazine

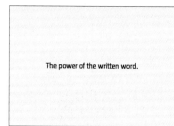

Agency:	Skandaali/Leo Burnett, Helsinki
Creative Directors:	Milla Monola Mirva Viitanen
Copywriter:	Markku Haapalehto
Art Director:	Minna Lavola
Production:	Elohopea
Director:	Olli Rönkä
Client:	Keltainen Pörssi Classified Ad Magazine, "Rich Friends"

A couple proudly show friends around their home. One of the guests admires their massive TV set. "Directly from Germany, €10,000," boasts the man of the house. The caption reveals the truth: "€900, from Finland." It's the same story with an antique chest of drawers, which the woman claims cost €15,000 from Sotheby's. "Truth: €300, from Finland." And the motorbike, supposedly bought in America for €30,000... Inside the house, the female guest says she met her boyfriend at the Opera. "Truth: personal ad." The spot is for a classified ads magazine.

Agency:	Kolle Rebbe, Hamburg
Creative Director:	Erik Hart
Copywriter:	Alexander Baron
Art Director:	Erik Hart
Production:	539090 Productions
Director:	Jürgen Nerger
Producers:	Claudia Geissler Henning Stamm Ana López
Client:	Die Tageszeitung Newspaper, "Come In"

Approaching a pair of double doors outside an office block, a man cunningly changes the stickers saying "pull" to "push". Then we watch what happens. A girl pushes the doors, but can't open them. A man arrives, and has the same problem. Soon a small group of people have gathered outside, furiously pushing the doors and looking angry at being kept outside the building. Nobody thinks of trying to pull. That's the power of the written word

Built for the kill.

NATIONAL GEOGRAPHIC CHANNEL

Now on National Geographic Channel.

SCHWEIZER ILLUSTRIERTE
CLOSER TO THE CELEBRITIES.

Agency:	Amsterdam Advertising, Amsterdam	Agency:	Wirz Werbung, Zürich
Creative Directors:	Darre van Dijk Piebe Piebenga	Creative Director:	Matthias Freuler
		Copywriter:	John Leuppi
Copywriter:	Piebe Piebenga	Art Director:	Rolf Kaelin
Art Director:	Darre van Dijk	Photographer:	Henrik Halvarsson
Illustrator:	Fulco Smit Roeters	Client:	Schweizer Illustrierte
Client:	National Geographic Channel		

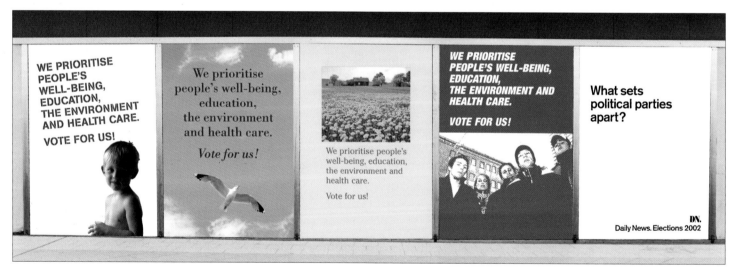

278   Media

Agency:	King, Stockholm	A Swedish sports reporter seems woefully
Production:	Acne Film	unqualified to interview Soren Akeby and Zoran
Client:	Sportsbladet,	Lukic, the coaches behind the country's biggest
	"Soren & Zoran"	football team, Djurgerdens IF. He asks: "OK –
	& "Christopher"	so a game is 90 minutes long?" The baffled

men confirm that he is correct. In the next spot, a reporter is poised to interview Christopher Andersson. He says: "Congratulations Christopher. You won tonight, it must feel great." "Yes, it feels wonderful," replies the football star. "Thanks," says the reporter, ending the interview. Want to know more about soccer? Turn to Sportsbladet.

Agency:	Lowe Brindfors, Stockholm
Creative Director:	Johan Nilsson
Copywriter:	Johan Nilsson
Art Director:	Patrick Waters
Client:	Dagens Nyheter Newspaper

The colour and typography of each of these posters are similar to those of real political parties in Sweden; the Social Democrats, the Conservatives, the Green party etc.

PREMIER LEAGUE has started. Only on CANAL+

PREMIER LEAGUE has started. Only on CANAL+

PREMIER LEAGUE has started. Only on CANAL+

Agency:	Storåkers McCann, Stockholm
Copywriter:	Emma Berg Raune
Art Director:	Håkan Liljemärker
Photographer:	Calle Stolz
Client:	Canal+ Pay TV

280	Media

Agency:	Grey Worldwide, Oslo	A family are watching TV together – and the parents look seriously bored by the raucous cartoons on the screen. Mum and dad give each other a certain glance, and then begin kissing in front of their children. Moving into a passionate embrace, they snog like teenagers. Disgusted, their kids leave the room. The parents go back to their seats and change the channel. Canal Digital – take control.
Copywriter:	Sverre Hytten	
Art Director:	Tom Nissen	
Production:	Kraftwerk Prod.	
Directors:	Ubbe Hovind	
	Steiner Borge	
Client:	Canal Digital, "Making Out"	

Agency:	Leo Burnett & Target, Bucharest	As an elderly couple drive along a country road in their ancient car, the woman finds a spare steering wheel under the passenger seat. Her husband has replaced it. For fun, she childishly plays with it. When they overtake a smart yellow car, its driver glances at her. The woman quickly twists her fake steering wheel as if she's going to slam him off the road. Fooled, the yellow car driver hits the brakes. Bored? Watching Antena 1 TV might be a better way of entertaining yourself.
Creative Director:	Bogdan Naumovici	
Production:	Abis	
Director:	Radu Muntean	
Producer:	Laura Georgescu-Baron	
Client:	Antena 1 TV Channel, "Steering Wheel"	

FEAST YOUR EYES.

Why go for second best?

Agency:	Fagan Reggio Del Bravo, Rome	Agency:	LG&F, Brussels
Creative Directors:	Paolo Del Bravo	Creative Director:	Christophe Ghewy
	Patrizio Marini	Copywriters:	Philip Vandenberghe
Copywriter:	Emanuele Madeddu		Eric Piette
Art Director:	Patrizio Marini	Art Directors:	Iwein Vandevyver
Photographer:	Mario Polidori		Benoit Hilson
Client:	Anna Fashion Magazine		Henry Scott
		Photographer:	Frank Uyttenhove
		Client:	Vacature Newspaper

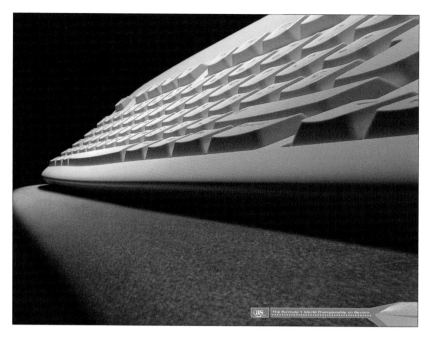

282 Media

Agency:	Umwelt Advertising, Copenhagen	Agency:	Ruiz Nicoli, Madrid
Client:	Information Newspaper	Creative Directors:	Paco Ruiz-Nicoli
			Nacho Esteire
		Copywriter:	Jose Luis Marrazzo
		Art Directors:	Cesar Lopez
			Chema Bercial
		Client:	AS Online Sports Magazine

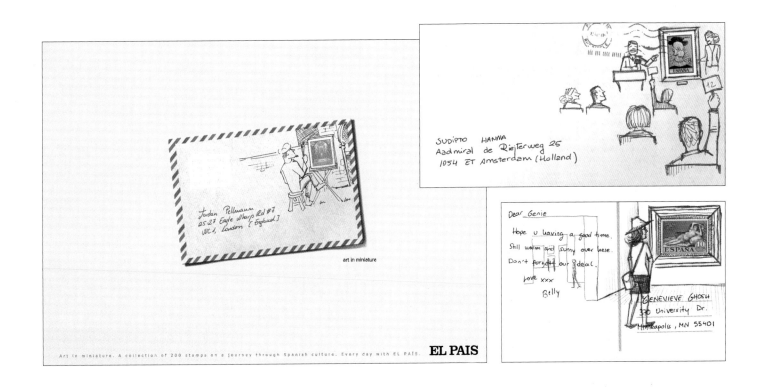

art in miniature

EL PAÍS

On TV politicians should really do what they know best.

Politics.

PUBLIC SENAT

Political satellite channel

Agency:	Contrapunto, Madrid
Creative Directors:	Antonio Montero
	Juan Silva
Art Director:	Lorena Marti
Client:	El Pais Newspaper

Agency:	BDDP & Fils, Paris
Creative Director:	Olivier Altmann
Copywriter:	Pierre Louis Messager
Art Director:	Frédéric Royer
Production:	Dans le Sud
Producers:	Christine Bouffort
	Géraldine Fau
Client:	Public Senat TV
	Channel, "The Song"

The spot shows clips of politicians – including Boris Yeltsin, former French president Valéry Giscard D'Estaing and French culture minister Jack Lang – performing excruciatingly bad song and dance routines on TV, presumably to impress the public. The caption says: "On TV, politicians should do what they do best. Politics." The ad is for a political satellite TV channel.

Agency:	RKCR/Y&R, London
Creative Directors:	Mike Boles
	Jerry Hollens
Copywriter:	Andy Clough
Art Director:	Richard McGrann
Production:	Gorgeous Enterprises
Director:	Chris Palmer
Producers:	Ciska Faulkner
	Claudio Gorini
Client:	The Times London
	Film Festival, "Director"

"Once you're happy with your character, if you feel you can improvise, go for it…" In this spot, we meet a deluded but likeable chap who believes he is a film director. From toddlers playing in the park to senior citizens, street artists and even pigeons, everyone has a part in his imaginary blockbuster. "I need to see that symbiosis between man and machine," he tells a forklift driver. Or to a pair of bemused Japanese tourists: "Have you been to hair and makeup?" The Times BFI London Film Festival is bringing film to the public.

8 m 95. World Long-Jump Record.

JUST IMAGINE.

WORLD ATHLETICS CHAMPIONSHIPS, PARIS 2003.

Agency:	Louis XIV DDB, Paris
Creative Director:	Bertrand Suchet
Copywriter:	Olivier Apers
Art Director:	Hugues Pinguet
Photographer:	Philippe Plantrose
Client:	World Athletics Championships 2003

286   Recreation & Leisure

286   Recreation & Leisure

Agency:	180 Amsterdam
Creative Director:	Peter McHugh
Copywriter:	Andy Fackrell
Art Director:	Andy Fackrell
Production:	Park Pictures, New York
Director:	Lance Acord
Producers:	Jackie Kelman-Bisbee Deannie Blank Sid Daffarn Peter Cline
Client:	Adidias, "Wake Up Call"

Young women emerge onto their balconies after being awoken by a football thudding against the side of their hotel. They are surprised to see a team of female Chinese footballers practising in the park below. They try to look unimpressed as the Chinese perform a series of synchronised tricks for their benefit. The display is a veiled threat, as the onlookers are the US women's soccer team, who beat the Chinese to the 1999 World Cup. Can they do the same in 2003? (In fact China was knocked out by Canada in the quarter finals, and the US lost to Germany in the semis.)

Agency:	DDB, Amsterdam
Creative Directors:	Michael Jansen Bas Korsten
Copywriter:	Bas Korsten
Art Director:	Michael Jansen
Production:	In Your Eye Films
Director:	Jonathan Herman
Producers:	Machiel van der Heyden Chantal Gulpers
Client:	De Lotto, "Women"

Wives seem strangely impressed by their husbands' lacklustre attempts to please them. "Some flowers!" "A gold-coloured bracelet!" One man delights his partner by taking her to a fast food joint on their 25th wedding anniversary. Another "transforms" the cupboard under the stairs into a "sewing room". The voiceover says: "Enjoy your wife's simple enthusiasm while you still can." If you win the lottery, she will be a millionaire's wife – and a lot harder to please. "A white one?" says a newly rich wife, disappointed by her husband's gift of a giant yacht.

Agency:	FHV BBDO, Amstelveen
Creative Director:	David Snellenberg
Copywriter:	Mark Muller
Art Director:	Christian Borstlap
Ilustrator:	Christian Borstlap
Client:	Natura Artis Magistra Zoo

A picture says more than
a thousand words.

Oh, really? Then please
paint the sentence
you just said!

3rd international
literature festival
berlin

www.literaturfestival.com

Agency:	TBWA\Germany, Berlin		**Agency:**	McCann-Erickson, Frankfurt
Creative Directors:	Kurt-Georg Dieckert		**Copywriter:**	Milos Lukic
	Stefan Schmidt		**Art Director:**	Tim Böhm
Copywriter:	Stefan Schmidt		**Client:**	Karlsruhe Low Budget
Art Director:	Stefan Schmidt			Film Festival
Photographer:	Attila Hartwig			
Client:	Berlin International			
	Literature Festival			

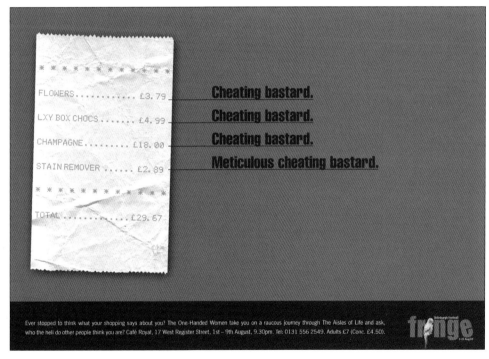

Agency:	Leo Burnett, Prague	**Agency:**	Frame C, Glasgow
Creative Director:	Basil Mina	**Creative Directors:**	Martin Gillan
Copywriters:	Michael Yee		Doug Cook
	Pavel Dufka	**Copywriter:**	Martin Gillan
	Jiri Pleskot	**Art Director:**	Doug Cook
Art Director:	Michael Martin	**Photographer:**	Phil Sanderson
Client:	Prague	**Client:**	Edinburgh Fringe Show,
	Museum of Communism		One Handed Women

the Jewel Box

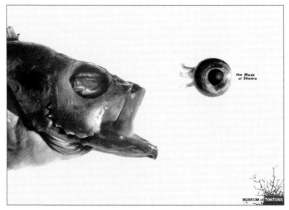

the Mask of Shame

the Rectal Plough

the Rack

MUSEUM of TORTURE

290   **Recreation & Leisure**

Agency:	Leo Burnett, Prague
Creative Director:	Basil Mina
Copywriter:	Jen Robinson
Art Directors:	Paul Stoeter
	Hunter Fine
Photographer:	Nikola Tacevski
Client:	Prague
	Museum of Torture

ANIMALS ARE BACK IN THE CITY.

Agency:	Leo Burnett, Prague	**Agency:**	Leo Burnett, Prague
Creative Director:	Basil Mina	**Creative Director:**	Basil Mina
Copywriter:	Vera Cesenkova	**Copywriter:**	Vera Cesenkova
Art Director:	Jiri Langpaul	**Art Director:**	Jiri Langpaul
Photographer:	Goran Tacevski	**Production:**	Filmservice
Client:	Prague Zoo	**Director:**	Tomas Barina
		Producer:	Premysl Grepl
		Client:	Prague Zoo, "Carwash" & "Feeding"

Stuck in a traffic jam, a driver is surprised when a massive shower of water sprays his windscreen. An elephant's trunk appears, and completes the job of cleaning the windscreen. The man winds down the window and hands the elephant a banknote. The trunk grasps it and retreats. "Animals are back in the city," says the caption. After heavy floods in Prague, many animals at the city zoo were temporarily transferred to other homes. But now they are back.

In the second execution, a man and a woman sit on a park bench. The woman throws out breadcrumbs for the sparrows. But the man chucks out two enormous chunks of raw meat. Suddenly, the shadow of an enormous pair of wings falls over them, and we hear the cry of a bird of prey. Animals are back in the city.

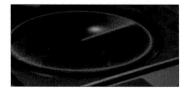

Agency:	Gimla, Stockholm	**Agency:**	McCann-Erickson, Dublin
Creative Director:	Johan Hellström	**Creative Directors:**	Jonathan Stanistreet
Copywriter:	Johan Hellström		Shay Madden
Art Director:	Pelle Lundquist	**Copywriter:**	Jason Hynes
Production:	Forsberg & Co.	**Art Director:**	Keith Doyle
Director:	Tomas Jonsgården	**Production:**	Russel Avis
Client:	Silva Navigation	**Director:**	Damien O'Donnell
	Equipment,	**Producers:**	Russ Russell
	"The Captain"		Genie Dorman
		Client:	Heineken Green
			Energy Music Festival,
			"Kitchen"

In the Irish Sea, the US battleship Montana has spotted a blip on its radar screen. A crew-member radios the offender, ordering it to divert course to avoid a collision. But the Irish voice refuses. The Montana's captain snatches the radio and repeats the order. The Irish voice says: "I'm not moving anything. You change YOUR course." The captain bellows: "This is the 2nd largest vessel in the North Atlantic fleet. You will divert 15 degrees north or I will be forced to take measures to ensure the safety of this ship!" After a pause, the Irishman replys: "This is a lighthouse, mate." Silva – serious navigation equipment.

Wannabe rock band The Transformers – the word "struggling" is too good for them – have bad news for their bass player. Sitting round his kitchen table, they tell him that he's out of the band. Just then, his mum enters with a basket of washing. She's infuriated by the news: "He IS The Transformers! He's more talented than you three put together!" The other members of the group relent. But can The Transformers make it to the Heineken Green Energy Festival – Dublin's biggest indie music fest? It looks unlikely.

Agency: G7, Warsaw
Creative Directors: Przemek Bogdanowicz
                      Maciek Kowalczuk
Copywriter: Maciek Kowalczuk
Art Director: Przemek Bogdanowicz
Client: Polish Scrabble
                      Federation

Agency:	Lowe Brindfors, Stockholm		**Agency:**	Leo Burnett, Prague
Creative Director:	Johan Nilsson		**Creative Director:**	Basil Mina
Copywriter:	Monica Hultén		**Copywriter:**	Michael Yee
Art Directors:	Magnus Löwenhielm		**Art Director:**	Paul Stoeter
	Mitte Blomqvist		**Photographer:**	Nikola Tacevski
Client:	Folkoperan Opera		**Client:**	Delroy's Gym

OFFICIAL SPONSOR OF THE 60TH TOUR DE POLOGNE FIAT

Agency:	Leo Burnett, Warsaw	Agency:	Publicis, Frankfurt
Creative Director:	Darek Zatorski	Creative Directors:	Michael Boebel
Copywriter:	Darek Szablak		Gert Maehnicke
Art Director:	Lukasz Ufnalewski		Andreas Redlich
Client:	Fiat, Tour de Pologne	Copywriter:	Hasso von Kietzell
	Sponsorship	Art Director:	Alan Vladusic
		Client:	Fitness Company

Joe **Pinhead** Peters never visited the **National Galleries of Scotland**. So his brain shrank. If only he could turn back the clock. And remember where he lives.

Robert **Finger Bob** Todd developed an extra finger playing arcade games. He likes it, but his friends think it's odd. "If only he'd discovered the **National Galleries of Scotland**" they say, "instead of the arcade."

Tony **The Bat** Moore bumps into things. Walls, lamp posts, that kind of thing. The **National Galleries of Scotland** could help open his eyes, but he's not interested. He prefers wearing cushions.

Lee **Luggsy** Bennett liked music, not art. He never went to the **National Galleries of Scotland**. He now travels the country, preaching the dangers of using your ears more than your eyes.

296   **Recreation & Leisure**

Agency:	The Union Advertising Agency, Edinburgh
Creative Directors:	Simon Scott
	Andrew Lindsay
Copywriter:	Phil Evans
Art Director:	Guy Vickerstaff
Photographer:	Victor Albrow
Client:	National Galleries of Scotland

Agency:	J. Walter Thompson, Madrid
Creative Director:	Paco Segovia
Copywriters:	Paco Segovia
	Silvio Panizza
Art Directors:	Andres Linares
	Fran Lopez
Photographer:	Pepe Abascal
Client:	Prado Museum
	Fellowship Foundation

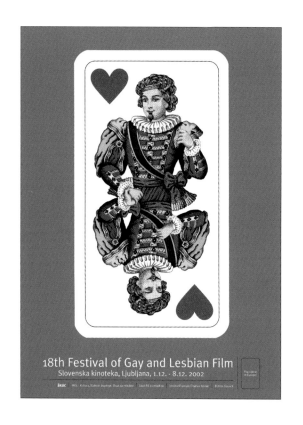

18th Festival of Gay and Lesbian Film
Slovenska kinoteka, Ljubljana, 1.12. - 8.12. 2002

WE'VE GOT RUGBY IN OUR BLOOD. AND VICE VERSA.

THE BORDERS. WHERE RUGBY REALLY LIVES.
THE BORDERS v GLASGOW. FRIDAY OCT 4TH 7.30PM NETHERDALE, GALASHIELS.

I HAD A COUSIN THAT WENT TO A FOOTBALL MATCH ONCE.
BUT THAT SIDE OF THE FAMILY WERE ALWAYS WEIRD.

THE BORDERS. WHERE RUGBY REALLY LIVES.
THE BORDERS v MADRID 2012. FRIDAY OCT 18TH 7.30PM NETHERDALE, GALASHIELS.

Agency:	Mayer McCann, Ljubljana		**Agency:**	The Bridge, Glasgow
Creative Director:	Marko Majer		**Copywriter:**	Martin Gillan
Copywriter:	Boštjan Pavletič		**Art Director:**	Doug Cook
Art Director:	Boštjan Pavletič		**Photographer:**	David Boni
Client:	Ljubljana Gay & Lesbian Film Festival		**Client:**	The Borders Rugby Team

Agency:	Storåkers McCann, Stockholm	We are being addressed by Samir, a fan of contemporary art. "I really like this place," he enthuses, almost at a loss for words. "It's so…inspirating. It's so fantastic. The energy is so positive." The camera pans back to show us a room containing nothing but a stool and a bag of cement. The caption reads: "The Moderna Museum. Not every-one knows we've moved." The modern art museum has a new address.	Agency:	Spillmann/Felser/ Leo Burnett, Zürich
Copywriter:	Mia Cederberg		Creative Director:	Martin Spillmann
Art Director:	Klaudia Carp		Copywriter:	Peter Brönnimann
Production:	Pettersson Åkerlund		Art Directors:	Dana Wirz
Directors:	Jesper Hiro			Patrik Rohner
	Christoffer Diös		Photographer:	Stefan Minder
Producer:	Magnus Theorin		Client:	Swisscom
Client:	Moderna Museum, "Samir"			Corporate Sponsorship

Advertising Photography

Photographer: Marc Gouby
Creative Director: Erik Vervroegen
Copywriter: Eric Helias
Art Director: Jorge Carreño
Agency: TBWA\Paris
Client: Sony PlayStation 2

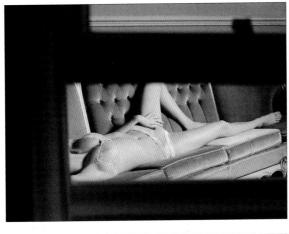
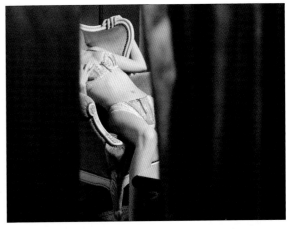

Photographer: Rankin
Agency: The Glue Society, Sydney
Client: Elle MacPherson Intimates

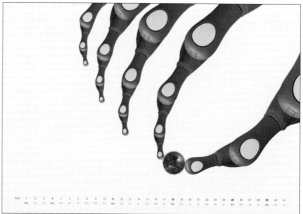

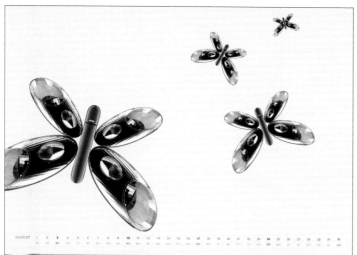

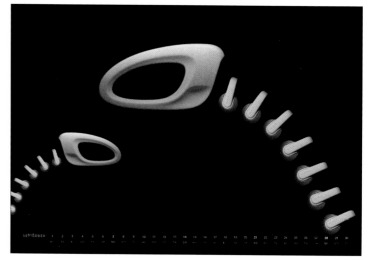

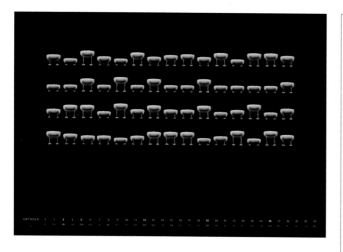

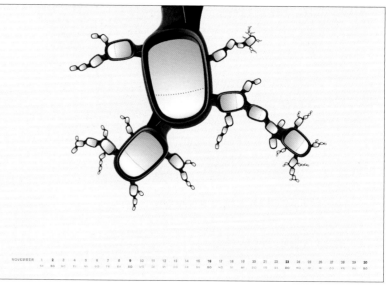

302   **Advertising Photography**

Photographer:	Matthias Baumann
Creative Directors:	Kai Roeffen
	Wolfgang Bahle
Copywriters:	Donald Tursman
	Olaf Moessler
Art Director:	Rainer Schmidt
Agency:	TBWA\Germany, Berlin
Client:	Nissan 2003 Calendar

Photographer:	Andreas Bitesnich
Creative Directors:	Kurt-Georg Dieckert
	Stefan Schmidt
Copywriters:	Athanassios Stellatos
	Helge Bloeck
Art Director:	Gritt Pfefferkorn
Agency:	TBWA\Germany, Berlin
Client:	Behinderten-Sportverband
	Berlin Handicapped Sports

Photographer:	Christopher Thomas
Creative Directors:	Benjamin Lommel
	Harald Wittig
	Carsten Heintzsch
Copywriter:	Stefan Craul
Art Director:	Anne Henkel
Agency:	Saatchi & Saatchi, Frankfurt
Client:	Audi A3

UNEXPECTED VIEW: VILNIUS
WITH TRAVELING AGENCY "GINTARINE SALA"

UNEXPECTED VIEW: BERLIN
WITH TRAVELING AGENCY "GINTARINE SALA"

Photographer:	Markku Lähdesmäki	Photographer:	Ruslanas Baranauskas
Copywriters:	Ville Norra	Creative Director:	Kazimiras Bangaitis
	Samuli Vapaasalo	Copywriter:	Svetlana Simakova
Art Directors:	Ville Norra	Art Director:	Ruslanas Baranauskas
	Samuli Vapaasalo	Agency:	Efendi Art Studio, Vilnius
Agency:	McCann, Helsinki	Client:	Gintarine Sala
Client:	APU Magazine		Travel Agency

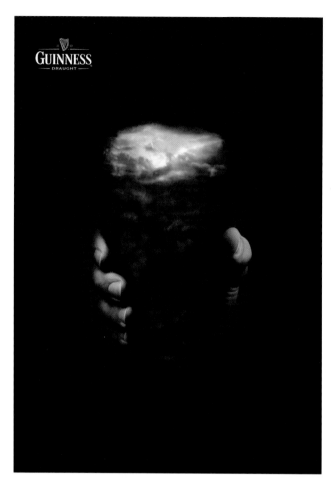

Photographer:	Marc Gouby	Photographer:	Nadav Kander
Creative Director:	Anne de Maupeou	Art Director:	Grant Parker
Copywriter:	Benoît Sahores	Agency:	DDB, London
Art Director:	Cédric Haroutiounian	Client:	Heal's Furniture Store
Agency:	CLM BBDO, Paris		
Client:	Guinness Beer		

Photographer:	Jaap Vliegenthart
Creative Director:	Martin Boomkens
Copywriter:	Ivar van den Hove
Art Director:	Bert Kerkhof
Agency:	Euro RSCG BLRS, Amstelveen
Client:	Citroën C2

Agency:	Saatchi & Saatchi, Vienna
Creative Director:	Ingeborg Frauendorfer
Copywriter:	Christoph Reicher
Art Director:	Alexander Kowatschitsch
Client:	Mobilkom Austria, A1 Mobile Images MMS Promotion

This weekend edition of the Austrian newspaper Der Standard was published without any pictures. Readers were invited to download the missing images on their mobile phones. By using the new medium in this way, Der Standard was even able to provide pictures that were unavailable when the paper went to press.

DER STANDARD

Sa./So., 25./26. Jänner 2003 | Österreichs unabhängige Tageszeitung | Herausgegeben von Oscar Bronner | € 1,10

Graz wählt: Erster Test für Stärke der VP
Seite 10, Kommentar Seite 40

Irakkonflikt

THEMA Neue Spaltung in Europa Seite 2, ALBUM Seiten A1–A3
Intellektuelle verteidigen Alten Kontinent Seiten 31 und 39
Henryk M. Broder: Kanzler Schröder wird es billiger geben S. 39
Kopf des Tages US-Minister Donald Rumsfeld, Kommentar S. 40

„MMS2" per SMS an 0664/222 3 999 senden und das Bild kommt per MMS direkt auf Ihr Handy.

Galt als heimlicher Herrscher Italiens: Fiat-Ehrenpräsident Giovanni Agnelli. Foto: Reuters

Giovanni Agnelli 1921–2003

Turin – Italien trauert um Giovanni Agnelli (81). Der Fiat-Ehrenpräsident ist am Freitag einem Krebsleiden erlegen. Während einer Übergangsphase wird Agnellis jüngerer Bruder Umberto das Steuer des Großunternehmens übernehmen. Danach könnte der Lieblingsneffe des Patriarchen, der 26-jährige John Philip Elkann, an die Spitze des Konzerns rücken. (red) **S. 24**

HEUTE

Wahl gescheitert Erneut erhielt kein Kandidat für das Amt des tschechischen Präsidenten die erforderliche Mehrheit. **Seite 6**

Euro in Hochform Der Euro hat gegenüber dem Dollar ein Dreijahreshoch markiert, die Aktienkurse stürzten ab. **Seite 22**

Wissenschaft Spezial Alles, was dem Menschen nützt, kann Fortschritt sein: Der britische Bioethiker Tom Shakespeare über Klonbabys und Gesichtsverpflanzung. **ALBUM Seite 4**

Crossover	11, 12
Sport	19, 20
Kultur	31, 32
Kommunikation	38
Wissenschaft	38
Kolumne Günter Traxler	39
Szenario	
Watchlist	33
Theater-Programm	34
Kino-Programm	34, 35
TV, Switchlist	36, 37
Abo-Service	0810 20 30 40

BÖRSE

New York (Schluss)	8131,00 –
Frankfurt (DE, Schluss)	2717,82 –
Wien (ATX, Schluss)	1187,79 +
€ (in US-Dollar)	1,0846 +
€-Anleiherendite	3,516 –
Gold, London (in $)	364,10 +
Investment-Fonds S. 26, 29, 30	
Börsenkurse auf	S. 26 + 27

WETTER

Morgens ist es noch vielfach bewölkt. Im Lauf des Tages lockern die Wolken dann auf und die Sonne kommt öfters durch. Die Höchstwerte erreichen –2 bis + 4 Grad. **Seite 15**

Chancen für große Koalition sinken: Heftige Wortgefechte

Gehrer: „Doppelspiel der SP", Prammer: „Kein friss, Vogel, oder stirb"

Wien – Noch vor dem möglichen Eintritt in Regierungsverhandlungen nächste Woche fliegen zwischen SPÖ und ÖVP nun die Fetzen: Die SPÖ habe in den Sondierungsgesprächen so viele Hürden aufgebaut, „dass sie sich selbst nicht mehr bewegen kann", kritisiert Schüssel-Stellvertreterin Elisabeth Gehrer im STANDARD-Gespräch. Sie vermutet ein „Doppelspiel". Das Angebot der ÖVP, über das Wochenende weiterzuverhandeln, lehnte die SP ab.

Denn diese habe von der „Friss, Vogel, oder stirb"-Methode der ÖVP die Nase voll, wie Vizechefin Barbara Prammer dem STANDARD verriet. Womit es vorerst keinen weiteren schwarz-roten Termin gibt. Bedingung der SPÖ ist, dass die ÖVP keine weiteren Sondierungsgespräche mehr führt. Nächste Woche sind noch eine schwarz-blaue und eine schwarz-grüne Runde geplant.

Indes brodelt die Gerüchteküche: So soll SP-Vizechef Michael Häupl bei Bundespräsident Thomas Klestil ein Schreiben der schwarz-roten Gespräche angedeutet haben.

Die SPÖ veröffentlichte am Freitag Pläne der ÖVP, die diese in den Sondierungsgesprächen präsentiert hatte: Demnach soll es ab 2009 Frühpension wegen langer Versicherungsdauer mehr geben. (red) **Seiten 8 und 9 Kommentar Seite 40**

24 Seiten
KARRIERENSTANDARD Seiten K1 bis K24
8 Seiten IMMOBILIEN Seiten A1 bis A8
Wortanzeigen Seiten 16 bis 18

Radikale Palästinenser unterstützen Saddam

„MMS1" per SMS an 0664/222 3 999 senden und das Bild kommt per MMS direkt auf Ihr Handy.

Bombenattrappen und vermummte Gesichter: Mitglieder der militanten Palästinenserorganisation Hamas demonstrierten am Freitag in Gaza für Saddam Hussein. Donnerstagnacht erschossen Hamas-Aktivisten bei Hebron drei israelische Soldaten. Die israelische Armee marschierte daraufhin in Gaza ein, Apache-Kampfhubschrauber feuerten Raketen auf die Stadt. Bei Nablus wurden zwei Palästinenser getötet, die laut Armeeangaben versucht hatten, einen israelischen Stützpunkt anzugreifen. Foto: Epa

USA kündigen Beweise gegen Bagdad an

Washington/Bagdad/Wien – Die USA haben wenige Tage vor dem Bericht der UN-Waffeninspektoren im Sicherheitsrat angekündigt, „sehr überzeugende" Beweise für die Existenz von Massenvernichtungswaffen im Irak vorlegen zu wollen. Der US-Staatssekretär für Abrüstungsfragen, John Bolton, erklärte Freitag, dazu zählten vor allem ballistische Langstreckenraketen, deren Besitz dem Irak seit dem Golfkrieg 1991 verboten ist.

Im Streit um einen Irakkrieg zwischen Deutschland und Frankreich auf der einen und der US-Regierung auf der anderen Seite hat sich der deutsche Bundeskanzler Gerhard Schröder die Unterstützung des russischen Präsidenten Wladimir Putin zugesichert. Der Konflikt sei politisch im Rahmen der UNO zu lösen, legten die beiden Politiker in einem Telefongespräch fest. Der EU-Außenpolitikbeauftragte, Javier Solana, rief indes die EU-Staaten und die USA auf, sich nach dem Irakstreit zu beruhigen.

Österreichs Verteidigungsminister Herbert Scheibner nannte es „problematisch", die unterschiedlichen Positionen innerhalb der demokratischen Staatengemeinschaft offen auszutragen. Nur eine geschlossene Haltung könne den nötigen Druck auf Regime wie das des Saddam Hussein erzeugen. (red) **Irak Seiten 5 und 8**

Jetzt kommt Gebühr auf alle Flugtickets

Weitere Airlines kündigen den Reisebüros und folgen der AUA bei Zusatzgebühr ab April

Wien – Neue Gebühren sind offenbar ansteckend: Nachdem vor einer Woche die Austrian Airlines mit der Einführung einer Gebühr von 18 Euro für das Ausstellen eines Tickets vorpreschten, ziehen jetzt die meisten anderen Airlines nach. Hintergrund der neuen Flugticketgebühr ist die Kürzung der Provision, die von AUA und anderen Airlines bisher an Reisebüros für die Ausstellung der Tickets bezahlt wurde. Wie berichtet, einigte sich die AUA vor wenigen Tagen mit den Reisebüros darauf, nur noch fünf statt sieben Prozent Provision zu zahlen; im Gegenzug wird eine Art Ausgabezuschlag von 18 Euro eingeführt, der sowohl von der AUA selbst als auch den Reisebüros beim Kauf zusätzlich zum Flugpreis verrechnet wird. Dazu kommt noch die Flughafengebühr.

Nunmehr haben auch Lufthansa, KLM, SAS, Alitalia und andere Airlines ihre Verträge mit den Reisebüros gekündigt. Erwartet wird eine neue Regelung mit kleinerer Provision und zusätzlicher Ticketgebühr. Experten bezeichnen den Schritt als indirekte Preiserhöhung, da eine Anhebung der Ticketpreise am Markt nicht möglich sei. (red) **Seite 21, Kommentar Seite 40**

Alte Neue Welt

1940, als England in höchster Not war – Frankreich am Boden, Hitler am Ärmelkanal –, hielt Winston Churchill seine historische Rede: „... wir werden an den Stränden kämpfen, wir werden an den Landungsstellen kämpfen, wir werden auf den Feldern und in den Straßen kämpfen, wir werden in den Hügeln kämpfen, wir werden niemals aufgeben." Und zwar so lange, „bis die Neue Welt, mit all ihrer Macht und Stärke nach vorne tritt, um die Alte Welt zu retten und zu befreien". Churchill wusste, dass England und Europa trotz alles Heroismus ohne die USA verloren waren. Die Amerikaner haben dann Westeuropa 40 Jahre lang vor dem Kommunismus geschützt, zur Befreiung Osteuropas und zur deutschen Vereinigung massiv beigetragen und noch vor wenigen Jahren den Völkermord in Bosnien und im Kosovo beendet, wozu die Europäer nicht imstande waren. Alte Geschichten, gewiss. Und Bush ist ein Cowboy. Und Rumsfeld ist ein alter Reaktionär, der glaubt, eigentlich sei er Präsident der USA. Am Ende aber, wenn es um die fundamentalen Werte geht, dann stehen auf der einen Seite die Demokratien der Alten und der Neuen Welt und auf der anderen Seite die Barbarei. Wie 1940.

RAU

Dichand und WAZ einig: Doppelführung

Wien – Herausgeber Hans Dichand und Erich Schumann, Geschäftsführer der WAZ (Westdeutsche Allgemeine Zeitung), haben sich am Freitag auf die künftige Führungsstruktur der Kronen Zeitung geeinigt. Dichand hat seinen Wunsch durchgesetzt: Sohn Christoph wird ab 1. Februar neuer Krone-Chefredakteur. Der deutsche 50-Prozent-Eigentümer WAZ darf im Gegenzug einen geschäftsführenden Chefredakteur wählen. Für diese Funktion kommen die stellvertretenden Krone-Chefredakteure Christoph Biro und Georg Wailand sowie Klaus Hermann, Chef der Oberösterreich-Krone, in Frage. (red) **Seite 38**

Where are the pictures?

A perfect communication requires pictures. The A1 MMS service makes such a perfect communication possible for you. With the MMS you can even [...] sounds on your [...] With the A1 MM [...] scriptions your mobile turns to an information pool. By the way, the missing pictures in today's [...]

STANDARD [...] 'kidnapped' [...] T-Mobil [...] with [...] 0664 [...] picts [...] imm [...] scre [...] free, [...]

GZ: 02Z030924T · P.b.b. Verlagspostamt 1010 Wien · Nr. 4277 · Adresse: 1010 Wien, Herrengasse 19–21 · Tel. 01/531 70 · http://derStandard.at · International: € 1,60 / sfr 2,50

Agency:	Family, Edinburgh	**Agency:**	Lowe Forever, Stockholm	We've stopped selling eggs from caged
Creative Directors:	Kevin Bird	**Creative Director:**	Jack Wahl	hens. Try standing in this cage with 7
	David Isaac	**Copywriter:**	Björn Colliander	people and you'll understand why. Coop
Copywriter:	David Isaac	**Art Director:**	Jörgen Lindström	- a small step towards happier hens.
Art Director:	Kevin Bird	**Client:**	Coop Konsum,	
Photographer:	David Isaac		Free-Range Eggs	
Client:	Scottish National Party			

be pathetic
for the rest of your life
or take a peek at

seznamka.cz

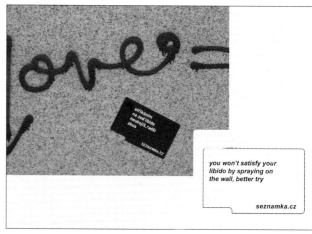

you won't satisfy your
libido by spraying on
the wall, better try

seznamka.cz

← teorii jsi
zvládnul, co takhle
trochu praxe?

SEZNAMKA.CZ

you mastered
the theory, how about
a little practice?

seznamka.cz

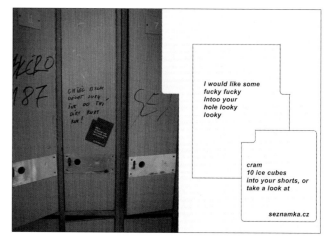

I would like some
fucky fucky
Intoo your
hole looky
looky

cram
10 ice cubes
into your shorts, or
take a look at

seznamka.cz

Agency:	Publicis, Frankfurt	To bring home the effects of malnutrition in underdeveloped countries, a sticker was placed on the grip bars in municipal buses. Drawing a shocking analogy between the spindly bar and an emaciated youngster, the text reads: "Now you can grasp how thin the thigh of a starving child is."
Creative Directors:	Michael Boebel	
	Dirk Bugdahn	
	Hadi Geiser	
Copywriter:	Hadi Geiser	
Art Director:	Dirk Bugdahn	
Photographers:	Hendrik Hohmann	
	Christoph Mager	
Client:	World Vision	

Agency:	Euro RSCG, Prague	These Seznamka stickers were distributed through bars and restaurants to be used wherever obscene graffiti was to be found. The idea was to refer the graffiti's author to the dating website as a better place to satisfy his or her sexual desires.
Creative Director:	Eda Kauba	
Copywriter:	Ondrej Soucek	
Art Director:	Tereza Eschlerova	
Client:	Seznamka	
	Online Dating Service	

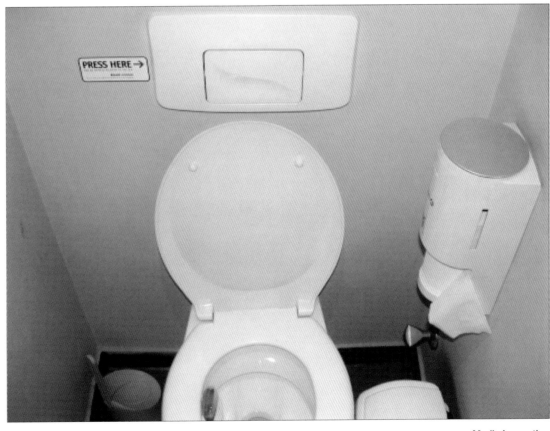

Agency:	Heye & Partner, Hamburg	The title of the book is Iraq's Cultural
Creative Director:	Reinhard Crasemann	Treasures. The text on the inside back
Copywriter:	Candan Sasmaz	cover explains how they are in jeopardy
Art Director:	Michael Theuner	as a result of the war.
Client:	UNESCO Fundraising	

Agency:	H&C Leo Burnett, Beirut	Press here for an express delivery to the sea.
Creative Director:	Bechara Mouzannar	Join us to take action against the pollution of
Copywriter:	Sheila-Anne Johnston	our coast.
Art Directors:	Malak Beydoun	
	Mazen Kerbaj	
Client:	Sea Lebanon, Coastline	
	Preservation Society	

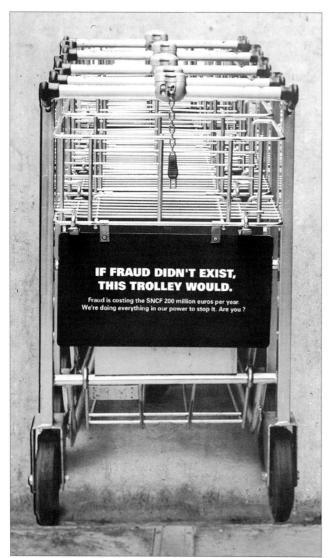

IF FRAUD DIDN'T EXIST,
THIS TROLLEY WOULD.

Fraud is costing the SNCF 200 million euros per year.
We're doing everything in our power to stop it. Are you ?

IF FRAUD DIDN'T EXIST, THIS TOILET WOULD.

Fraud is costing the SNCF 200 million euros per year.
We're doing everything in our power to stop it. Are you ?

IF FRAUD DIDN'T EXIST,
THIS SOCKET WOULD.

Fraud is costing the SNCF 200 million euros per year.
We're doing everything in our power to stop it. Are you ?

IF FRAUD DIDN'T EXIST, THIS BENCH WOULD.

Fraud is costing the SNCF 200 million euros per year.
We're doing everything in our power to stop it. Are you ?

Agency:	TBWA\Paris
Creative Director:	Erik Vervroegen
Copywriter:	Cécile Guais
Art Director:	Laurent Bodson
Photographer:	Oliver Reindorf
Client:	SNCF
	(French National Railways),
	Fraud Awareness

Agency: TBWA\Paris
Creative Director: Erik Vervroegen
Copywriter: Benoit Leroux
Art Director: Philippe Taroux
Photographer: Marc Gouby
Client: Amnesty International

AVOID TODAY

Dallas
UK Gold, 4.25am

At Southfork everything had to be bigger. Including, apparently, the furnishing faux pas - gold fixtures, acres of flock and antiqued leather. Surrounded by all that 'early 80s oil sheik', it's no wonder Sue Ellen hit the bottle. Or that Bobby spent a year in the shower. Whoever shot JR was probably aiming at the decorator. They could have just shot down to Martin & Frost.

Martin & Frost
Be discerning. We are.
130 Mcdonald Road Edinburgh EH7 4NN

AVOID TODAY

Dallas
UK Gold, 4.25am

At Southfork everything had to be bigger. Including, apparently, the furnishing faux pas - gold fixtures, acres of flock and antiqued leather. Surrounded by all that 'early 80s oil sheik', it's no wonder Sue Ellen hit the bottle. Or that Bobby spent a year in the shower. Whoever shot JR was probably aiming at the decorator. They could have just shot down to Martin & Frost.

Martin & Frost
Be discerning. We are.
130 Mcdonald Road Edinburgh EH7 4NN

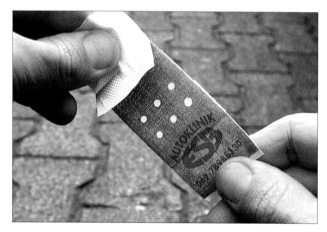
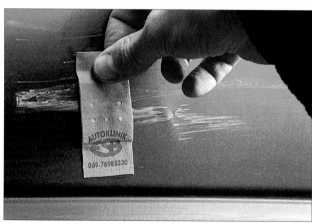

314 **Media Innovation**

Agency:	Family, Edinburgh	One of several ads that appeared on consecutive days in a weekly TV guide. In each one Martin & Frost offered their opinions on the furniture featured in that day's primetime show.
Creative Directors:	Kevin Bird	
	David Isaac	
Copywriter:	Gregor Findlay	
Art Director:	Kevin Colquhoun	
Photographer:	Richard Mountney	
Client:	Martin & Frost Furniture Stores	

Agency:	Change Communication, Frankfurt	The plasters advertised a garage that specialises in repairing and spraying damaged cars. Large plasters were placed on the walls of ramps in multi-storey car parks and smaller plasters were used on dented and scratched cars around the city centre.
Copywriter:	Gunther Brodhecker	
Art Directors:	Boris Aue	
	Kersten Meyer	
Client:	ESB Autoklinik Garage	

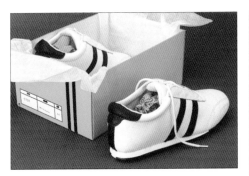

Agency:	Euro RSCG MRT, Lisbon	No matter what your angle of vision,
Creative Director:	Jorge Teixeira	these Big Brother lenticular posters
Copywriter:	Marcelo Lourenço	gave the impression of following you
Art Director:	Pedro Bexiga	on the city streets.
Photographer:	Francisco Prata	
Client:	Big Brother 4 TV show	

Agency:	Ruiz Nicoli, Madrid
Creative Director:	Paco Ruiz-Nicoli
Copywriter:	Carlos Yuste
Art Director:	Jesús Martín-Buitrago
Client:	Ayuda en Accion, Non-Profit Organisation Against Child Labour

TRIPLE DISTILLED FOR EXTRA SMOOTHNESS

Agency:	BDS Beechwood, London	To communicate the smooth flavour and
Creative Director:	Derek Hayes	taste of Jameson Irish Whiskey these
Copywriter:	Simon Hipwell	magazine ads were printed on simulated
Art Director:	Simon Wakeman	sand-paper.
Client:	Jameson Irish Whiskey	

Agency:	1576 Advertising, Edinburgh	These metal plaques were attached
Creative Director:	Adrian Jeffery	to trees off the fairways to reach
Copywriter:	Adrian Jeffery	those golfers who were most in need
Art Director:	David Reid	of lessons from the local pro.
Client:	Nairn Dunbar Golf Club	

Agency:	Saatchi & Saatchi, Amsterdam	To promote the annual IDFA documentary film festival, the strip of lights that runs across the Museum Square in Amsterdam was transformed into a movie reel. The first scene of Michael Moore's "Bowling for Columbine", which opened the festival, was reproduced on transparent material and stretched 300 metres between the Rijksmuseum and the Concertgebouw. The lamps under this strip literally 'illuminated' the film.	**Agency:**	Zapping, Madrid
Creative Director:	Edwin Kopper		**Creative Directors:**	Uschi Henkes
Copywriter:	Robin Zuiderveld			Urs Frick
Art Director:	Marq Strooy		**Copywriter:**	David Palacio
Client:	IDFA Documentary Film Festival		**Art Directors:**	Uschi Henkes
				Esther Abengozar
			Client:	Tennis Masters Madrid

Agency:	Harrison Troughton Wunderman, London	In order to target the banking sector, IBM identified managers at 17 top banks in the UK. At 4am on the day of the mailing, the agency customised first editions of the Financial Times for the individuals concerned. The papers were then delivered to the banks before dawn. When the executives got into work, they discovered an ad specifically about themselves in the newspaper.
Creative Director:	Steve Harrison	
Copywriter:	Rob Kavanagh	
Art Director:	Tony Haigh	
Client:	IBM, Financial Times Mailing	

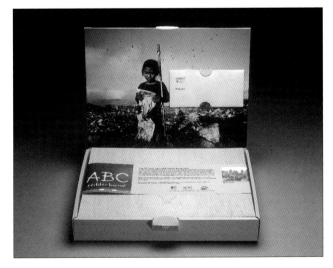

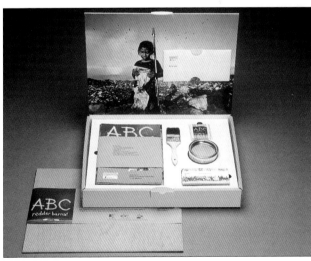

Agency:	OgilvyOne Worldwide, London	Stamp collectors in the UK received a mysterious envelope. On it was written: "Everything we know about you can be written on the back of a stamp." Inside was a huge postage stamp. The back of the stamp featured a questionnaire that would enable Royal Mail to find out more about collectors and their interests. The stamp has now become a collectors' item in its own right.
Creative Directors:	Cordell Burke Rick Sear	
Copywriter:	Mark Davies	
Art Director:	Charlie Wilson	
Client:	Royal Mail Stamps	

Agency:	MRM Partners Worldwide (McCann), Oslo	The theme of this campaign was: ABC Saves the Children. First, a mailing urging schools to help raise funds for the education of Third World kids was sent out to school heads. A message on a small blackboard invited teachers to apply for classroom kits. When the kits arrived, they contained plywood and blackboard paint so the school children could make their own blackboards and use them at their own school bazaars to raise money for the charity.
Creative Director:	Jan Petter Ågren	
Copywriter:	Ole Kristian Ellingsen	
Art Director:	Anette Waage Mohn	
Client:	Save the Children	

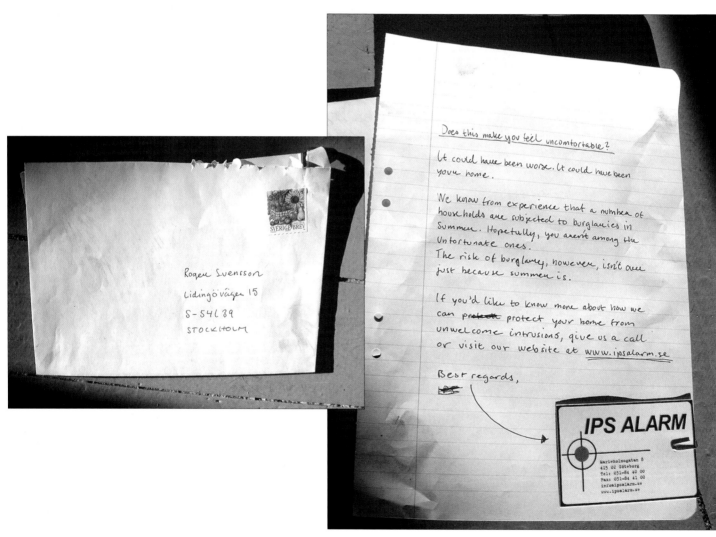

Direct Marketing

Agency: Lowe Brindfors, Stockholm
Creative Director: Johan Nilsson
Copywriter: Monica Hultén
Art Directors: Magnus Löwenhielm
Mitte Blomqvist
Photographers: Susanne Björkman
J. H. Engström
Dennis Blomberg
Gabriel Uggla
Client: Folkoperan Opera, Press & VIP Invitation

Sponsors and VIPs in the arts community of Stockholm were invited to the opera with this criminally inventive package. The opera was The Masked Ball – based on the murder of King Gustav III in 1792. So it was quite natural that the first mailing was a summons to attend the reconstruction of the crime, while the second looked like a police file: complete with post-mortem details of the victim, fingerprints and mug shots of the suspects.

Agency: Milk, Gothenburg
Copywriters: Ola Sandell
Torkel Norling
Anders Holmström
Art Director: Andreas Bergendahl
Client: IPS Alarm Systems

A handwritten, dirty, partly opened letter arrives at the targeted households. The recipients feel violated – who has been reading their mail? However, a polite message inside says: "We apologise for scaring you, but it could have been your home." The mailing is about the importance of installing an effective alarm system.

Agency:	Pemberton & Whitefoord, London	A fake newspaper unwraps to reveal some fish and chips, together with salt, vinegar and a wooden fork. But the fish and chips are not greasy, as they're simply photographs. The shots were taken by photographer James Murphy for a book by famous British seafood chef Rick Stein.	Agency:	Happy Forsman & Bodenfors, Gothenburg	This book promoting a paper supplier was sent out to art directors and printers. As well as tempting them with the company's Amber Graphic stock, it was also quite useful, as the splats and splashes on its pages could be downloaded free from the company's website.
Creative Director:	Simon Pemberton		Creative Director:	Anders Kornestedt	
Art Director:	Simon Pemberton		Copywriter:	Björn Engström	
Photographer:	James Murphy		Art Directors:	Lisa Careborg	
Client:	James Murphy Photography			Andreas Kittel	
			Client:	Arctic Paper, Book of Splashes	

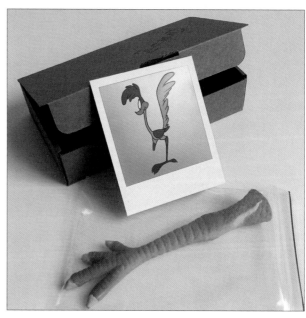

Agency:	OgilvyOne Worldwide, London	
Creative Directors:	Colin Nimick Harvey Lee	
Copywriter:	Colin Nimick	
Art Director:	Harvey Lee	
Client:	Royal Mail Special Delivery	

To convey the efficiency of the Royal Mail, 200,000 business customers received a freshly cut carnation, with a note informing them that it was just one of 80 million special deliveries made that day. Each pack contained a relevant case study, depending on the sector the recipient worked in.

Agency:	D'Adda, Lorenzini, Vigorelli, BBDO, Milan
Creative Directors:	Giovanni Porro Stefano Campora
Copywriter:	Francesco Poletti
Art Director:	Serena Di Bruno
Client:	Turner Broadcasting System, Cartoon Network Invitations

When TV station Cartoon Network organised a party, it had to come up with a funny invitation. So guests received an Acme box containing a Polaroid of a well-known cartoon character – and a body part in a plastic bag! On the back of the Polaroid, recipients were told by the "kidnappers" that if they wanted to see their favourite character alive, they should come to the party.

Agency:	OgilvyOne Worldwide, Frankfurt	Logistics is the art of delivering the right thing at the right time. To draw attention to its service and to invite potential clients to an exhibition stand, logistics solutions provider SAP sent out this box – which looked like it contained an elegant bottle of wine. In fact, it held a bottle of vinegar. The accompanying letter said: "We were planning on sending you wine from quite an exquisite year. Unfortunately, we received the wrong delivery". In a second mailing, a chocolate Santa Claus arrived for Easter. Hence the importance of logistics…
Creative Director:	James Langton	
Copywriter:	Heiko Krassmann	
Art Director:	Katrin Wendt	
Client:	MySAP Service Provider	

Agency:	Arc, London	As the Ulysee is Fiat's biggest vehicle, seating up to seven people, an entire family can enjoy its spaciousness and comfort. And when does the entire family travel together? Of course: when they are going on holiday. Hence this mailing of a beach towel and postcards urging families to enjoy a holiday experience all year round.
Creative Directors:	Graham Mills	
	Jack Nolan	
Copywriter:	Aaron Martin	
Art Director:	Garry Munns	
Illustrator:	Metin Salih	
Client:	Fiat Ulysee	

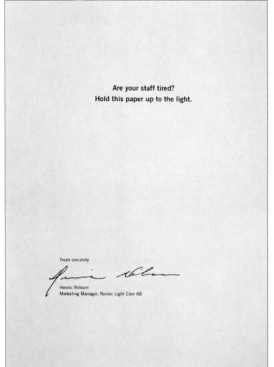

Agency:	Clara, Karlstad	"Are your staff tired?" asked the headline on this	
Copywriter:	Niclas Hallgren	(apparently) otherwise blank sheet of paper.	
Art Director:	Olle Olsson	"Hold this paper up to the light." Once held up	
Client:	Nordic Light Care	to a lamp, faint grey writing emerges. The newly	

Agency: Clara, Karlstad
Copywriter: Niclas Hallgren
Art Director: Olle Olsson
Client: Nordic Light Care

"Are your staff tired?" asked the headline on this (apparently) otherwise blank sheet of paper. "Hold this paper up to the light." Once held up to a lamp, faint grey writing emerges. The newly visible text explains that lack of sunlight often causes fatigue in office environments – and that a special lamp emitting light similar to that of the sun is the solution.

Agency: OgilvyOne Worldwide, Frankfurt
Creative Director: Christine Blum-Heuser
Copywriter: Susanne Lippert
Art Director: Christine Schmidt
Client: Dresdner Bank

This mailing suggested that moving your corporate account to Dresdner Bank is like embarking on a fitness regime for your company. And so inside the blender, the package contained everything the recipients needed for creating their own fitness drink.

Agency:	Utsikt Kommunikation, Stockholm	The Foundation for Respect works with troubled children, adolescents and adults. It	**Agency:**	Claydon Heeley Jones Mason, London	The Guardian published a series of reports on the state of the UK's public services,

Agency: Utsikt Kommunikation, Stockholm
Creative Director: Fredrik von Essen
Illustrator: Jenny Ljungqvist
Client: Foundation for Respect, Christmas Cards

The Foundation for Respect works with troubled children, adolescents and adults. It helps to put their lives back on track when things have gone wrong. The problems can include drugs, alcohol, violence, vandalism or bullying. This self-explanatory Christmas card is part of an annual fund-raising campaign.

Agency: Claydon Heeley Jones Mason, London
Creative Directors: Dave Woods
Pete Harle
Copywriters: Darren Crew
Gary McNulty
Art Director: Simon Haslehurst
Client: The Guardian Newspaper

The Guardian published a series of reports on the state of the UK's public services, using the town of Enfield as a representative sample. To alert Enfield's citizens to the article about healthcare services in their district, they were sent this mailing in the shape of a sticking plaster.

Agency:	Zapping, Madrid	
Creative Directors:	Uschi Henkes	
	Manolo Moreno Marquez	
	Urs Frick	
Art Director:	Gabriel Hueso	
Client:	Buena Vista International, "La Fiesta" Press Mailing	

Why send a bag of garbage to film critics at newspapers and magazines? To promote a low-budget Spanish film called La Fiesta ("The Party"). The whole film revolves around the titular event, at which people drink, talk, dance, get drunk, and have sex. The film ends when the party does, so viewers don't have to see the mess left behind. But some of the items in the garbage bag may evoke memories of cleaning up with a hangover.

Agency:	Fritz Reklambyra, Sundsvall
Copywriter:	Annika Bellander
Art Director:	Ulf Nilsson
Client:	Hew Saw

To thank customers for coming to a trade fair, this company – which provides cutting equipment for sawmills – sent out a bread knife. "We have a saw for every purpose," said the copy. A second mailing a few days later contained a loaf of dark Swedish rye bread, to symbolise a tree trunk. A later invitation to another trade fair contained breadsticks, designed to represent smaller trees. The company was launching a product designed to cut smaller timber at the event.

Agency:	DEC, Barcelona	**Agency:**	Harrison Troughton Wunderman, London
Creative Director:	Valen Soto	**Creative Director:**	Steve Harrison
Copywriter:	Helena Marzo	**Copywriter:**	Steve Harrison
Art Director:	Valen Soto	**Art Director:**	Steve Harrison
Client:	Fundació Èxit	**Client:**	NABS
			Christmas Canvases

Fundació Èxit is a charity helping young people without resources to find work. Potential employers received this box with an upside-down cap in it. "I'm not asking for charity," said the message. "Please turn this box over to turn my life around." When recipients did so, the cap appeared the right way up, with the message: "Yes, I am asking for work." A follow-up mailing contained a single euro coin, with the message: "It can be charity…or a salary."

This mailing was sent out by NABS (the National Advertising Benevolent Society), the UK's advertising industry charity. To raise money, NABS sent out blank canvases, with the words: "This is the White Christmas everyone is dreaming of." Leading industry personalities were urged to fill the blank space with their own Christmas designs, paintings or scribbles which were then auctioned. The operation enjoyed a 23% response and canvases by the likes of Sir Martin Sorrell raised several thousand pounds for the charity.

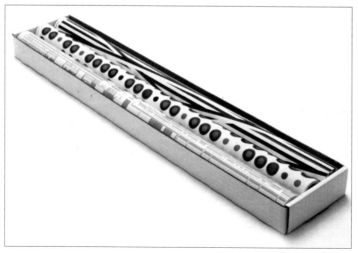

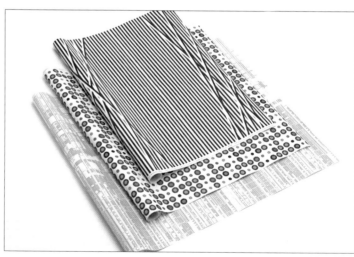

Agency:	Eigen Fabrikaat, Amstelveen	Most companies have too many computer servers. Consolidation would provide more efficient results. Cap Gemini Ernst & Young offers this service in partnership with IBM. The "less is more" theme was expressed to businesses using this mailing, which explained: "We have removed all excess paper from this letter. It is a way of attracting your attention, and ensuring that this mailing is more effective. The same is true for server consolidation."
Creative Directors:	Henk Seelt	
	Paul van 't Veld	
Copywriter:	J-P Nieuwerkerk	
Art Director:	Jan Willem Baggerman	
Client:	Cap Gemini Ernst & Young Server Consolidation Service	

Agency:	Happy Forsman & Bodenfors, Gothenburg	Wrapping paper is useful around Christmas time, so recipients were probably delighted to get this gift box of jazzy styles from paper company Arctic.
Creative Director:	Anders Kornestedt	
Copywriter:	Björn Engström	
Art Directors:	Andreas Kittel	
	Lisa Careborg	
Illustrator:	Lara Bohinc	
Client:	Arctic Paper	

Agency:	ADK Europe, Amsterdam	This "DVD cleaner" packaging actually contained a ball of steel wool. The mailer directed at the press and trade announced the launch of TDK's new scratchproof DVDs.
Creative Director:	Dan Mawdesley	
Copywriter:	Evert-Jan Scherpenzeel	
Art Director:	Hesling Reidinga	
Illustrators:	Ben Koch	
	Brian Florea	
Client:	TDK scratchproof DVDs	

Agency:	Wunderman, Vienna	This direct mail with a spirit of adventure was designed to turn a test drive into a voyage of discovery. Recipients were urged to test drive the new Land Rover Discovery in the most unusual landscapes they could imagine, collect samples of the terrain, and mail it back to their dealer. The driver who sent in the most original sample won a trip to Utah in the United States. The mailing encouraged drivers to appreciate the Discovery in its natural environment – not in a showroom.
Creative Director:	Peter Skudnigg	
Copywriter:	Daniel Schwarz	
Art Director:	Maw Wagner	
Client:	Land Rover Discovery	

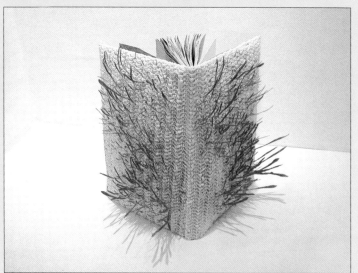
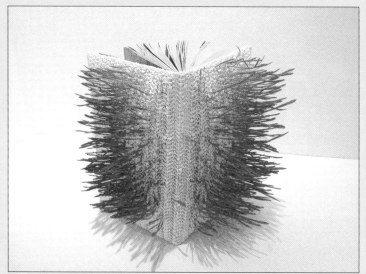

330 **Publications**

Agency:	Zapping, Madrid
Creative Directors:	Uschi Henkes
	Urs Frick
Copywriters:	Urs Frick
	Mercedes Lucena
Art Directors:	Uschi Henkes
	Ana Casanova
	Marcos Fernandez
Client:	Buena Vista International, "The Jungle Book 2" Press Book

This press book was published for the premier of the Disney movie, the Jungle Book 2 in Spain. The book was delivered to critics, journalists and media people. The cover was made from special paper containing seeds which grew within a few days when they were watered, then the book changed into a genuine jungle (book).

Flower

Teddy

Tree

House

Agency:	Futura DDB, Ljubljana	Agency:	TBWA\Germany, Berlin
Creative Directors:	Vital Verlič	Creative Directors:	Kurt-Georg Dieckert
	Žare Kerin		Stefan Schmidt
Copywriter:	Žare Kerin	Copywriter:	Helge Bloeck
Art Director:	Žare Kerin	Art Director:	Boris Schwiedrzik
Photographer:	Janez Štravs	Graphic Designer:	Christine Taylor
Client:	Mura Fashion	Illustrator:	Susann Greuel
	Catalogue	Client:	Sony PlayStation 2

STUFFED ROAST MEAT IN WINE

75 dg rib roast no bones, stuffing: 2 pears, 5dg raisins without kernels, lemon juice, 12 dg one-day-old rolls, 2 tablespoons milk, 5dg butter, 1 egg, 1 yolk, parsley, salt, pepper, 4 tablespoons oil, 5 dg dried bacon, 1 onion bulb, 1 bundle soup vegetables (carrot, parsley, celery), 2 dl white wine, pepper grains, bay leaf, vinegar, 1 Vegeta tablespoon, First prepare the stuffing: cut pears and raisins (if necessary moist them before) in cubes and sprinkle over with lemon juice. Cut rolls into cubes and sprinkle with 2 tablespoons of milk. Mix butter (3dg) foamy with yolk and egg to combine and add bread and fruit cubes. Add salt, pepper, add freshly chopped parsley and mix well. Then prepare meat: Cut it into length and open like a book, so to get a big steak. Batter well, add pepper and sprinkle with Vegeta. Arrange the stuffing over the meat and roll firmly. Tie with thread and sprinkle with salt. Roast the meat all over in a hot oiled tin. Fry bacon, onions and vegetables separately in a pan and add to meat. Add a little vinegar and wine, add bay leaf and pepper grains. Cover with aluminium foil and bake in a pre-heated oven on 200°C for 60 minutes. Before baked , remove the foil and brown, add the wine left and water if necessary. Remove from oven, remove thread and slice it. Arrange on a warm plate and baste with strainer run sauce mixed with butter. As trimming serve potato dough horns.

FRIED CUTLETS WITH MUSHROOMS

8 small pork cutlets, salt, pepper, frying oil, 4dg butter, 20 dg mushrooms, 1 clove of garlic, parsley, 1 dl wine, 1 dl cream, 1 Vegeta teaspoon, hot pepper, Cut cutlets in ends, batter them. Sprinkle salt, pepper and fry on hot oil on both sides. Fry sliced mushrooms separately on hot butter. Add Vegeta, chopped garlic, hot pepper, add water and wine. Leave to boil shortly, add cream mixed with Gussnel. Baste fried hot cutlets with this sauce and sprinkle with chopped parsley. As trimming serve string noodles or potato croquettes.

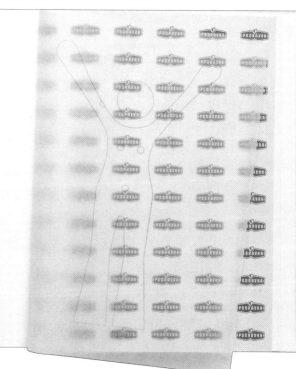

Agency:	Memac Ogilvy, Jeddah	Agency:	Bruketa & Žinić, Zagreb
Creative Director:	Marino Corazza	Creative Directors:	Davor Bruketa
Copywriter:	Fitna Nazer		Nikola Žinić
Art Director:	Edward Roxas	Copywriters:	Davor Bruketa
Client:	Volvo XC90 SUV Brochure		Nikola Žinić
		Art Directors:	Davor Bruketa
			Nikola Žinić
		Photographer:	Marin Topic
		Client:	Podravka Food Company Annual Report

Aluminium foil and greaseproof paper enhance the presentation of this food company's annual report. Perforations along the edges of the pages also allow readers to discover recipes under the financial tables.

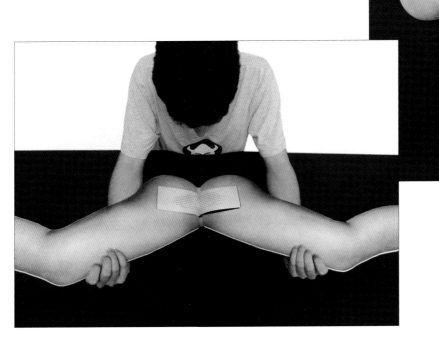

Agency:	Zapping, Madrid	**Agency:**	Weigertpirouzwolf, Hamburg
Creative Directors:	Uschi Henkez	**Creative Directors:**	Kay Eichner
	Manolo Moreno Marquez		Michael Reissinger
	Urs Frick	**Copywriters:**	Manuel Kruck
Copywriters:	Mercedes Lucena		Jonas Bernschneider
	Virginia Mosquera	**Art Director:**	Marc Leitmeyer
Art Directors:	Victor Gomez	**Photographer:**	Hans Starck
	Marcos Fernandez	**Client:**	Endless Pain Tattoo
Client:	S2 Internacional		& Piercing Studio,
	"Golfos y Picardias",		Christmas Calendar
	Erotic Movie Press Book		

This Christmas calendar was produced by Endless Pain, a famous tattoo and piercing studio on the Reeperbahn in Hamburg. Like a traditional German Weihnachts calendar, users could anticipate Christmas by opening a small window each day. Inside each window they discovered the full range of intimate body decorations that Endless Pain offers its clients.

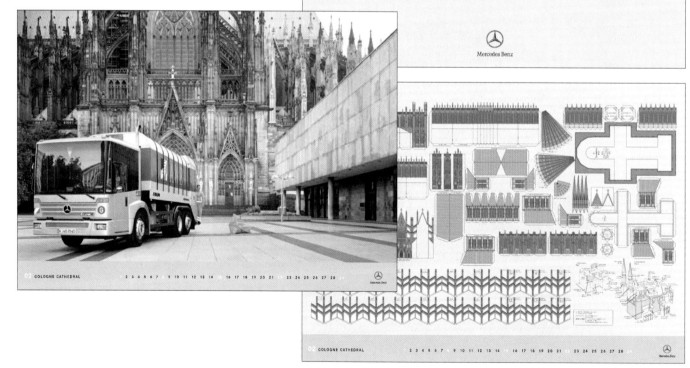

Agency:	Åberg & Co, Stockholm
Creative Director:	Klas Björkhagen
Copywriter:	Peter Kandimaa
Art Director:	Max Åberg
Photographer:	Mattias Edwall
Illustrator:	Lasse Åberg
Client:	Färdlektyr Anthology
	of Short Stories

Färdlektyr (Travel Reads) is an anthology of short stories distributed to teenagers in Sweden by the Swedish public transport authorities. The main objective is to inspire high school students to read and write, while instilling an affinity for public transport. This is the fifth edition. Each year, eight of Sweden's leading writers submit a short story. The book also contains stories and poems by students who can also publish their texts on the Färdlektyr website.

Agency:	H2E Hoehne Habann
	Elser, Ludwigsberg
Creative Directors:	Jens Schmidt
	Peter Herrmann
Copywriter:	Patric Velten
Art Directors:	Raimund Niederwieser
	Thomas Maguin
Photographer:	Marc Trautmann
Illustrator:	Hans Dieter Lahe
Client:	Mercedes-Benz
	Commercial Vehicles
	Calendar 2004

The calendar features Mercedes-Benz commercial vehicles against the backdrop of twelve world-famous European buildings and monuments which are shown from unconventional viewpoints. Instead of concentrating on their public façade, the photographer reveals the lesser-known aspects of these sights – the ones which are more usually seen from the wheel of a commercial vehicle. As a bonus, each month is complemented by a second page featuring a cut-out model of the building which can be assembled.

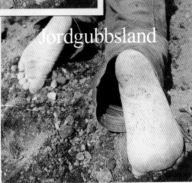

Ordets makt

Agency:	Catch Advertising,	**Agency:**	Ruth, Stockholm	To demonstrate the power of the written
	Wiesbaden	**Creative Director:**	Magnus Ruthström	word this brochure contained a number
Creative Director:	Christine Götzl	**Copywriter:**	Tosse Sund	of images each reproduced on three
Art Director:	Katharina Fröhlich	**Art Director:**	Magnus Ruthström	consecutive pages with different texts.
Photographer:	Michael Link	**Photographers:**	Nina Ericson	The picture shown above takes on different
Client:	Anja Gockel London,		Björn Lindberg	meanings with the words, Afghanistan,
	Birdland Catalogue		Gunnar Smoliansky	Woodstock and strawberry fields.
			Kenneth Hellman	
		Client:	Journalistgruppen	
			Brochure	

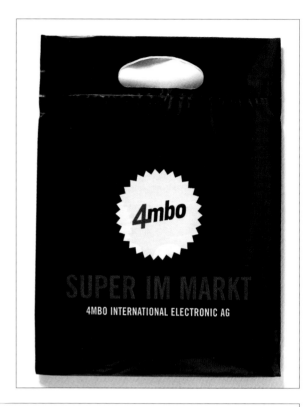

Agency:	Sorec-Media, Moscow	To help relieve stress and inject a little	**Agency:**	Strichpunkt, Stuttgart	4MBO sells low-cost high-tech products via

<table>
<tr><td>Agency:</td><td>Sorec-Media, Moscow</td><td>To help relieve stress and inject a little</td></tr>
<tr><td>Creative Director:</td><td>Gregory Fedorov</td><td>pleasure into their daily routines, recipients</td></tr>
<tr><td>Copywriter:</td><td>Natalia Graifer</td><td>of this calendar could 'pop' each day. If</td></tr>
<tr><td>Art Director:</td><td>Vladimir Gorshkov</td><td>this did not do the trick, they could turn to</td></tr>
<tr><td>Client:</td><td>Self-Promotion</td><td>the bottle of vodka that was protected by</td></tr>
<tr><td></td><td>Bubblewrap Calendar</td><td>the bubblewrap.</td></tr>
</table>

<table>
<tr><td>Agency:</td><td>Strichpunkt, Stuttgart</td><td>4MBO sells low-cost high-tech products via</td></tr>
<tr><td>Creative Director:</td><td>Jochen Rädeker</td><td>big supermarket chains. The annual report</td></tr>
<tr><td>Copywriters:</td><td>Uli Sackmann</td><td>features the 4MBO clients by using their</td></tr>
<tr><td></td><td>Jochen Rädeker</td><td>plastic shopping bags with word-plays on</td></tr>
<tr><td>Art Director:</td><td>Kirsten Dietz</td><td>each store name.</td></tr>
<tr><td>Client:</td><td>4MBO Annual Report</td><td></td></tr>
</table>

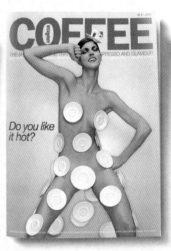

Agency:	Armando Testa, Turin	Agency:	Armando Testa, Turin
Creative Directors:	Maurizio Sala	Creative Director:	Guido Avigdor
	Michele Mariani	Art Directors:	Andrea Lantelme
Art Director:	Camilla Nannavecchia		Teresa Gennuso
Photographer:	Gregory Colbert	Photographer:	Jean-Baptiste Mondino
Client:	Gregory Colbert	Client:	Luigi Lavazza Coffee
	Photography Exhibition Brochure,		
	"Ashes & Snow"		

Agency:	Lowe Brindfors, Stockholm
Creative Directors:	Johan Nilsson
	Magnus Löwenhielm
Art Directors:	Magnus Löwenhielm
	Eva Elgström
	Elin Renck
	Jakob Brundin
Illustrator:	Jakob Brundin
Client:	Tiger of Sweden

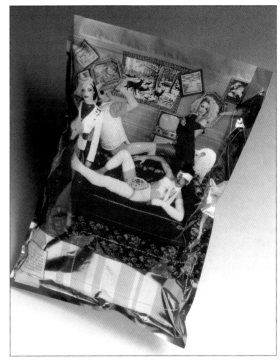

Agency:	McCann-Erickson, Tel-Aviv	**Agency:**	EnVision, Århus
Creative Director:	Alon Seifert	**Creative Director:**	Kim Karmark
Art Director:	Ayala Eilat	**Copywriter:**	Kim Karmark
Photographer:	Yaki Halperine	**Art Director:**	Jesper Hansen
Client:	ESC Mobile Phones	**Client:**	Cocio Chocolate Milk

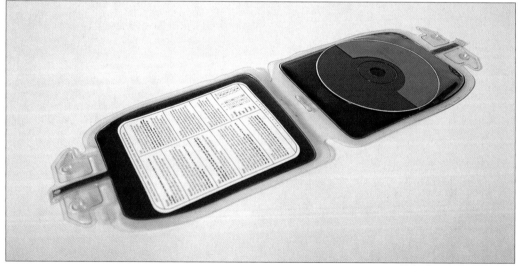

Agency:	Embrink Design, Stockholm	**Agency:**	Ventilator, Bled
Creative Director:	Rossen Lingbell	**Designer:**	Sašo Dornik
Art Director:	Hans Embrink	**Client:**	Siddharta Rh-,
Client:	Reimersholms,		"Blood Bag", CD Cover
	Sthlm Aquavit		

Agency:	Batllegroup/La Sal, Barcelona	**Agencies:**	Turner Duckworth, London & San Francisco
Creative Directors:	Enric Batlle Àngela Giró	**Creative Directors:**	David Turner Bruce Duckworth
Art Directors:	Enric Batlle Àngela Giró	**Designers:**	Christian Eager David Turner Mark Waters
Client:	Comodynes Cosmetics	**Typographer:**	Christian Eager
		Illustrators:	Christian Eager Anthony Biles
		Client:	Poppets Chocolates

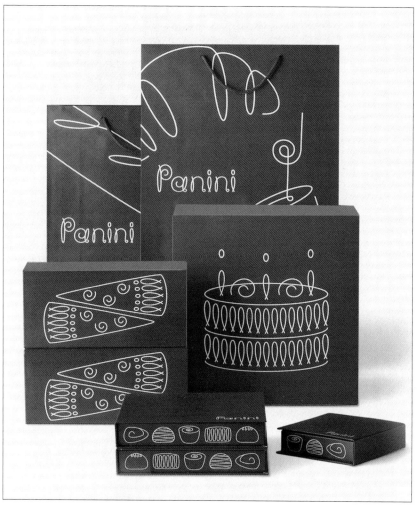

Agency:	Lewis Moberly, London		**Agency:**	Cusidó Comella, Barcelona
Creative Director:	Mary Lewis		**Creative Directors:**	Josep Cusidó
Designers:	Sonja Frick			Jordi Comella
	Hideo Akiba		**Copywriter:**	Ricardo Quemades
Illustrator:	Fiona Verdon-Smith		**Art Director:**	Jordi Comella
Client:	Grand Hyatt Dubai,		**Graphic Designers :**	Joan Puig
	Panini Café & Bakery			David Comella
				Silvia Molas
			Illustrator:	Jose Ramon Domingo
			Client:	Nestlé Caja Roja Chocolates

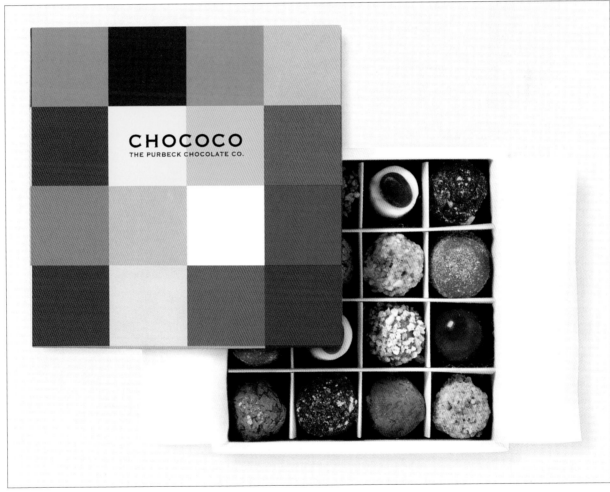

Agency:	Pearlfisher, London	Agency:	Pearlfisher, London
Creative Director:	Karen Welman	Creative Director:	Karen Welman
Production Manager:	Darren Foley	Production Manager:	Darren Foley
Client:	Bees Knees Honey	Client:	Chococo Chocolates

Packaging Design

Agencies:	Turner Duckworth, London & San Francisco	Agency:	K2 Design, Athens
Creative Directors:	David Turner Bruce Duckworth	Creative Director:	Yiannis Kouroudis
		Art Director:	Chrysafis Chrysafis
Designers:	David Turner Luke Snider	Client:	Korres Natural Skin Care Range
Typographers:	David Turner Jonathan Warner		
Client:	Truce Alcoholic Drink		

Agency:	Catch Advertising, Wiesbaden	Agency:	Design Kontoret Silver, Stockholm
Creative Director:	Mario Dzalto	Creative Director:	André Hindersson
Art Director:	Christian Stocker	Copywriter:	Mathias Abrahamsson
Client:	Smoodoo Soft Drink	Art Directors:	Eva Elgström
			Jonas Ström
		Client:	H&M Christmas Packaging

346 **Packaging Design**

Agency:	Blackburn's, London	Agency:	Batllegroup/La Sal, Barcelona
Creative Director:	Matt Thompson	Creative Directors:	Enric Batlle
Art Director:	John Blackburn		Àngela Giró
Client:	Up a Gum Tree	Art Directors:	Enric Batlle
	Australian Wine		Àngela Giró
		Client:	Sensilis Sun Advantage

Agency:	SWE, Schumacher Wessman & Enander, Stockholm	Agencies:	Turner Duckworth, London & San Francisco
Creative Director:	Greger Ulf Nilson	Creative Directors:	David Turner
Copywriter:	Mattias Jersild		Bruce Duckworth
Art Director:	Greger Ulf Nilson	Designers:	Bruce Duckworth
Photographer:	Dawid		Janice Davison
Client:	Vinzavod Bulgarian Wines	Client:	Liz Earle
			Aromatherapy Bath Oils

Illustration & Graphics

Agency:	k2 Design, Athens
Creative Director:	Yiannis Kouroudis
Designers:	Yiannis Kouroudis
	Chrysafis Chrysafis
	Dimitra Diamanti
Client:	Olympic Games Pictograms,
	Athens 2004

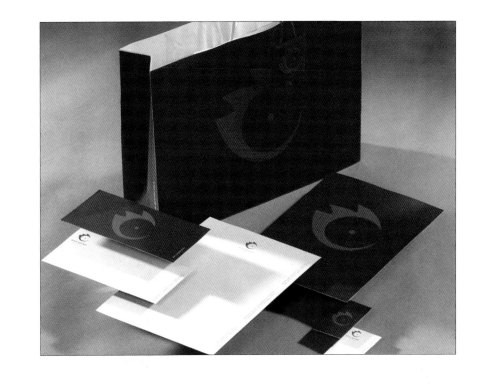

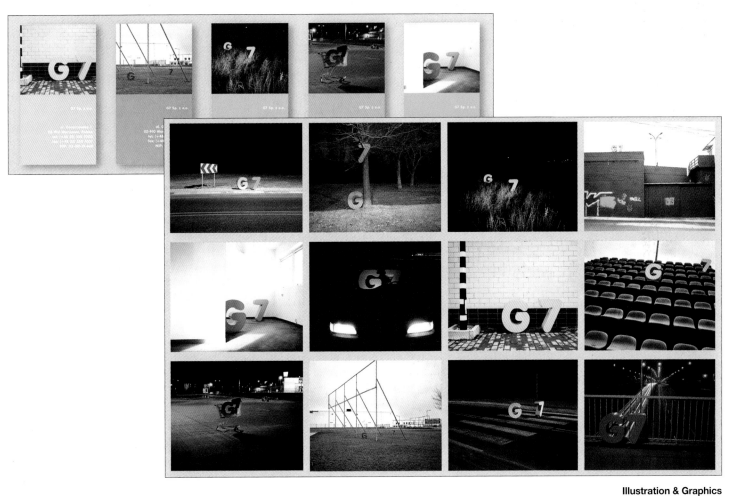

Agency:	Catch Advertising, Wiesbaden	Agency:	G7, Warsaw
Creative Director:	Christine Götzl	Creative Directors:	Przemek Bogdanowicz
Art Director:	Katharina Fröhlich		Maciek Kowalczuk
Photographer:	Michael Link	Copywriters:	Artur Dynowski
Client:	Anja Gockel,		Szymon Saliñski
	Birdland Logo	Art Directors:	Artur Dynowski
			Szymon Saliñski
		Photographer:	Szymon Roginski
		Client:	G7, Logos &
			Business Cards

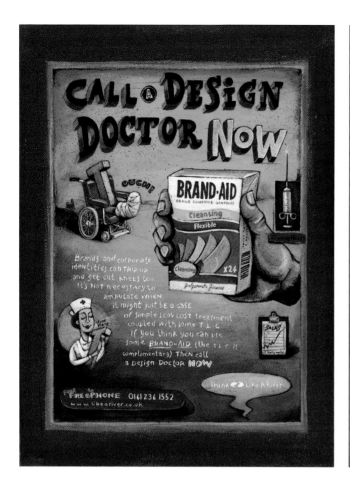

Agency:	Like A River, Manchester		**Agency:**	Change Communication, Frankfurt
Creative Directors:	Rob Taylor		**Creative Director:**	Julian Michalski
	Peter Rogers		**Copywriter:**	Michael Bell
Copywriter:	Rob Taylor		**Art Director:**	Michael Bell
Art Director:	Rob Taylor		**Client:**	Liane's Retrotapeten
Illustrator:	Simon Henshaw			(Retro Wallpaper),
	Andy O'Shaughnessy			Letterheads
Client:	Like A River,			
	Self-Promotion			

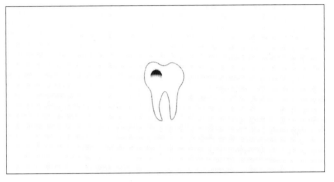

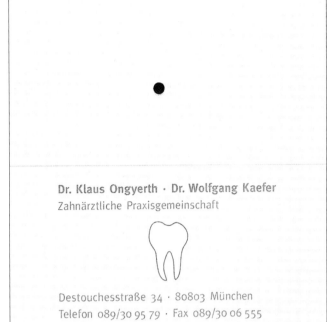

Dr. Klaus Ongyerth · Dr. Wolfgang Kaefer
Zahnärztliche Praxisgemeinschaft

Destouchesstraße 34 · 80803 München
Telefon 089/30 95 79 · Fax 089/30 06 555

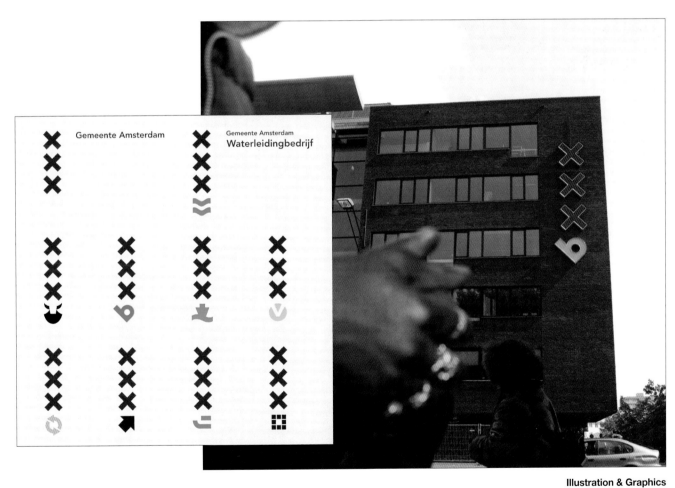

Gemeente Amsterdam

Gemeente Amsterdam
Waterleidingbedrijf

Agency:	Serviceplan Gruppe, Munich	**Agencies:**	Eden Design & Communication, Amsterdam
Creative Director:	Ekkehard Frenkler		Thonik, Amsterdam
Art Director:	Daniela Bardini	**Creative Directors:**	Edo Van Dijk
Client:	Dr. Klaus Ongyerth &		Jan Brinkman
	Dr. Wolfgang Kaefer		Thomas Widdershoven
	(Dentists), Business		Nikki Gonnissen
	Card	**Client:**	City of Amsterdam,
			Identity Programme

The new Amsterdam house style regrouped 55 city districts and services under a common visual theme.

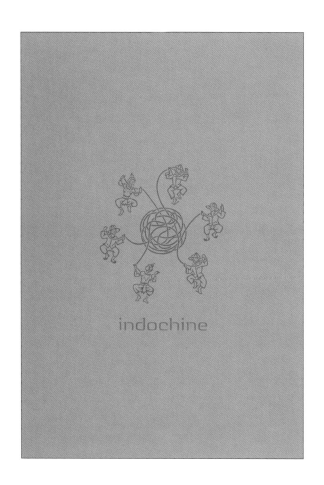

Agency:	Lewis Moberly, London		Agency:	Leo Burnett, Prague
Creative Director:	Mary Lewis		Creative Director:	Basil Mina
Designer:	Bryan Clark		Copywriter:	Michael Yee
Illustrator:	Graham Evernden		Art Director:	Michael Martin
Client:	Grand Hyatt Dubai,		Photographer:	Michael Martin
	Indochine Restaurant Logo		Client:	Amnesty International

A trip to Sweden.
Design exhibition at the
Swedish Embassy in
Tokyo, October 5-15th.
スウェーデンへの旅

A trip to Sweden.
Design exhibition at the
Swedish Embassy in
Tokyo, October 5-15th.
スウェーデンへの旅

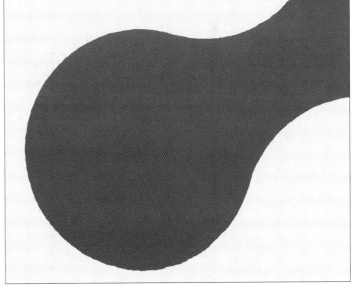

A trip to Sweden.
Design exhibition at the
Swedish Embassy in
Tokyo, October 5-15th.
スウェーデンへの旅

Agency:	Kitchen, Madrid
Creative Directors:	Araceli Iranzo
	Jose Carnero
	Juan Lassalle
Client:	Wind Production Company

Agency:	BVD, Blidholm Vagnemark
	Design, Stockholm
Creative Director:	Susanna Nygren Barrett
Art Director:	Susanna Nygren Barrett
Illustrator:	Susanna Nygren Barrett
Client:	SMI Swedish Furniture Industry
	Association

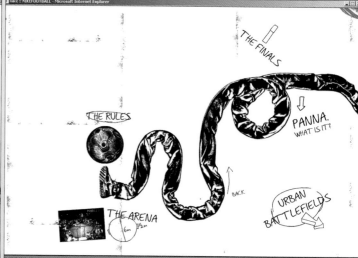

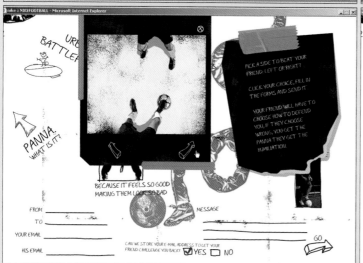

Agency:	Framfab Denmark, Copenhagen
Creative Director:	Lars Bastholm
Copywriter:	Thomas Robson
Art Director:	Rasmus Frandsen
Producer:	Sara Trier
Client:	Nike Footaball, Panna K.O.

Panna is Amsterdam street slang for playing the ball through the legs of your opponent. If you make a Panna you're a hero – if you get one, you're humiliated. Panna K.O. is a one-on-one knock-out competition. Games last 3 minutes – or until someone gets a Panna. On the website, you can view the finals, watch the moves of top players, download screen savers and play the game online with friends.

Agency:	Framfab Denmark, Copenhagen	
Creative Director:	Lars Bastholm	
Copywriter:	Rhiannon Davies	
Art Directors:	Lars Cortsen	
	Robert Thomsen	
Producer:	Sara Trier	
Client:	Nike Women	

Nike's lean and sweaty website allows women to choose gear, get exercise and training tips, and watch a film on how to get fit in just four weeks!

Agency:	Framfab Denmark, Copenhagen
Creative Director:	Lars Bastholm
Copywriter:	Jamie McPhee
Art Director:	Damian Claassens
Producers:	Jesper Kjaer
	Lars-Bo Heidemann
Client:	Nike Freestyle

Reintroducing us to the Nike stick man who enthralled us in a series of ads, this site shows us how to make all his moves. It also gives details about the stars and – most importantly – tells us how to get hold of their gear.

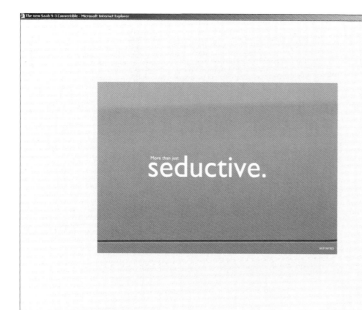

Agency:	Lowe Tesch, Stockholm	Saab's print campaign "More than a
Creative Director:	Johan Tesch	convertible" used three ads focussing on
Project Managers:	Nils Lindhe	different aspects of the 9-3 Convertible:
	Anna Axelsson	design, individuality and versatility. Each
Copywriter:	Paul Jackson	ad featured a website address, and those
Art Directors:	Patrik Westerdahl	who were tempted by the car could continue
	Tim Scheibel	their Saab experience on the internet.
Flash Designers:	Marcus Johansson	
	Niklas Fransson	
Photographer:	Adrian Burt	
Illustrator:	Niklas Fransson	
Producer:	Anna Axelsson	
Client:	Saab 9-3 Convertible	

Agency:	Lowe Tesch, Stockholm	While it contains all the expected elements
Creative Director:	Johan Tesch	of a site devoted to an automobile – lots
Project Manager:	Nils Lindhe	of facts and figures and the ability to zoom
Copywriters:	Paul Jackson	in on selected details – this showcase for
	Tom Eriksen	the Saab 9-3 Aero includes built-in
Art Director:	Patrik Westerdahl	"interference". The idea is that the new car
Flash Designers:	Marcus Johansson	is so fast and innovative that even your web
	Neil Jedrzejewski	browser has trouble keeping up.
	Niklas Fransson	
Photographer:	Adrian Burt	
Client:	Saab 9-3 Aero	

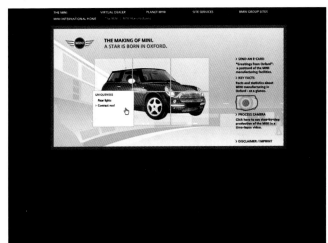

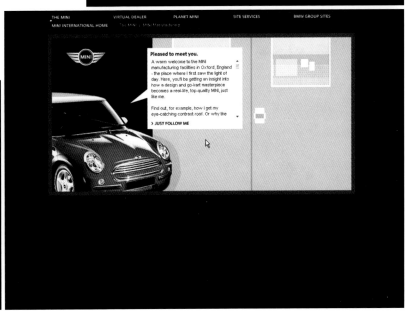

Agency:	BBDO InterOne, Hamburg	An art theft in Barcelona was the setting for this Mini Mission. A story created by thriller writer Val McDermid formed the basis of the site. Users could access detective Sam Cooper's notebook, log in to the database S.O.L.V.E.D. and discover all facts necessary to start their investigation. The story then continued in real-life: after submitting online applications, 84 "detectives" were recruited to solve the case on the streets of Barcelona – behind the wheels of Mini Coopers.
Creative Director:	Sandra Schittkowski	
Copywriter:	Oliver Bentz	
Designer:	David Hoffmann	
Technical Director:	David Athey	
Programmers:	Eric Funk	
	Oliver Rebbin	
	Eva Sürek	
	Nicole Kengyel	
	Andreas Wellhausen	
Producer:	Sven Heckmann	
Client:	Mini, "Mission Mini"	

Agency:	BBDO InterOne, Hamburg	"How does the Mini become a Mini?" – In response to Mini fans' interest in the processes behind the scenes at the Mini manufacturing facilities and in order to reinforce Mini customers' long-term enthusiasm for the brand, the answer to this question is provided in full by the international online special "Mini Manufacturing". A virtual tour of the Mini factory in Oxford, England, shows how the little cars are brought into the world. Including history, trivia and behind-the-scenes info.
Creative Directors:	Sandra Schittkowski	
	Martin Gassner	
Copywriters:	Stephen James	
	Oliver Bentz	
	Silke Gottschlack	
	Anke Schenk	
Art Director:	Margit Schröder	
Illustrators:	Stefan Schulz, Meike Ufer	
Programmers:	David Athey, Eva Sürek	
	Rico Marquardt	
Producer:	Oliver Rosenthal	
Client:	Mini, "Mini Manufacturing"	

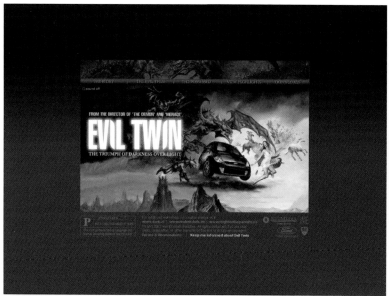

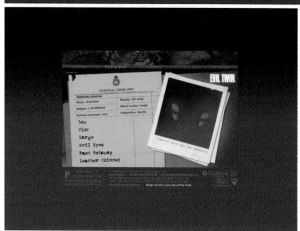

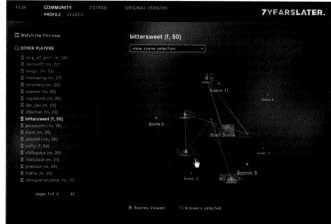

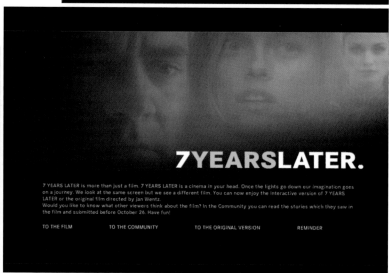

Internet Sites

Agency:	Wunderman Interactive, London
Creative Directors:	Simon Milliship Richard Last
Designer:	Richard Barrett
Client:	Ford Sport Ka, "Evil Twin"

This dark and gothic site promotes the Ford Sportska – positioned here as the "evil twin" of the Ford Ka, that nifty little runabout traditionally bought by women. The accent of the site is unmistakably masculine, with a horror film poster of a homepage, mug shots of "possessed" owners, and short clips portraying the Ka behaving in an evil manner.

Agency:	Scholz & Volkmer, Wiesbaden
Creative Director:	Heike Brockmann
Project Manager:	Christoph Kehren
Copywriter:	Andreas Henke
Art Director:	Jenny Fitz
Director:	Jan Wentz
Programmer:	Thorsten Kraus
Flash Programmer:	Duc-Thien Bui
Client:	Mercedes-Benz, "7 Years Later"

The site takes the form of a short psychological drama directed by Jan Wentz. A story of jealousy and adultery – with lots of shots of the glossy Mercedes – the film is interactive, allowing users to splice the 13 scenes together as they like. Users are presented with a choice at the end of each scene, and the decisions they take affect the outcome of the film.

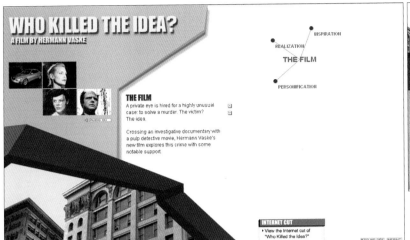

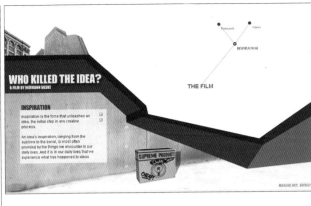

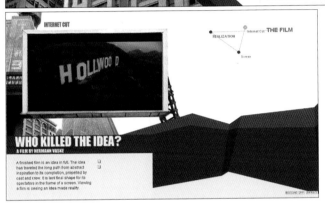

Agency:	BBDO InterOne, Hamburg
Creative Director:	Simone Ashoff
Copywriter:	John Dubois
Art Director:	Mike John Otto
Designers:	Jochen Roehling
	Achim Janes
Technical Director:	Thomas Feldhaus
Programmers:	Eric Funk
	Rico Marquardt
	David Loehr
	Jan Mankopf
Client:	BMW Series 5

A host of detective movie clichés are entertainingly disinterred in "Who Killed the Idea?", a film directed by Hermann Vaske with support from BMW. Presented on an explorative website accompanying its development – and featuring the BMW 5 Series – the movie recounts the investigation of a murder with a very unusual victim: the idea.

Agency:	Forsman & Bodenfors, Gothenburg
Copywriters:	Jacob Nelson
	Filip Nilsson
	Jesper Lövkvist
Art Directors:	Mathias Appelblad
	Anders Eklind
	Martin Cedergren
	Andreas Malm
	Mikko Timonen
Designer:	Lars Johansson
Client:	Volvo XC 90

Potential buyers of the Volvo XC90 SUV are invited on a virtual tour through the countryside of Sweden – with the chance to find out about the car's road holding, safety and entertainment capabilities along the way.

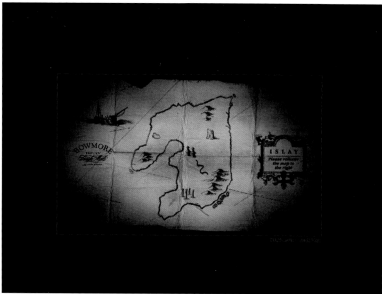

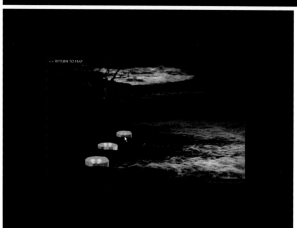

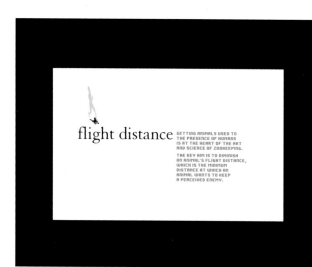

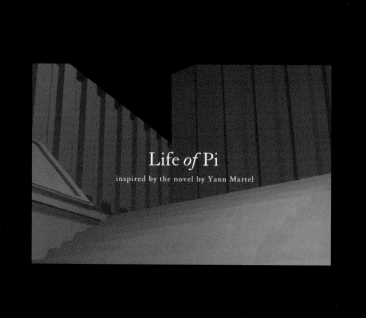

Agency:	Citigate Smarts, Edinburgh	An online game transports users to the mysterious island of Islay – home of Bowmore whisky – first virtually, and then in reality if they solve all the clues and win the competition. With a treasure map, spooky locations and plenty of riddles, the site has all the ingredients of a classic adventure.
Creative Director:	Pete Martin	
Copywriter:	Colin Montgomery	
Art Director:	Ben Craig	
Photographer:	Roben Antoniewicz	
Client:	Bowmore Whisky	

Agency:	Hoss Gifford, Glasgow	A combination of game and animation allows users to become Pi – or Piscine Molitor Patel, to give him his full name – the hero of Yann Martel's 2002 Man Booker Prize winning book, Life of Pi. The site features scenes from Pi's life: the Pondicherry Zoo where he grew up; the ship on which his parents try to transport animals across the Pacific Ocean; and the lifeboat in which he is stranded with a Bengal tiger after a shipwreck.
Creative Director:	Hoss Gifford	
Copywriter:	Yann Martel	
Art Director:	Hoss Gifford	
Illustrator:	Hoss Gifford	
Production:	Screenbase, Edinburgh	
Director:	Hoss Gifford	
Producer:	Peter Collingridge	
Client:	Canongate Press, "Life of Pi"	

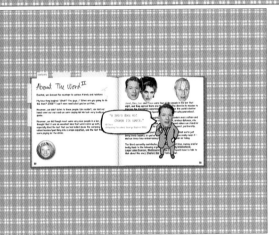

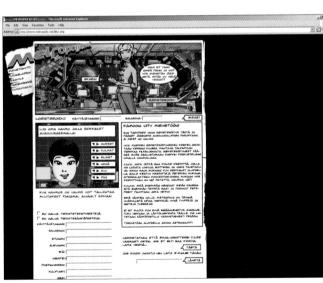

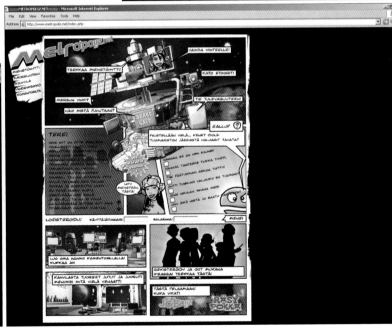

Agency:	Atmosphere Cph, Copenhagen	This site uses a book-style format to tell us – most amusingly – about the services offered by The Word, a Danish-to-English translation, subtitling and copywriting agency.	
Creative Directors:	Carsten Gottshalck Vigh Tobias Smidt-Fibiger		
Copywriter:	Greg Hanscomb		
Art Directors:	Søren Nørgaard Chaga Signe Bruun		
Illustrator:	Søren Nørgaard		
Client:	The Word Translation Agency		

Agencies:	Nitro FX, Helsinki Contra, Helsinki	This Manga style site enables users to meet various cool cartoon characters on a metallic space station. It is designed to attract young people to the metal industry – not an obvious career choice.	
Creative Directors:	Tuomas Harju Jussi Loytokorpi		
Client:	Metropoliz Metal Industry		

Agency:	Springtime, Stockholm	On entering the Absolut site visitors are presented with three separate rooms. The first room, Absolut Display, takes over with a rolling series of trailers on the brand's latest events. In Absolut Reality, users can delve into the world of mixing and tasting with the six Absolut flavours. Each flavour is featured through recipes, short films and games and experimental tools. Absolut Campaigns features the latest Absolut advertising from around the world and delves deep into the communications activities of a world-class brand.
Creative Director:	Mårten Ivert	
Project Manager:	Ola Spännar	
Copywriter:	Marika Jarislowski	
Art Director:	Ted Persson	
Designers:	Jesper Klarin	
	Oskar Sundberg	
Photographer:	Per Erik Hagman	
Technical Director:	Otto Giesenfeld	
Production:	Pixshift	
Producer:	Magnus Wålsten	
Client:	Absolut Vodka	

Agency:	Springtime, Stockholm	The Absolut Vanilia micro site tells the story of hip singletons Alexa and Jason and their separate nights out – leading to the moment when they meet. Users follow the story by dragging the mouse across the screen, which unreels in a series of glamorous images supported by cheesy dialogue. But the most compelling part of the site is the "Pick-up line generator". Click to get a great chat-up line or put-down, such as: "I like a man who can make me laugh, but that shirt isn't what I had in mind."
Creative Director:	Staffan Bane	
Project Managers:	Andreas Jerat	
	Mattias Järnemar	
Copywriters:	Linda Sandberg	
	Steve Strid	
Art Directors:	Niklas Peterson	
	Jörgen Jöralv	
Designer:	Dan Lindgren	
Technical Director:	Otto Giesenfeld	
Production:	Projector	
Producer:	Ola Spännar	
Client:	Absolut Vodka, "Vanilia"	

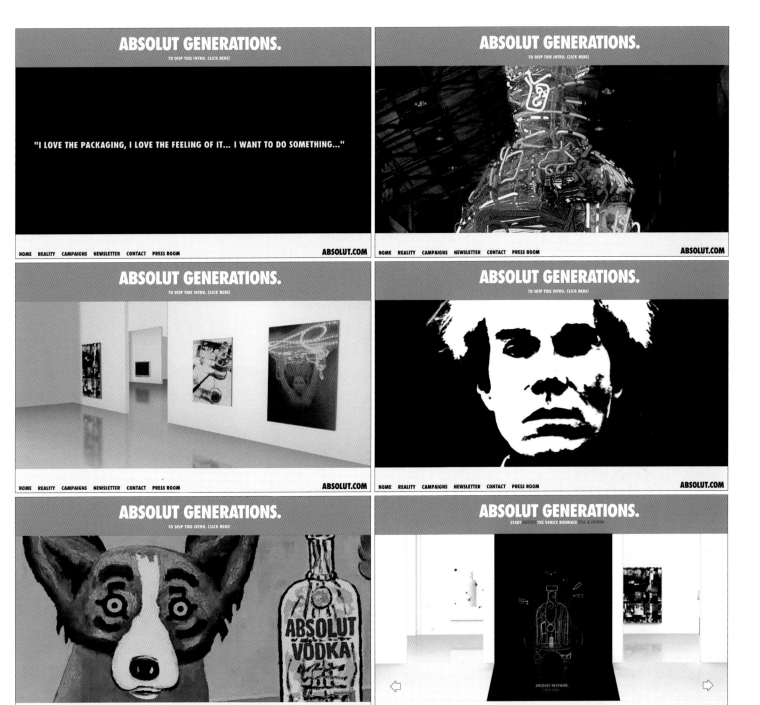

Agency:	Springtime, Stockholm
Project Manager:	Andreas Jerat
Copywriter:	Dan MacDougal
Art Director:	Ted Persson
Graphic Designer:	Jesper Klarin
Photographer:	Per-Erik Hagman
Technical Director:	Otto Giesenfeld
Production:	Pixshift
Flash Designers:	Oskar Sundberg
	Mårten Ivert
	Tomas Forsberg
Producer:	Magnus Wålsten
Client:	Absolut Vodka, "Generations"

The Absolut Generations website strengthens the brands' involvement with contemporary art via their exhibition at the 2003 Venice Biennale. Absolut paired up two generations of artists, a known artist with his or her chosen protégé, to create various pieces of contemporary art. Included is an interactive piece of art which melts computer technology with sonic art into a "sound film" in which Absolut bottles are used to create a virtual landscape, taking the shape and appearance of buildings. Visitors are invited to contribute and interact with the work of art by inputting personal data.

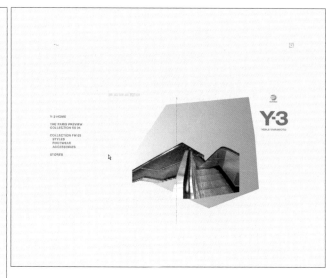

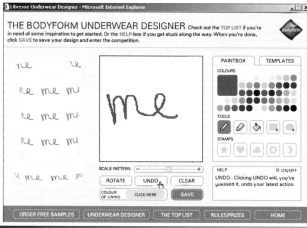

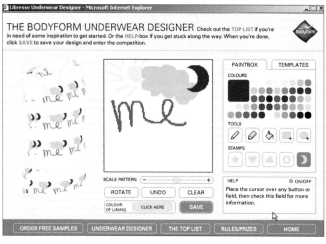

Agency:	Neue Digitale, Frankfurt	The site was designed to promote Y-3, a sportswear brand created by adidas and fashion designer Yohji Yamamoto. Kaleidoscopic images collide to form stills of models wearing the clothes, reflecting the brand's eclectic personality. Users can also access a gallery of snapshots from Paris Fashion Week.
Creative Director:	Olaf Czeschner	
Copywriters:	Roland Grossmann	
	Katarina Steinijans	
Art Director:	Rolf Borcherding	
Programmers:	Marius Bulla	
	Jens Steffen	
Producer:	Kater Haak	
Client:	Adidas Sport Style Y-3	

Agency:	Forsman & Bodenfors, Gothenburg	Using various drag and click tools, users could enter a competition to design their own colourful underwear. Winners received a real-life recreation of their entries.
Copywriter:	Jesper Lövkvist	
Art Directors:	Lars Johansson	
	Lotta Ågerup	
Designer:	Lars Johansson	
Production:	Ceruna	
	Raketspel	
Producer:	Mathias Appelblad	
Client:	Libresse	
	Sanitary Towels	

THÁI-CÔNG MY PARENTS
Eine Hommage an die Mode, die Fotografie und das Leben

DEUTSCH   ENGLISH

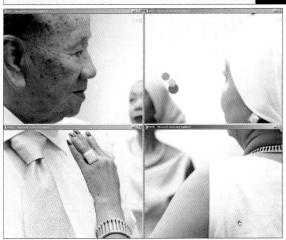

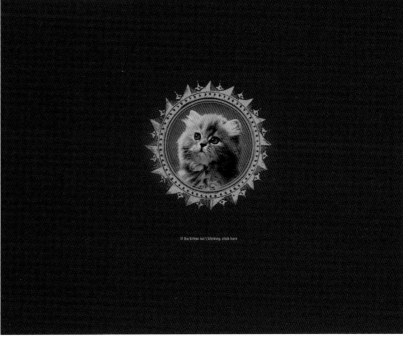

Agency:	Nordpol+ Hamburg Agentur Für Kommunikation, Hamburg	Fashion stylist Thái Công persuaded leading international photographers to shoot pictures of his parents modelling designer clothing and jewellery. Through the website, users could stage their own virtual "exhibition" of the results. The real exhibition, held in Hamburg in summer 2002, showed how clothing and photography affect our perceptions of individuals and their personalities.	
Creative Director:	Ingo Fritz		
Art Director:	Gunther Schreiber		
Designers:	Dominik Anweiler Mark Höfler		
Client:	Thái Công Fashion, "My Parents"		

Production Co.:	Gorgeous Enterprises, London
Creative Director:	Chris Palmer
Copywriter:	Tom Carty
Art Director:	Frank Budgen
Designer:	Katharina Leuzinger
Technical Directors:	David Buckley
	Steven Tilkin
	Robert Bader
	Tony Volfe
Producers:	Mark Iremonger
	Piero Frecobaldi
Client:	Gorgeous

This literally Gorgeous website – from the production company of the same name – features kitsch photographs of kittens. But click on their collars and you can access the reels of some extremely famous directors: Frank Budgen, Peter Thwaites, Ben Seresin, Tom Carty and Chris Palmer.

Agency:	TBWA\Germany, Berlin
Creative Director:	Kai Roeffen
Copywriter:	Donald Tursman
Art Director:	Rainer Schmidt
Illustrator:	Christian Borstlap
Client:	SVF, Self-Defense Classes for Women

The pop up reveals a pretty cartoon girl with a slender physique: but try and click on her with the mouse, and she deftly kicks or punches the arrow away with killer karate blows. The ad was for a women's self defence class.

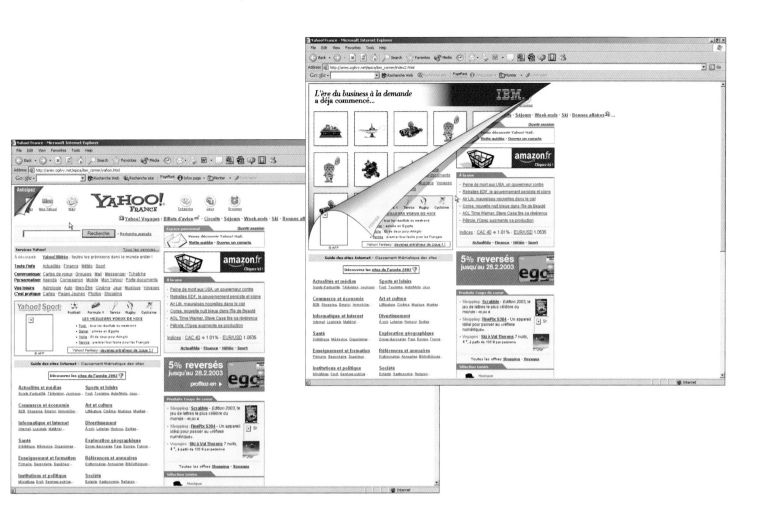

Agency:	OgilvyOne Worldwide, Paris	This promotion enabled users to "peel back" their search engine homepage to reveal a series IBM related icons underneath. Then they could click on the binoculars to look into the future, or use the time machine to discover ways of undoing the errors of the past. The magic lamp provided a business genie, while a vial of magic powder promised to add technological sparkle to their company. Finally, the universal business adaptor enabled businesses to work together.	
Creative Director:	Pepijn Vlasman		
Copywriters:	Thomas Baker		
	Richard Woodruff		
Art Directors:	Jérome Muguet		
	Jean Christophe Hemez		
Producers:	Christophe Beuve		
	Samantha Mary		
Client:	IBM e-Business on Demand		

Agency:	Neue Digitale, Frankfurt	These pop-ups from Nitro Snowboards tell a story. The folks at Nitro have been receiving ransom notes: "Send me a Nitro Youth Brigade 1.59 (your new board) and your mom comes home alive…" The pop-up shows us a copy of the note and a photo of a plastic bag with a severed finger in it! But it goes on to tell us that blackmail won't work. If we want a new board, we'll have to wait for the launch.	
Creative Director:	Olaf Czeschner		
Copywriter:	Roland Grossmann		
Art Director:	Rolf Borcherding		
Client:	Nitro Snowboards		

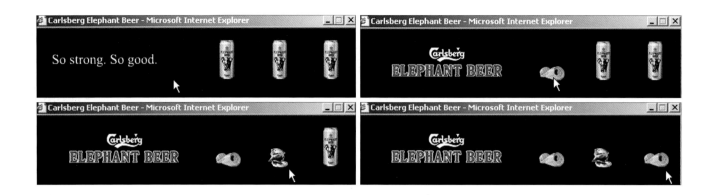

Agency:	TBWA\Germany, Berlin	After users clicked on the banner, the cans
Creative Director:	Kai Roeffen	of Elephant beer were crushed by an un-
Copywriters:	Gerd Turetschek	seen force – and the entire web page
	Siegfried Palomba	shuddered with the impact.
Art Directors:	Gerfried Grunke	
	Knut Burgdorf	
	Ben Teismann	
Illustrators:	Christiane Licht	
	Melanie Probstmayer	
Production:	Digerati, Munich	
Client:	Carlsberg Elephant Beer,	
	"Dizzy"	

Agency:	The Bearded Lady DDB,	To invite advertising agencies to a seminar
	Stockholm	on internet advertising, web specialists The
Copywriter:	Magnus Ericsson	Bearded Lady created personalised pop-
Art Director:	Andreas Dahlqvist	ups. When the targeted agencies visited
Producer:	Johan Öbrink	Aftonbladet (the most popular newspaper
Client:	Aftonbladet,	on the web in Sweden) the regular ads were
	"Freakshow"	replaced by spoof ads for their biggest
		clients. (For instance, Leo Burnett saw a
		spoof McDonald's ad promoting the new
		Murdah Burgah.) What the agencies did not
		know was that they were the only ones to
		see these ads. The implication was that the
		web makes one-to-one marketing possible.

reality sucks.
films are cool.

more
than
56th movies
edinburgh
international   ticket hotline
                 0131 623 8030
film
festival   find your movies with
in association with Film Four   suggest-o-tron
14-25 august 2002

 Online Films   369

Agency:	Hoss Gifford, Glasgow	This film promoting the Edinburgh Film
Creative Director:	Hoss Gifford	Festival shows an animated figure
Copywriter:	Hoss Gifford	performing various stunts – being fired out
Art Director:	Hoss Gifford	of a cannon, dangling from a helicopter, and
Illustrator:	Hoss Gifford	jumping from a tall building into a swimming
Production:	Eiff	pool – before suddenly finding himself in a
Director:	Hoss Gifford	boring, real-life street. The figure studies his
Producer:	Richard Baker	bland surroundings and scratches his head,
Client:	Edinburgh	bemused. Reality sucks. Films are cool.
	International Film Festival,	
	"Reality Sucks"	

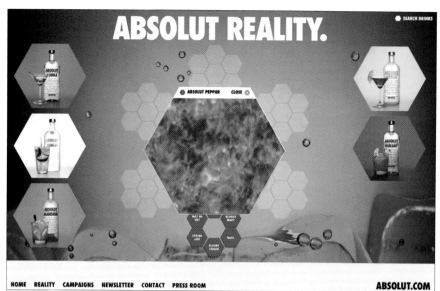

370   **Online Films**

Agency:	Springtime, Stockholm
Project Manager:	Charlotta Larsson
Copywriter:	Marika Jarislowsky
Art Director:	Marten Ivert
Flash Designer:	Mårten Ivert
Technical Director:	Otto Giesenfeld
Production:	Pixshift
Producer:	Magnus Wålsten
Client:	Absolut Vodka, "Peppar"

This short animated film from Absolut tells a fable about the power of the pepper. "My grandmother told me how the peppers laughed as they set fire to the tongues of strangers," it relates, as a series of exotic images unfold. The film uses fiery colours and passionate Spanish music to evoke the emotions imparted by drinking Absolut Peppar.

Agency:	Springtime, Stockholm
Project Manager:	Charlotta Larsson
Copywriter:	Marika Jarislowsky
Art Director:	Marten Ivert
Flash Designer:	Mårten Ivert
Technical Director:	Otto Giesenfeld
Production:	Pixshift
Producer:	Magnus Svensson
Client:	Absolut Vodka, "Mandarin"

Once again, a charming animated tale saturates us with exotic images, this time urging us to recall the fresh taste of mandarins – as used in Absolut's flavoured vodka. Like the drink, the film contains hints of sweetness and warmth.

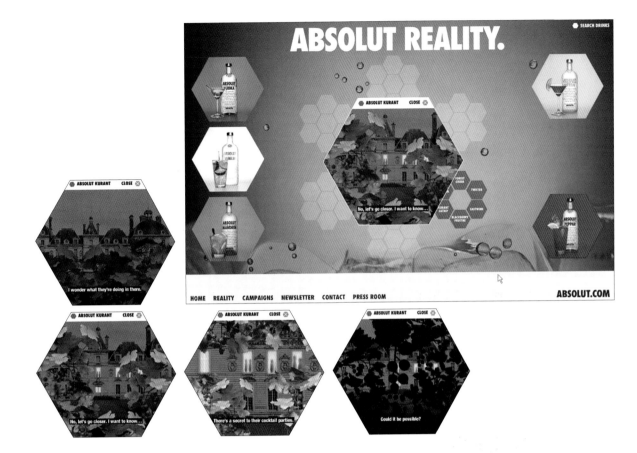

Agency:	Springtime, Stockholm	This time, Absolut's web film transports us to a mysterious mansion under a purple sky. From the cover of redcurrant bushes, we peer at silhouettes in its lighted windows. Why are the cocktail parties at the mansion so popular? Could it have something to do with redcurrant flavoured vodka?
Project Manager:	Charlotta Larsson	
Copywriter:	Marika Jarislowsky	
Art Director:	Marten Ivert	
Flash Designer:	Mårten Ivert	
Technical Director:	Otto Giesenfeld	
Production:	Pixshift, Stockholm	
Producer:	Magnus Wålsten	
Client:	Absolut Vodka, "Kurant"	

Agency:	Robert/Boisen & Like-Minded, Copenhagen	To promote the annual advertising festival in Cannes, this web film was not a film at all. In fact, those who clicked on it were told: "Sorry, this film is in Cannes." Using viral marketing, the film was sent out by email to people working in the ad industry.
Creative Director:	Michael Robert	
Copywriter:	Joachim Nielsen	
Art Director:	Michael Nyrop-Larsen	
Illustrator:	Andy Dymock	
Client:	Cannes Lions Festival	

Agency:	Loose Moose, London	Want to know what's really going on under your big toenail? Take a look at this gross but groovy animated film from Loose Moose. A trio of evil characters let rip on their host's skin until being zapped by a curative cream. The film for a fictitious client was made to demonstrate the production company's computer graphics capabilities.
Creative Director:	Ken Lidster	
Animators:	Dotti Colvin	
	John Shearlock	
Illustrator:	Peter Williamson	
Production:	Loose Moose	
Director:	Ken Lidster	
Producer:	Glenn Holberton	
Client:	Loose Moose,	
	"Simalip"	
	Viral Commercial	

Agency:	141 Portugal/Bates	Guronsan is a popular medicine used to combat various excesses – such as alcohol, cholesterol, stress and smoking. In this viral film, sent out to a targeted database by email, fake boy's band The Excesses are wiped out by a giant tube of Guronsan while performing their latest hit.
	Red Cell, Lisbon	
Creative Director:	Susana Albuquerque	
Copywriter:	João Galhardas	
Art Director:	Rui Pedro	
Production:	Bambú, Lisbon	
Directors:	Pablo Seron	
	Catarina Matos	
Producer:	Cristina Pryce	
Client:	Guronsan	
	Hangover Medicine	

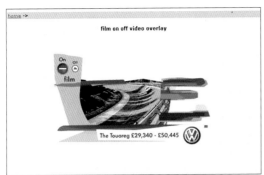

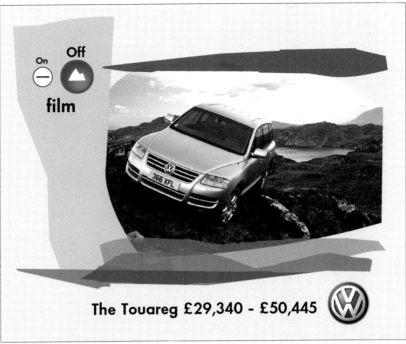

Agency:	Tribal DDB, London	The Volkswagen Toureg is equally at home
Creative Directors:	Sam Ball	on or off the road – as those watching this
	Dave Bedwood	film could see. Simply by clicking "on" or
Copywriters:	Sam Ball	"off" buttons, they could switch between
	Dave Bedwood	two simultaneously running strands of
Art Directors:	Sam Ball	footage showing the car performing on a
	Dave Bedwood	racetrack, or in rugged and mountainous
Producers:	Robin Grant	terrain.
	Sally Gallagher	
Client:	Volkswagen Touareg	

Agency:	The Bearded Lady DDB, Stockholm	To promote the Covert Strike video game, the agency created a fake home shopping
Copywriter:	David Sundin	film. A harmless-looking salesman
Art Director:	Andreas Dahlqvist	demonstrates a knife that's so sharp, "you'll
Production:	Too Much Too Soon	cut yourself on the handle". As incentives,
Director:	Mattias Sandström	buyers are also offered a free pistol,
Client:	IGI 2 Video Game, "Covert Strike"	handgrenades and a host of other lethal items – all for the price of the video game.

Agency:	Forsman & Bodenfors, Gothenburg
Copywriters:	Jacob Nelson
	Filip Nilsson
	Jesper Lövkvist
Art Directors:	Mathias Appelblad
	Anders Eklind
	Martin Cedergren
	Andreas Malm
	Mikko Timonen
Designer:	Lars Johansson
Client:	Volvo XC 90 Launch

For the launch of the Volvo XC90 SUV, the agency devised an integrated campaign that revolved around the web. Print ads, posters, TV spots and ads on websites all directed potential customers to the car's website. Once on the site, they could take a compelling virtual drive through the Swedish countryside in the new vehicle (see also page 359).

Agency:	Forsman & Bodenfors, Gothenburg
Copywriter:	Johan Olivero
Art Directors:	Mathias Appelblad
	Martin Cedergren
	Mikko Timonen
	Anders Eklind
Designer:	Lars Johansson
Client:	Volvo XC SUVs

In order to promote the rugged Volvo XC70 and XC90 SUVs, ads on websites warned users that they risked getting fat and lazy in front of their computer screens. Why not burn a few more calories? By clicking on the ads, users learned that if they test-drove the Volvo, they could enter a competition that might win them a week-long holiday of cross-country driving, skiing, climbing, hiking (and plenty of socialising!) on the Volvo Cross-Country Expedition.

Agency:	Edge Communication, Brussels
Creative Directors:	Serge Dielens
	Miss Gazzoline
	Maja Vanderborst
	Chantal Richez
Art Director:	Miss Gazzoline
Director:	Serge Dielens
Client:	Lipton Ice Green Tea

To launch Lipton's Iced Green Tea in Belgium, Edge Communication chose the Hawaiian island of Kauai – one of the greenest islands on the planet – to reflect the relaxing and health-giving properties of the drink. This would be explained via web pop-ups leading to the new internet site. The site offered users the chance to win a holiday in Kauai. But before the campaign began, underground 'buzz' was created by distributing cans of tea to style leaders via gallery openings and fashion shows. There were also Green events in leading Belgian nightclubs and advertorials in trendy magazines.

Agencies:	OgilvyOne Worldwide, London OgilvyInteractive Worldwide, London	**Agency:**	Joshua Agency, London
Client:	IBM, Wimbledon Sponsorship	**Creative Directors:**	Mitch Levy Helen Weddle
		Copywriter:	Christian Clark
		Art Directors:	Rod Clausen Richard Morgan
		Photographer:	Carl Warner
		Client:	The London Eye, Observation Wheel

The objective of the campaign was to show UK companies how IBM supports the Wimbledon tennis tournament with technology that could be relevant to their businesses. The campaign showcased IBM's role at Wimbledon via traditional media (outdoor, press and direct mail) as well as screen savers, emails (to Financial Times subscribers) – and a banner providing live match results, statistics, news and images. The banner also delivered Radio Wimbledon live. The campaign ran during the Wimbledon Championships in 2003.

An animated internet spot shows a giant figure marching across the London skyline, and coming to rest on the South Bank of the Thames. "See London differently," says the tagline, inviting users to click for more information, or book online. The London Eye, the tallest observation wheel in the world. The web advertising was part of an integrated campaign that also used press, poster and email ads.

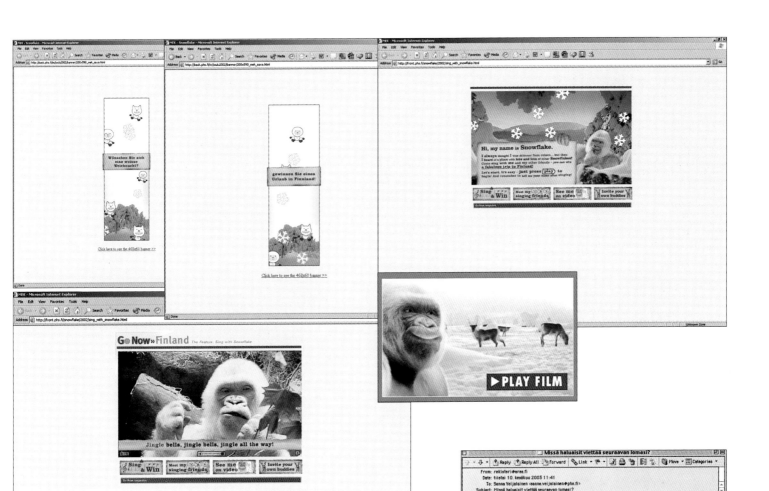

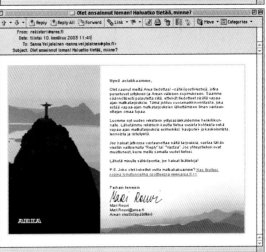

Agencies:	PHS\Interactive, Helsinki TBWA\PHS, Helsinki	The Finnish Tourist Board had a problem… everybody associated Finland with Santa, or with other clichés such as saunas and naturism. To change perceptions, the agency recruited Snowflake, the albino gorilla from Barcelona Zoo. In two viral email films, Snowflake explained that he felt out of place. He dreamed of visiting Finland, the land of many snowflakes. Those who enjoyed the ads were directed to a website where they could sing Christmas carols with Snowflake, and enter a competition to win a holiday in Finland.
Creative Directors:	Markku Rönkkö Zoubida Benkhellat	
Project Managers:	Mimmu Pekkanen Mika Koivula	
Copywriters:	Marjo Taura Heikki Paatelma	
Art Directors:	Panu Tuomela Eeva-Maria Kautia	
Animator:	Mari Tolkkinen	
Design:	PHSi Technical Team	
Client:	Finnish Tourist Board	

Agency:	PHS\Interactive, Helsinki	Most travel agencies assume you already know where you want to go. But Finnish travel agency Area feels that its job is to find the place that matches your dreams. To explain this concept, the agency created a travel search engine, allowing customers to describe the atmosphere and experiences they sought. The search engine then recommended three destinations. Customers were directed to the site through print ads and targeted emails. Once there, they could order a catalogue, win a trip to Lisbon, or even book their desired trip.
Copywriter:	Henna Lekka	
Art Director:	Sanna Vijalainen	
Animation:	Mari Tolkkinen	
Technical Director:	Sakari Kimmo	
Production Mgr:	Mimmu Pekkanen	
Tech. Developers:	Samuli Tivinen Jyrki Lappalainen	
Planner :	Susanna Sucksdorff	
Client:	Area, Finnish Travel Agency	

Actual viewing size

Find what you want, access 70,000 clips from 7 collections
See every detail, view footage at 480x360 pixel resolution
Improve your pitch, download non-watermarked preview files
Meet your deadlines, download broadcast quality

A man dreamt that he made a film overnight.

He'd had the same dream several times, but tonight it felt different, he could see more images quickly and clearly.

One idea flowed after another. Everything fell into place.

When the morning came, he found that all he had dreamt was true.

gettyimages.com/film

gettyimages®

AARÖE, Stefan 147
ABASCAL, Pepe 297
ABBOTT MEAD VICKERS BBDO, London 31, 110, 111, 128, 250, 275
ABBY NORM, Stockholm 147, 156
ABENGOZAR, Esther 317
ÅBERG & CO, Stockholm 334
ÅBERG, Lasse 334
ÅBERG, Max 334
ABIS, Bucharest 280
ABRAHAMSSON, Mathias 345
ABRAMS, Vincent 73
ABSOLUT VODKA 362, 363, 370, 371
ACHATZ, Sven 81
ACNE FILM, Stockholm 36, 38, 278
ACORD, Lance 286
ADAMSON, Anna 101
ADELSTÅL, Johan 122
ADIDA, Benjamin 205
ADIDAS 249, 257, 286, 364
ADK EUROPE, Amsterdam 175, 329
ADVICO YOUNG & RUBICAM, Zürich 23, 37, 41, 76, 169, 190
AEBI, Jean Etienne 84, 100
AEMMER, Jürg 238
AERTS, Peter 265
AFTONBLADET 368
ÅGERUP, Lotta 184, 364
AGF INSURANCE 98
ÅGREN, Jan Petter 319
AGUADO, Mikel 255
AGUILAR, Victor 122
AHA PUTTNERBATES,Vösendorf 222
AHMED, Sam 168, 222, 227
AHMED, Shahir 168
AHOUYEK, Rachid 253
AIDSHILFE FRANKFURT 140
AIMAQ RAPP STOLLE, Berlin 53, 223, 263,
AIMAQ, André 53, 263
AIME, Sébastien 98
AIR FRANCE 69
AIR, Brussels 120
AIRAGHI, Paolo 160
AIRBUS 240
AJANS ULTRA, Istanbul 161
ÅKERHUST, John 61, 186
ÅKERLUND, Pettersson 299
AKIBA, Hideo 342
ALAS, Mert 263
ALBERT, Thierry 104, 180, 181, 213
ALBERTS, David 177
ALBROW, Victor 296
ALBUQUERQUE, Susana 372
ALCARRIA, Mikel 255
ALFA LAVAL 242
ALFARO, Juan Ramon 87
ALLAN, Pål 206
ALLAN, Stewart 129
ALLDAYS 178
ALLIANZ 97
ALLISON, John 46
ALLSOP, Nick 196
ALMÉN, Robert 156
ALTMANN, Olivier 20, 45, 104, 110, 180, 181, 213, 242, 283
ALTMANN, Rosemarie 71
AMELINE, Yoann 212
AMERICAN AIRLINES 79
AMEYE, Alex 86
AMICHAY, Gideon 153, 178, 232
AMIGOS DE LA TIERRA, 116
AMMANATH, Manoj 234
AMNESTY INTERNATIONAL 107, 118, 120, 313, 352
AMPE, Peter 102, 103, 129, 182, 270
AMSTERDAM ADVERTISING, Amsterdam 121, 277
ANDERS SKOG FILMS, Gothenburg 176
ANDERSEN, Peter 88
ANDERSON JORGENSEN, Per 214
ANDERSON, Stuart 22
ANDERSSON, Christer 59
ANDERSSON, David 60
ANDERSSON, Patrik 52
ANDRÉ, Philippe 212
ANDREASSEN, Egil Alv 150
ANDREASSON, Hans-Erik 253
ANDREWS, Justin 57
ANIMAL PEACE 114
ANJA GOCKEL 335, 349
ANNA FASHION MAGAZINE 281
ANR.BBDO, Gothenberg 253
ANTENA 1 TV CHANNEL 280
ANTHONY, Richard 134
ANTONETTI, Emiliano 71
ANTONIEWICZ, Roben 360
ANWEILER, Dominik 365
APAV 125
APERS, Olivier 285
APERS, Tom 86
APPELBLAD, Mathias 359, 364, 374, 375
APU MAGAZINE 305
ARAGÃO, Chico 228
ARC, London 50, 130, 323
ARCTIC PAPER 321, 328
AREA TRAVEL AGENCY 377
ARGUS FILM, Budapest 16
ARIAGNO, Federica 114
ARIEL 162, 164
ARIEYE, Lilach Gur 178
ARLA 40
ARMANDO TESTA, Turin 337
ARNELL, Vaughan 220
ARQUE, Aureli 267, 268
ARRIAGADA, Alejandro 203
ARRIAZU, Victor 66
ARSENOAIEI, Emilian 235
ARTCORE, Amsterdam 72
AS SPORTS MAGAZINE 282
ASFA ASSOCIATION 110
ASHOFF, Simone 359
ASKELÖF, Oscar 142, 145, 184, 185
ASSADIAN, Chermine 240
ASSOCIACAO AUTO MOBILIZADOS 108
ASTORGA, Alberto 24, 74, 203
ASTORGUE, Eric 61
ATES, Erdem Sinan 161
ATHEY, David 357
ATKINSON, Pete 195
ATMOSPHERE CPH, Copenhagen 361
ATRIA FOODS 21
AUDI 202, 203, 204
AUE, Boris 314
AUERSWALD, Thomas 140
AULD, Chris 129
AVE 74
AVIGDOR, Guido 337
AVIS, Russel 153
AXA BELGIUM 231
AXELSSON, Anna 356
AYUDA EN ACCION 315
AZEMARO, Francis 62
BABA FILM, Istanbul 125
BABINET, Rémi 61, 69, 212, 263
BABUSCIO, Benito 206, 207
BACARDI 44
BADER, Robert 365
BAEKKEN, Carl 150
BAGGERMAN, Jan Willem 328
BAGNOLI, Riccardo 160
BAGOLA, Aljosa 188
BAHLE, Wolfgang 225, 302
BAHRMANN, Ole 130
BAILEY, Chris 30
BAKER, Richard 369
BAKER, Thomas 367
BAKKER, Sander 99
BALL, Alex 59
BALL, Sam 373
BALLANCE, Fergal 196
BAMBÚ, Lisbon 236, 372
BANASZUK, Bruno 240
BANDITS, Paris 61
BANE, Staffan 362
BANGAITIS, Kazimiras 305
BANI, Arno 116
BAÑOS, Cristina 74
BARANAUSKAS, Ruslanas 305
BARDINI, Daniela 351
BARDOU-JACQUET, Antoine 194
BARINA, Tomas 291
BARLAS, Deniz 125
BARON, Alexander 276
BARRETT, Richard 358
BARROTE, Jorge 125
BARRY, Ted 153
BARRY, Tony 33, 158
BARTELS, Ingmar 233
BARTHUEL, Antoine 44, 98, 151, 189, 260
BARTON, Anna 116
BASORA, Josep Mª 196
BASTHOLM, Lars 354, 355
BATALLA, Jose Mª 165
BATES INTERNATIONAL ADVERTISING, Barcelona 97
BATES RED CELL, Lisbon 372
BATES, Oslo 150, 202
BATI, Ali 65
BATLLE, Enric 341, 346
BATLLEGROUP/LA SAL, Barcelona 341, 346
BAUMANN, Matthias 302
BAUMANN, Willem 37, 41
BAYALA, Carlos 256
BAYRAKTAR, Birol 204
BBDO INTERONE, Hamburg 357, 359
BBDO, Berlin 223
BBDO, Denmark 20
BBDO, Düsseldorf 29
BBDO, Vienna 214
BBDO/PENTAMARK, Copenhagen 214
BDDP & FILS, Paris 20, 45, 104, 110, 180, 181, 213, 242, 283
BDS BEECHWOOD, London 316
BEAGLE, Amsterdam 72
BEATE-UHSE 272
BEATTIE, Trevor 46, 134, 248, 270, 271
BEAUCHAMP, Luke 44
BEAUREGARD, Xavier 180, 242
BECEDAS, Jesus 268
BECK, Florian 114
BECK, Miro 238
BEDI SOHAL, Komal 222, 227
BEDWOOD, Dave 373
BEES KNEES 343
BEHAEGHEL, Vincent 56, 57,149, 218
BEHINDERTEN SPORTVERBAND BERLIN 134, 303
BEKA 159
BELDARRAIN, Iñigo 255
BELFORD, Paul 31, 275
BELGACOM 152
BELHAVEN 50
BELL, Michael 350
BELLANDER, Annika 328
BELLEGRADE, Emmanuel 117
BELLISSON, Florence 61
BELLON, Damien 104, 180, 181, 213
BELSER, Tim 263
BELVAUX, Remy 63, 218
BEN DOV, Shira 40
BENDITO, Iñaki 267, 268
BENGTSSON, Carl 244
BENKER, André 274
BENKHELLAT, Zoubida 234, 252, 377
BENNETT, Marc 179, 186
BENSON, Russell 33
BENTON, Anthea 48
BENTZ, Oliver 357
BENZER, Christof 222
BERCIAL, Chema 282
BERG RAUNE, Emma 279
BERGENDAHL, Andreas 320
BERGKVIST, Markus 146, 185
BERGKVIST, Masse 214
BERGMANN, Daniel 162
BERGSTRÖM, Niklas 126
BERGSTRÖM, Pelle 158
BERLIN INTERNATIONAL LITERATURE FESTIVAL 288
BERNE, Leo 57
BERNSCHNEIDER, Jonas 333
BERTRAM, David 57
BERTRAND, Patrick 244
BESTAGNO, Francesco 255
BETC EURO RSCG, Paris 61, 69, 212, 263
BETHKE, Wiebke 200
BEUVE, Christophe 367
BEXIGA, Pedro 315
BEYDOUN, Malak 311
BIANCO 265
BIELER, Torstein 28
BIERNACKA, Teresa 154
BIG BROTHER 315
BIG DEAL DDB, Oslo 34, 38, 148, 150
BIG PRODUCTION, Paris 110
BILES, Anthony 341
BIOMETAL 244
BIRD, Kevin 314, 309
BISLEY 226
BITESNICH, Andreas 134, 303
BIWALD, Bärbel 243
BJØLBAKK, Stig 68, 148
BJÖRKHAGEN, Klas 334
BJÖRKMAN, Susanne 320
BJORNSSON, Sverrir 192
BLACKBURN, John 346
BLACKBURN'S, London 346
BLACKLEY, Cam 31, 275
BLANC, Guillaume 141
BLANK, Deannie 286
BLECKER, Olaf 132
BLES, Michiel 72
BLINK PRODUCTIONS, London 72
BLOECK, Helge 134, 249, 303, 331
BLOM, Jimmy 177
BLOMBERG, Dennis 320
BLOMBERG, Fredrik 50
BLOMQVIST, Mitte 35, 294, 320
BLONDELL, Joakim 35, 140
BLUM-HEUSER, Christine 324
BLUSH DESSOUS 254
BMW 213, 359
BOB, Helsinki 239, 260
BOBST, Christian 76
BODIN, Frank 238
BODSON, Laurent 312
BOEBEL, Michael 63, 114, 206, 295, 310
BOEKELS, Stefan 71
BOGDANOWICZ, Przemek 178, 293, 349
BOGENSPERGER, Beate 81
BÖHINC, Lara 328
BÖHM, Tim 288
BÖHM, Uwe 223
BOIL, Santiago 24
BOJAGO, Delphine 22
BOKEMEYER, Henriette 136
BOLD\TBWA, Oslo 88
BOLES, Mike 216, 284
BONAVIA, Fulvio 17, 237
BOND, Fredrik 216, 250
BONI, David 298
BONOMINI, Enrico 108
BONRIPOSI, Federico 17
BOOMKENS, Martin 307
BORCHERDING, Rolf 364, 367
BORGE, Steinar 150, 280
BORGIONS, Mark 182
BORSTLAP, Christian 287, 366
BOSCH, Pep 196
BOSMA, Arno 121
BOTTA, Sabine 32
BOTTEZ, Katrien 102, 103, 182, 270
BOUFFORT, Christine 104, 110, 283
BOURSIN 39
BOUYAHIA, Safia 263
BOVILL, Chris 46
BOWMORE WHISKY 60
BRAAM, Sanne 94
BRADBURY, David 50, 130
BRADY, Dave 42
BRAJDIC, Damir 193
BRAND, Sonja 84
BRANTAS, Ulf 38
BRATUSA, Peter 151
BRAZIER, Paul 110, 111, 250
BREDENDIECK, Jörg 97
BRENNICKE, Jörgen 262
BREUNIG, Andreas 223
BREZINA, Christian 214
BRINKMAN, Jan 351
BRISSARD, Xavier 26
BRITISH GAS 158
BRITISH GLASS 241
BROCKFELD, Timm 136
BROCKMANN, Heike 358
BRODHECKER, Gunther 314
BRODZINSKA, Joanna 137
BRÖNNIMANN, Peter 76, 249, 299
BROSSMANN, Igor 135
BROVELLI, Fabrice 61, 212
BROWN, James 162
BROWN, Rob 186
BROWN, Stuart 257
BRÜCK, Nestori 21
BRUGUER PAINTS 164
BRUKETA & ZINIC, Zagreb 24, 332
BRUKETA, Davor 24, 332
BRUNDIN, Jakob 338
BRUUN, Chaga Signe 361
BUCCINO, Valter 170
BUCKLEY, David 365
BUDGEN, Frank 259, 365
BUDIS 64
BUENA VISTA INTERNATIONAL 326, 330
BUGDAHN, Dirk 206, 310
BUGGG FILMS, London 271
BUI, Duc-Thien 358
BUJTAS, Attila 52
BULIK, Michal 137
BULLA, Marius 364
BULMERS CIDER 49
BUNDESVERBAND TIERSCHUTZ 113
BUNDESVEREINIGUNG LEBENSHILFE 136
BUNGAY, Bil 248, 270, 271
BURGAUD, Pierre-Dominique 262
BURGDORF, Knut 368
BURGER KING 81
BURGER, Peter 19
BURKE, Cordell 319
BURNS, Kirsty 208
BURT, Adrian 356
BUSCHE, Nils 224
BUTLER, Tom 42
BUTTER, Düsseldorf 228
BUTZBACH, Simone 228
BVD, BLIDHOLM VAGNEMARK DESIGN, Stockholm 353
BYRNE, Mike 259
CAFÉ DEL MONDO 65
CAJA ROJA 342
CAKE FILMS, Paris 240
CALANT, Marco 124, 239
CALEDONIAN LANGUAGE SCHOOL 238
CALVÉ 19
CAMP DAVID, Gothenburg 146
CAMPBELL, Dave 49
CAMPBELL, Mike 210
CAMPORA, Stefano 157, 322
CANAKCI, Gurkan 125
CANAL DIGITAL 280
CANAL+ 279
CANNES LIONS FESTIVAL 371
CANONGATE PRESS 360
CAP DE VILLE, Germaine 86
CAP GEMINI ERNST & YOUNG 328
CAPRA, Hilde 71
CARDA, Leos 90, 181
CAREBORG, Lisa 321, 328
CARLSBERG 368
CARNERO, Jose 353
CARP, Klaudia 101, 299
CARRASCO, Julia 196
CARREÑO, Jorge 171, 172, 173, 300
CARSON, Ben 220, 221
CARTY, Tom 259, 365
CASANOVA, Ana 330
CASELL, Peter 264
CASINI, Alessia 71
CASOLARI, Carole 212
CASSINA 157
CATCH ADVERTISING, Wiesbaden 335, 345, 349
CAVALLONE, Carlo 253, 256
CAYENNE, Milan 17
CAZALS, Jean 22
CE CRUICKSHANK, James 226
CEDERBERG, Mia 101, 299
CEDERGREN, Martin 359, 374, 375
CENTRAAL BEHEER 94, 102
CERKEZ, Robert 265
CERUNA 364
CESAR, F.A. 220, 221
CESENKOVA, Vera 107, 291
ÇETINTÜRK, Murat 65
CFPE 234
CHALKLEY, Yvonne 110
CHANEY, Richard 153
CHANGE COMMUNICATION, Frankfurt 314, 350
CHANT, Rick 39
CHAPUIS, Emeric 44
CHARITY, Charity 188
CHARVAT, Martin 106
CHATER-ROBINSON, Simon 212
CHAUVIN, Nicolas 98
CHÁVARRI, Jaime 55
CHEMISTRY, Dublin 153, 235
CHESTER, Craig 193
CHIO 32
CHIRILA, Tudor 166
CHOCOCO 343
CHRYSAFIS, Chrysafis 344, 348
CHUDALLA, Thomas 220
CHUK, Chuk 178
CHUPA CHUPS 27
CITIGATE SMARTS, Edinburgh 360
CITROËN 307
CITY OF AMSTERDAM 351
CIZL, Nenad 167
CLAASSENS, Damian 355
CLAESSON, Fredrik 138
CLAN CAMPBELL 45
CLARA, Karlstad 324
CLARK, Ben 54, 58
CLARK, Bryan 352
CLARK, Christian 376
CLARKE, Alan 177
CLAUSEN, Rod 376
CLAYDON HEELEY JONES MASON, London 325
CLEARASIL 184
CLEMMOW HORNBY INGE, London 54, 58, 59, 158, 266, 268, 274
CLINE, Peter 286
CLM BBDO, Paris 26, 51, 56, 57, 85, 116, 149, 218, 306
CLOUGH, Andy 284
CNAPD 118
CNP INSURANCE 98
COBO, Eva 112
COCA-COLA 63
COCIO 339
COEMAN, Marvu 104
COFFRE, Christophe 22
COHEN,Yisrael 139
COHIBA, Martinique 244
COLBERT, Gregory 337
COLENS, Sophie 184
COLIN, Emmanuel 199
COLLIANDER, Björn 309
COLLIER, Kate 33, 48
COLLINGRIDGE, Peter 360
COLLINS, Damon 33
COLOMBO, Alberto 71
COLOMER, Pepe 196
COLQUHOUN, Kevin 314
COLVIN, Dotti 372
COMELLA, David 342
COMELLA, Jordi 342
COMODYNES 341
COMTE, Daniel 23, 190
COMVIQ 144, 146
CONDESSA, Vasco 108
CONDOR COMMUNICATIONS, Zürich 96
CONTRA, Helsinki 361
CONTRAPUNTO, Madrid 95, 215, 283
COOK, Doug 289, 298
COOP KONSUM 309
COOP SWISS BANK 96
CORAZZA, Marino 332
CORNARA, Guido 90, 207, 272
CORNELIS, Herlinde 39
CORNELISSEN, Martin 94, 102
CORTSEN, Lars 355
COURADJUT, Olivier 45
COUTELLE, Stéphane 189
CRAIG, Ben 360
CRAIGEN, Jeremy 196, 197
CRAMER, Kim 144, 146, 176
CRASEMANN, Reinhard 311
CRAUL, Stefan 304
CREW, Darren 325
CROFT, Dave 153
CROLL, Diane 46, 134, 248
CTS 71
CUCIUC, Tudor 235
CUDE, Jonathan 259
CULLEN, John 49
CURRAN, Anne Marie 153
CURTIS, Hal 259
CUSIDÓ COMELLA, Barcelona 342
CUSIDÓ, Josep 342
CVETNIC, Andrej 167
CZAR.NL, Amsterdam 102
CZESCHNER, Olaf 364, 367
D'ADDA, LORENZINI, VIGORELLI BBDO, Milan 157, 213, 261, 322
DAENEN, Vincent 167
DAFFARN, Sid 286
DAGENS NYHETER 278
DAGIEL, Wojtek 193
DAHLBERG, Fredrik 185
DAHLIN, Petrus 262
DAHLQVIST, Andreas 368, 373
DAIMLERCHRYSLER 220, 221
DALIN, Carl 77, 100
DALLIES-LABOURDETTE, Béatrice 189
DALLMANN, Arndt 97
DANILOFF, Dimitri 171, 172
DANISH CANCER SOCIETY 131
DANS LE SUD, Paris 283
DAS, Tim 42
DAVID-MATHIO, Julie 117
DAVIDSON, Tony 194
DAVIES, Libby 58
DAVIES, Mark 319
DAVIES, Rhiannon 355
DAVISON, Janice 347
DAWID 347
DDB GERMANY, Berlin 200
DDB, Amsterdam 94, 102, 200, 286
DDB, Brussels 199, 209
DDB, Budapest 16
DDB, London 196, 197, 306
DDB, Milan 108, 237
DDFH&B/JWT, Dublin 42
DE BACKER, Dylan 112
DE BARY, Guillaume 149
DE BERNADINIS, Valerio 109
DE CASTELBAJAC, Vainui 26
DE CEUSTER, Philippe 67
DE DECKER, Chiara 86
DE FILIPPI, Stefano 109
DE LOTTO 286
DE MAUPEOU, Anne 26, 51, 56, 57, 85, 116, 149, 306
DE MULDER, Peter 103
DE ROOSE, Vincent 217

DE SCHIETTENT, Amsterdam 94
DE SOUZA, Joe 48
DE WITTE, Jean-françois 86, 239
DEC, Barcelona 327
DEJONGHE, Jan 86
DEL BRAVO, Paolo 281
DEL VALLE, Félix 215
DELAHAYE, Luc 267
DELANEY, Dominic 44
DELFGAAUW, Martien 198
DELHAIZE 86
DELHOMME, Bruno 69, 110
DELLA FAILLE, Jean-Charles 184
DELROY'S GYM 294
DELUC, Mathieu 85
DEMIRDELEN, Selim 125
DEMNER, Mariusz Jan 86
DEMNER, MERLICEK & BERGMANN, Vienna 86, 255
DEMUYNCK, Koen 67, 182, 270
DENNIS, Nigel 195
DERBYSHIRE FIRE SERVICE 130
DERMAUX, Olivier 116
DERTINGER, Yorck 81
DESCALS, Tomás 216
DESIGN KONTORET SILVER, Stockholm 345
DETARYOVA, Olga 135
DEUTSCHE KREBSHILFE 130
DEVARRIEUXVILLARET, Paris 262
DEXIA NETBANKING 102, 103
DFT 110, 111
DI BRUNO, Serena 322
DI GIAMBATTISTA, Catia 162
DIALECT 147
DIAMANTI, Dimitra 348
DIANA, Jaume 216
DICKENS, Mark 175
DIE SCHEINFIRMA, Hamburg 230
DIE TAGESZEITUNG 276
DIECKERT, Kurt-Georg 134, 174, 249, 288, 303, 331
DIEHL, Goesta 113
DIELENS, Serge 375
DIETER LAHE, Hans 334
DIETZ, Kirsten 336
DIFFERENT, Newcastle upon Tyne 129
DIGERATI, Munich 368
DIMENSIÓN, San Sebastien 255
DINESEN, Peter 64
DIOS, Kristoffer 101, 299
DIWADKAR, Nirmal 234
DIXON, Vincent 45,181, 242
DOH 128
DOHERTY, Orla 235
DOKTOROW, Kjell 52, 126
DOM & NIC 246, 253
DOMINGO, Jose Ramon 342
DORAN, Graham 241
DORMAN, Genie 292
DORNIK, Saso 340
DOYLE, Keith 292
DR. KLAUS ONGYERTH 351
DRAVET, Laurent 218
DREAM ICE CREAM 34, 38
DRESDNER BANK 324
DRIESEN, Tim 211, 245
DRUGGE, Catarina 156
DRUMMOND, Stephen 251
DU TOIT, Tertia 49
DUBOIS, John 359
DUCKWORTH, Bruce 341, 344, 347
DUCKWORTH, Martin 50, 130
DUETTMANN, Peter 206
DUFKA, Pavel 289
DUGUID, Patrick 134
DUNARD, Patrik 262
DUPONT, Pascal 141
DUPUY, Laurence 26
DURAND, Olivier 26
DUREX 181, 182
DURIAU, Emmanuel 217
DUVAL GUILLAUME, Brussels 32, 67, 102, 103, 152, 182, 270
DUVOUX, Laurent 20
DYMOCK, Andy 371
DYNAMO, Helsinki 141
DYNOWSKI, Artur 349
DZALTO, Mario 345
E45 BODY LOTION 186
EAGER, Christian 341
EASY CONDOMS 183
EDEN DESIGN & COMMUNICATION, Amsterdam 351
EDGE COMMUNICATION, Brussels 375
EDINBURGH FRINGE SHOW 289
EDINBURGH INTERNATIONAL FILM FESTIVAL 369
EDWALL, Mattias 334
EFENDI ART STUDIO, Vilnius 305
EFFEKT 244
EFTI, Gothenberg 253
EGG BANKING 104
EGHAMMER, Johan 184, 185
EHLBECK, Jan 105
EHRENSTRÄHLE & CO. BBDO, Stockholm 242
EHRENSTRÄHLE, Per 242
EHRLICH, Alexandra 222
EICHNER, Kay 333
EIFF 369
EIGEN FABRIKAAT, Amstelveen 328
EILAT, Ayala 339
EILOLA, Kari 260
EINARSSON, Stefan 192
EINIÖ, Antti 70, 105
EIZO MONITORS 228
EKBERG, Carl-Johan 77
EKLIND, Anders 158, 359, 374, 375
EKROS, Per 60
EKROS:BLOCK, Helsingborg 60
EL ALJ, Mehdi 273
EL PAIS 283
EL SIBARITA 92
ELBANK, Brock 31
ELECTROLUX 156, 168
ELGSTRÖM, Eva 338, 345
ELLE MACPHERSON INTIMATES 301
ELLINGSEN, Ole Kristian 319
ELOHOPEA, Helsinki 276
ELWOOD, Mark 111
EMBRINK DESIGN, Stockholm 340
EMBRINK, Hans 340
EMHOFF, Kerstin 258
ENDLESS PAIN 333
ENGHAGE, Jonas 176
ENGSTRÖM, Björn 158, 269, 321, 328
ENGSTRÖM, J. H. 320
ENVISION, Århus 339
ENZI, Markus 214
ERDMANN, Kristina 224
ERICSON, Nina 335

ERICSSON, Magnus 368
ERICSTAM, Jesper 68, 127
ERIKSEN, Tom 356
ERIKSSON, Peter 247
ERIKSSON, Ulf 38
ERKMAN, Arda 125
EROTIKA 93
ESB AUTOKLINIK 314
ESC MOBILE PHONES 339
ESCAT, Isabelle 63
ESCHLEROVA, Tereza 310
ESPIRITO SANTO, João 125, 132, 166
ESTEBAN, Santiago 254
ESTEIRE, Nacho 282
EURO RSCG BLRS, Amstelveen 307
EURO RSCG C&O, Paris 240
EURO RSCG MRT, Lisbon 228, 315
EURO RSCG PARTNERS, Barcelona 165
EURO RSCG PARTNERS, Madrid 112
EURO RSCG WORLDWIDE, Paris 212
EURO RSCG, Prague 115, 310
EURO RSCG, Stockholm 185
EURO RSCG, Zürich 238
EUROFAKTA 127
EUROSTAR 73
EVANS, Phil 296
EVERI, Timo 40, 70, 105
EVERKE, Christoph 226
EVERNDEN, Graham 352
EVIAN 61
EXTEBERRIA, Miki 95
EYMIEUX, Mario 151, 260
EZARU, Cosmin 47
FABRIKANT, Remy 43
FACKRELL, Andy 257, 286
FADDEN, Ray 235
FAGAN REGGIO DEL BRAVO, Rome 281
FAKTA 93
FALCO, Anthony 58, 59, 266, 268
FALK, Mattias 247
FALK, Stefan 127, 156
FALKENBERG, Leila 127
FALKENBERG, Thomas 93
FALLON, London 208
FAMILY, Edinburgh 309, 314
FANTI, Federico 114
FÄRDLEKTYR 334
FARLEY, Andrew 62
FAU, Géraldine 110, 283
FAULKNER, Ciska 284
FAUSSURIER, Pierre-Marie 65
FAUSTINO, Xerex 49
FCB PORTUGAL, Lisbon 108, 179
FCB/TAPSA, Madrid 267, 268
FEDOROV, Gregory 336
FELDHAUS, Elisabeth 228
FELDHAUS, Thomas 359
FELDSKOV JUUL, Ulrik 93
FELINA FILMS, Ljubljana 151
FELOT, Sandrine 199
FERENS, Stephan 98
FERNANDEZ, Marcos 330, 333
FERNANDEZ, Miquel 187
FERNÁNDEZ-MANÉS, Tony 74, 75
FERRARI, Pier Paolo 157, 213
FERRATER, José Manuel 75
FERRY SAUVAIRE, Laure 44
FHV BBDO, Amstelveen 30, 99, 287
FIALA, Alis 181
FIAT 219, 295, 323
FICHTEBERG, Gilles 217
FILM REPUBLIC, Warsaw 137, 178
FILMITALLI, Helsinki 21
FILMSERVICE, Prague 291
FINDEXA 150
FINDLAY, Gregor 314
FINE, Hunter 290
FINNISH TELEVISION LICENCE FEES 141
FINNISH TOURIST BOARD 377
FITNESS COMPANY 295
FITZ, Jenny 358
FIVE TV CHANNEL 270, 271
FJELLSTRÖM, Mikael 242
FLANTZ, Ohav 153
FLIMS LAAX FALERA 76
FLINTHAM, Richard 208
FLOR 165
FLOREA, Brian 329
FLORESCU, Bradut 166
FLUM, Noe 143, 145
FOECKING, Mareike 228
FOHR, Daniel 44, 98, 151, 189, 260
FOLEY, Darren 343
FOLKOPERAN 294, 320
FONT DEL REGÁS 67
FÖRCH, Suzanne 18
FORD 358
FORDHAM WHITE 91
FORENINGSSPARBANKEN 100
FORSBERG & CO, Stockholm 212, 292
FORSBERG, Patrik 212
FORSBERG, Tomas 363
FORSMAN & BODENFORS, Gothenburg 142, 144, 145, 146,
    158, 176, 184, 185, 269, 359, 364, 374, 375
FORSMAN, Staffan 269
FOSSA, Ugo 63
FOSTER, Richard 128
FOUBERT, Bernard 124
FOUNDATION FOR RESPECT 325
FOURNON, Jean-François 162
FRACCA, Cesare 93
FRAME C, Glasgow 289
FRAMFAB DENMARK, Copenhagen 354, 355
FRANCESCO BIASIA 261
FRANCIS, Mary 110, 248
FRANDSEN, Rasmus 354
FRANK, Oliver 223, 263
FRANKEL, Johnnie 46
FRANSSON, Niklas 356
FRAUENDORFER, Ingeborg 149, 308
FRAZER-SMITH, Chris 130
FRECOBALDI, Piero 365
FREDEBEUL, Stefan 223
FREDRICKS, Roger 124
FREED, Leonard 267
FREI, Lukas 92
FRENCH CONNECTION UK 248
FRENKLER, Ekkehard 351
FREULER, Matthias 83, 89, 277
FRICK, Sonja 342
FRICK, Urs 92, 116, 192, 317, 326, 330, 333
FRID, Emil 156
FRIEDLIN, Martin 92
FRIENDS 140
FRINDER, Martin 64

FRISTADS 253
FRITZ REKLAMBYRA, Sundsvall 326
FRITZ, Ingo 365
FRODLUND, Mattias 38
FRØGER, Loïc 117
FRÖHLICH, Katharina 335, 349
FROMM, Andreas 120
FUETER, Martin A. 96
FUJIFILM 170
FULCO SMIT ROETERS 277
FULL PAGE PRESS GROUP 239
FUNDACIÓ ÈXIT 327
FUNK, Eric 357, 359
FUTURA DDB, Ljubljana 101, 331
G7, Warsaw 178, 293, 349
GABRIJAN, Zoran 101
GACNIK, Mija 188
GAL, Amit 153
GALHARDAS, João 372
GALIA, Dirk 207
GALIANA, Jesús 187
GALINHA, Jérôme 240
GALLAGHER, Sally 373
GALOS, Viktor 32
GANG FILMS, Paris 26
GARBUTT, Chris 216
GARDINI, Mario 17
GARMANN, Tone 150
GARNER, Mike 153, 235
GARNIER 189
GAROLERA, Gerard 67
GARRIGA, David 67
GARRIGOSA, Joan 165
GASBARRO, Vincenzo 261
GASCON, Mario 27, 133
GASPAR, Nuno 163
GASSNER, Martin 357
GATSKY, Charlie 48
GB ICE CREAM 36
GEFEN PRODUCTIONS, Tel Aviv 178
GEFEN, Eyal 178
GEISER, Hadi 206, 310
GEISSBUEHLER, Nadine 236
GEISSLER, Claudia 276
GENNUSO, Teresa 337
GEORGESCU-BARON, Laura 280
GERKEMA, Sikko 94
GERLINEA 23
GERMANWINGS 78
GERNANDT, Anders 72
GEYER, Andreas 41
GHEWY, Christophe 159, 211, 231, 245, 281
GIDEN, Thomas 70
GIESENFELD, Otto 362, 363, 370, 371
GIFFORD, Hoss 360, 369
GIGLER, Claus 255
GILBERT, Christophe 32, 73, 118, 159, 199
GILERA, Stefano 108
GILL, Olivier 105
GILLAN, Martin 289
GIMLA, Stockholm 292
GINTARINE SALA 305
GIRO 555 121
GIRÓ, Àngela 341, 346
GITAM/BBDO, Ramat-Gan 208
GITTO, Vicky 213, 261
GLAESLE, Moritz 230
GLASS, Andy 213, 217
GLAUS, Nicole 144
GLAWION, Joachim 255
GLAXOSMITHKILNE 191
GLEJE, Jan 93
GNADINGER, Alexander 83
GNAEDINGER, Alexander 174
GOCKEL, Alexander 206
GOLAN, Ofer 208
GOLAN, Tzur 153
GOLDBRONN, Franck 260
GOLDEN PAGES 235
GOMEZ, Victor 192, 333
GONNISSEN, Nikki 351
GONZALEZ, Idoia 254
GOODEN, Matt 194
GOODSHIP, Amanda 216
GOODYEAR 224
GORGEOUS ENTERPRISES, London 259, 284, 365
GORINI, Claudio 284
GORSHKOV, Vladimir 336
GORSKA, Kartarzyna 137
GÖTEBORGS-POSTEN 269
GOTTSCHALK, Silke 357, 359
GOTTSHALCK VIGH, Carsten 361
GÖTZL, Christine 335, 349
GOUBY, Marc 44 ,51,172, 207, 300, 306, 313
GRABARZ & PARTNER, Hamburg 120, 198, 237
GRAÇA, Jaime 255
GRAF, Norbert 18
GRAFFITI BBDO, Bucharest 47
GRAIFER, Natalia 336
GRAINGER, Claire 241
GRAND HYATT DUBAI 342, 352
GRANGER, Tony 210
GRANSTRÖM, Jon 239
GRANT, Robin 373
GRAVINGEN, Anne 68
GREEN, Andy 59, 225
GREGORY COLBERT PHOTOGRAPHY 337
GREPL, Premysl 48, 106, 291
GREUEL, Susann 331
GREY WORLDWIDE, Dubai 49
GREY WORLDWIDE, Milan 160
GREY WORLDWIDE, Oslo 280
GREY WORLDWIDE, Rome 109
GREY WORLDWIDE, Stockholm 156
GREY, Brussels 184
GREY, Copenhagen 64
GREY, London 177
GROSSMANN, Roland 364, 367
GRUND, Christian 143, 145
GRUNKE, Gerfried 368
GUAIS, Cécile 312
GUASH, Marçal 216
GUBERMAN, Dario 66
GUERASSIMOV, Dimitri 85, 149
GUINNESS 47, 51, 306
GUINOT, Sandrine 273
GUIRAUD, Emmanuel 61
GULPERS, Chantal 286
GÜNES, Erol 224
GÜNTHER, Jean-Pascal 18, 264
GURONSAN 23
GUSTAFSSON, Stefan 122
GUT, Markus 236
GUTHRIE, Wayne 91
GUYE BENKER WERBEAGENTUR, Zürich 274

GV.COMPANY, Brussels 86
H FILMS, Milan 207
H&C LEO BURNETT, Beirut 311
H&M 345
H2E HOEHNE HABANN ELSER, Ludwigsberg 21, 113, 334
HAAK, Kater 364
HAAPALEHTO, Markku 25, 62, 276
HABERLAND, Heinke 228
HABOUSHA, Pascal 86, 217, 244
HACIENDA, Helsinki 25
HADANI,Yoram Ever 178
HADAS, Ishay 232
HAGMAN, Per Erik 362, 363
HAGWALL-BRUCKNER, Hedvig 212
HAHN, Frank 258
HAIBUN, Milan 93
HAIDER, Doris 78, 126, 152, 225
HAIGH,Tony 318
HAIN, Odile 190
HAISCH, David 96
HÅKANSON, Staffan 269
HAKLE 169
HAKTANIR, Guven 224
HALCON VIAJES 74
HALLDORSSON, Arnaldur 192
HALLGREN, Niclas 324
HALPERINE, Yaki 339
HALVARSSON, Henrik 277
HALVORSEN, Øystein 202
HAMER, Bent 34, 38
HAMM, Hubertus 78
HANEL, Johann Sebastian 249
HANEL, Sebastian 219
HANNETT, Ruth
HANSCOMB, Greg 361
HANSEL PRODUCTIONS 40
HANSEN, Jesper 20, 214, 339
HANSEN, Jimmy 64
HANSON, Jonas 214
HANSON, Wayne 205
HANSSON, Lars 38
HAPPEL, Uli 140
HAPPY DOG 18
HAPPY FORSMAN & BODENFORS, Gothenburg 321, 328
HARDIECK, Sebastian 226
HARJU, Tuomas 361
HARLAMOFF, Nicolas 62
HARLE, Pete 325
HARLEY DAVIDSON 223
HAROUTIOUNIAN, Cédric 51, 306
HARRIS, Elliot 220, 221
HARRISON TROUGHTON WUNDERMAN, London 318, 327
HARRISON, Dylan 196
HARRISON, Steve 318, 327
HARROLD MOTION PICTURE, Milan 170
HARRY NASH FILMS, London 250
HARSAGYI, Peter 32
HART, Carrie 142, 145
HART, Erik 276
HART, Michael 251
HARTMANN, Barbara 83
HARTWIG, Attila 288
HARVEY, Martin 195
HARVEY, Thomas 259
HASAN & PARTNERS, Helsinki 40, 70, 105, 155
HASFARI, Amir 208
HASHMI, Anna 210
HASLE, Andreas 102
HASLEHURST, Simon 325
HASLINGER, Joachim 86
HAWKES, Brian 195
HAYES, Derek 316
HAZAZAH, Amsterdam 19
HEAL'S 306
HECKMANN, Sven 357
HECTOR, Tony 220
HEFFELS, Guido 83, 130, 136, 243
HEIDEMANN, Lars-Bo 355
HEILEMANN, Kristoffer 233
HEIMAT, Berlin 83, 130, 136, 243
HEINEKEN 49, 53, 292
HEINTZSCH, Carsten 204, 304
HELIAS, Eric 171, 172, 173, 300
HELLMAN, Kenneth 335
HELLMAN, Oskari 229
HELLSTRÖM, Andreas 212
HELLSTRÖM, Johan 292
HEMEZ, Jean Christophe 367
HEMPEL, Stefan 78, 126, 225
HENAFF MEATS 20
HENKE, Andreas 358
HENKEL, Anne 304
HENKES, Uschi 92, 116, 192, 317, 326, 330, 333
HENNINGER, Heinz 189
HENNINGSSON, Melker 60
HENSHAW, Simon 350
HEREDIA, Javier Pastor 87
HERMAN, Jonathan 286
HERMAN, Robert 208
HERMANS, Veronique 118
HERNANDEZ, Francis 268
HERNANDO, Elena 24
HERNGREN, Felix 253
HERRERA, Maria Jesús 74
HERRMANN, Peter 21, 334
HERRMANN, Valentina 190
HERZOGGEISSLER 236
HEUEL, Ralf 120, 198, 237
HEVRON, Dudy 232
HEW SAW 326
HEYE & PARTNER, Hamburg 311
HGKZ 236
HIGGS, David 267
HILARIUS, Camilla 126
HILLAND, Guri N. 150
HILLER, Jost 29
HILSON, Benoît 159, 281
HINDERSSON, André 345
HINZEN, Markus 190
HIPWELL, Simon 316
HIRO, Jesper 101, 299
HIRRLINGER, Peter 78, 126, 225
HIRSCH, Pascal 22
HISSINK, Edward 72
HJALMAR, Björn 100
HJÄLMRUD, Berno 144
HK SININEN 25
HOBSON, Barney 39
HOEGAARDEN BEER 48
HOFFMANN, David 357
HOFFMANN, Thomas 265
HÖFLER, Mark 365
HOFMANN, Alexander 214
HOFSTEE, Christel 94
HOGREFE, Birgit 113

HOHLS, Kirsten 204
HOHMANN, Hendrik 310
HOLBERTON, Glenn 372
HOLCMANN, Paul 113
HOLDEN, Eric 212
HOLDSWORTH, Daniel 179
HOLLAND INTERNATIONAL 72
HOLLANDER, Eric 120
HOLLANDER, Nicolás 122, 123, 164
HOLLENS, Jerry 216, 284
HOLMGREN, Daniel 262
HOLMSTRÖM, Anders 320
HOLST, Marius 148
HOLT, Lars 150, 202
HOLTHUSEN, Corinna 243
HOME PIZZA 25
HOMOKI, Judith 254, 272
HONDA 194
HORNBACH 83, 243
HORNIMANS 66
HORTON, John 128
HORTS, Meritxell 67
HOSS GIFFORD, Glasgow 360, 369
HOURA.FR. 89
HOVIND, Ubbe 280
HOVLAND, Eirik 34, 38
HOWARD, William 136
HSCG, Amsterdam 264
HSI PRODUCTIONS, Culver City 258
HT MOBILE 151
HUBER, Klaus 226
HUESO, Gabriel 92, 116, 326
HUISMAN, Suzanne 19
HULTBERG, Christian 60
HULTÉN, Monica 35, 140, 204, 320
HUMO 270
HUNGRY MAN, Gothenburg 142, 145
HUNNICUT, Gabriela 125
HUNTER, Paul 258
HURST, Mark 44
HUTSON-FLYNN, Damon 186
HYNES, Jason 292
HYTTEN, Sverre 280
IBM 318, 367, 376
ICA 87
IDFA 317
IF INSURANCE 105
IGFM 120
IGI2 373
IGLESIA, Alejandro 74
IGNACIUK, Bartek 178
IGONI, Anu 260
IIVARI, Timo 239
IKEA 154, 155, 160
ILARIO, Danny 203
ILTERBERK, Bulent 224
IN BOCCA AL LUPO 255
IN YOUR EYE FILMS, Amsterdam 286
INFORMATION NEWSPAPER 282
INGE, Charles 54, 58, 59, 158, 266, 268, 274
INGESTEDT, Magnus 36, 244
INLINGUA 230
INTEGRACJA 137
INTERFLORA 80, 82
INTERPHARMA 190
INTERPOLIS 99
IPS ALARM SYSTEMS 320
IRANZO, Araceli 353
IREMONGER, Mark 365
IRÈNE, Paris 149
ISAAC, David 309, 314
ISBERG, Axel 38
ISHAY HADAS PRODUCTIONS, Tel Aviv 232
ISRAEL RADIO 232
ITEN, Mauko 23
ITI FILM STUDIO, Warsaw 137
IVAX CORPORATE 191
IVERT, Mårten 362, 363, 370, 371
J. WALTER THOMPSON, Barcelona 55,187
J. WALTER THOMPSON, Istanbul 125
J. WALTER THOMPSON, Lisbon 125, 132, 166, 236
J. WALTER THOMPSON, London 188
J. WALTER THOMPSON, Madrid 297
JABLANOVEC, Bojan 101
JACHMANN, Lina 200
JACKSON, Paul 356
JACOBSEN, Kerstin 254
JACQUES CHOCOLATE 32
JAMES MURPHY PHOTOGRAPHY 321
JAMES, Brian 62
JAMES, Stephen 357
JAMESON IRISH WHISKEY 316
JAN KNEIDING FINANCIAL SERVICES 105
JANE DAVIDSON 251
JANES, Achim 359
JANIS, Juraj 90
JANSEN, Joeri 30
JANSEN, Margret 120
JANSEN, Michael 102, 200, 286
JANSEN, Ruth 243
JANSSENS, Alain 152
JARISLOWSKI, Marika 362, 370, 371
JÄRNEMAR, Mattias 362
JBR McCANN, Oslo 124
JC DECAUX, 239
JEAN & MONTMARIN, Paris 65, 89
JEAN, Gérard 65, 89
JEDRZEJEWSKI, Neil 356
JEEP 214, 215
JEFFERY, Adrian 316, 362, 363
JERSILD, Mattias 347
JO! SCHMID, Berlin 208
JOAKIM & TOFT 141
JOHANSSON, Lars 359, 364, 374, 375
JOHANSSON, Marcus 356
JOHANSSON, Ulf 256
JOHN DOE WORLDWIDE, Stockholm 50
JOHN SMITH'S BITTER 46
JOHNSTON, Sheila-Anne 311
JOLY, Martine 141
JONES, Colin 210
JONES, Ivor 79
JONES, Nick 58
JONSGÅRDEN, Tomas 292
JORALV, Jörgen 362
JORGE, Carlos 215
JOSHUA AGENCY, London 376
JOSHUA HAIR SALON 90
JOURNALISTGRUPPEN 335
JUAREZ, Nacho 133
JUENGER, Nico 63
JULIUS MEINL 86
JUNCTION 11, Weybridge 191
JUNG VON MATT/LIMMAT, Zürich 92
JWT+H+F, Zürich 43
K2 DESIGN, Athens 344, 348
KACENKA, Peter 135
KAELIN, Rolf 277
KAIM, Peter 63
KALGARON 178
KANDER, Nadav 306
KANDIMAA, Peter 334
KANI, Yuki 61
KANTOR, Andrea 32
KARASEK, Jonas 135
KÄRKKÄINEN, Lasse 126
KARLBERG, Philip 140
KARLSRUHE LOW BUDGET FILM FESTIVAL 288
KARMARK, Kim 339
KARSAI, Marton 32
KARTBULIKKEN 88
KASSAEI, Amir 200
KATHE, Michael 215
KAUBA, Eda 115, 310
KAUTIA, Eeva-Maria 377
KAVANAGH, Rob 318
KAWASAKI 222
KAY, Ben 31, 275
KAZIMIR, Azar 91, 221
KEHREN, Christoph 358
KELDA 38
KELLY, Chris 46
KELMAN-BISBEE, Jackie 286
KELTAINEN PÖRSSI 276
KEMPTON, Garfield 266, 268
KENGYEL, Nicole 357
KERBAJ, Mazen 311
KERIN, Zare 331
KERKHOF, Bert 307
KERNER, Diether 105
KETTERER, Ronja 33
KEUNTJE, Hartwig 105
KEVYT OLO 62
KIEFER, Anna 136
KILDE, Christer 101
KIM'S SNACKS 28
KIMERA, Jasmine 246, 253
KIMMO, Sakari 377
KINDLER, Andreas 60
KING, Stockholm 66, 87, 183, 278
KINKEL-CLEVER, Eva 204
KIRSCHENHOFER, Bertrand 233
KISSA, Katrin 25
KITCHEN, Madrid 353
KITTEL, Andreas 321, 328
KJAER, Jesper 355, 362, 363
KLEINMAN, Daniel 46
KLEMP, Andreas 78, 126, 152, 225
KLINTH, Christer 126
KLUSZCZYNSKA, Iwona 193
KNSK, Hamburg 23
KNUDSEN, Per-Henry 34, 38, 148, 150
KNUTH, Klaus 225
KOCH, Ben 329
KOHAK, Jakub 106
KOHAN, Jozsef 52
KOIVULA, Mika 377
KOKONMÄKI, Niko 70
KOLLE REBBE, Hamburg 41, 136, 226, 230, 276
KOMOREK, Magda 178
KONTO BARIERY 135
KOOP, Marcel 81
KOOPMANS, Jan 102
KOPPER, Edwin 317
KORCEK, Vlado 64
KORNESTEDT, Anders 321, 328
KOROLCZUK, Jakub 164
KORRES 344
KORSTEN, Bas 102, 200, 286
KOSCHEL, Verena 29
KOSMICKI, Lukasz 137
KOSTGELD, Ralf 84
KOUROUDIS, Yiannis 344, 348
KOWALCZUK, Maciek 178, 293, 349
KOWATSCHITSCH, Alexander 149, 308
KRAFTWERK PRODUCTION, Oslo 150, 280
KRALLMANN, Andreas 226
KRASSMANN, Heiko 323
KRASUCKA, Joanna 154
KRAUS, Thorsten 358
KRAUSE, Doreen 272
KREJZLIK, Martin 208
KRIEG, Daniel 84
KRØIER, Kristel 265
KRUCK, Manuel 333
KRUG, Wolfgang 190
KRUGLIAK, Yvonna 208
KRUIJSEN, Jorn 19
KRZESLACK , Johannes G. 63, 114
KUBOTA 242
KUCERA, Marek 238
KUIJPERS, Joris 112
KUKLA, Filip 115
KUNTZ & MAGUIRE 33
KUNTZ, Tom 48
KURBASA, Tvrtko 151
KURNATOWSKI, Florian v. 243
KURZMEYER, Thomas 83
KVIEN MADSEN, Torbjørn 148
L'ORÉAL 189
LA FAUCI, Fabio 93
LA GLORIA, Barcelona 255
LADDH 119
LAFLEUR, Georges 39
LÄHDESMÄKI, Markku 70, 305
LAITINEN, Ari 141
LAMBIAGHI, Marco 252
LAMBORGHINI TRACTORS 245
LANAQUERA, Cesar 24
LAND ROVER 216, 217, 222, 329
LANDURIS TRUCKS 225
LANE, Jamie 170
LANGE, Patrice 237
LANGER, Matthias 207
LANGPAUL, Jiri 107, 291
LANGTON, James 323
LANTELME, Andrea 337
LANZ, Danielle 96,135
LAPPALAINEN, Jyrki 377
LARSSON, Charlotta 370, 371
LARSSON, Hakan 253
LARSSON, Juha 40, 70,105
LASSALLE, Juan 353
LASSIE FILM, Copenhagen 93
LAST, Richard 358
LAT DERMO FLASH 192
LATINOVIC, Vuk 90
LATTA 36
LAURHAMMER, Carina 124
LAURITZEN, Jørgen 150
LAVOLA, Minna 276
LDV/RED CELL, Antwerp 53, 265
LEAGAS DELANEY, Hamburg 132, 224
LEAL, Quito 196
LEBAS, Bernard 117
LECOQ, Stéphane 119
LEDER STOLL, 264
LEE FILMS INTERNATIONAL, Madrid 196
LEE JEANS 247
LEE, Harvey 322
LEGAMBIENTE 114
LEHTINEN, Petteri 25
LEITMEYER, Marc 333
LEKKA, Henna 377
LEMEL COHEN,Tel Aviv 139
LEMEL,Yossi 139
LEMOINE, Benoît 141
LEO BURNETT & TARGET, Bucharest 235, 280
LEO BURNETT ITALIA, Milan 71
LEO BURNETT, Paris 22
LEO BURNETT, Prague 48, 106, 107, 118, 289, 290, 291, 294, 352
LEO BURNETT, Stockholm 38
LEO BURNETT, Warsaw 137, 154, 169, 219, 295
LEPPANEN, Mira 234, 252
LEROUX, Benoit 313
LES CYCLOPES 151
LES DISSIDENTS, Paris 141
LES TÉLÉCRÉATEURS, Paris 98
LETARNEC, Patrice 151, 260
LEUPOLD, Andréa 69, 110
LEUPPI, John 277
LEUZINGER, Katharina 365
LEVI, Yoram 178
LEVIN, David 66
LEVY, Mitch 376
LEWIS MOBERLY, London 342, 352
LEWIS, Mary 342, 352
LG&F, Brussels 159, 211, 231, 245, 281
LIANE'S RETROTAPETEN 350
LIBERO DIAPERS 176
LIBRESSE 184, 185, 364
LICHT, Christiane 368
LIDSTER, Ken 372
LIDZELL, Anders 52
LIEBIG, Jana 132
LIEN, Jens 28
LIKE A RIVER, Manchester 350
LILJA, Niklas 25
LILJEMARKER, Håkan 279
L'ILLA DIAGONAL 87
LIMA, Cláudio 179
LINARES, Andres 297
LINDBERG, Björn 335
LINDFORS, Petra 127
LINDGREN, Dan 362
LINDHE, Nils 356
LINDSAY, Andrew 22, 138, 251, 296
LINDSTRÖM, Frederic 131
LINDSTRÖM, Jörgen 309
LINEA SPORTSWEAR 255
LINGBELL, Rossen 340
LINK, Michael 335, 340
LINNE WATER 66
LIPMANN, Camille 218
LIPPERT, Susanne 324
LIPTAK, Peter 41
LIPTON 375
LIZ EARLE AROMATHERAPY 347
LJUBLJANA GAY & LESBIAN FILM FESTIVAL 298
LJUNGQVIST, Jenny 325
LODGE, David 266, 268
LOEHR, David 359
LOELL, Keith 143, 144, 145
LÖFFLER, Tobias 83
LOMMEL, Benjamin 204, 304
LOOSE MOOSE, London 372
LÓPEZ DE OCHOA, Luis 254
LÓPEZ, Ana 230, 276
LÓPEZ, Cesar 282
LÓPEZ, Fran 297
LÓPEZ, Isabel 123
LOTHIAN & BORDERS FIRE BRIGADE 138
LOTZE, Simon 120
LOUIS VUITTON 263
LOUIS XIV DDB, Paris 98, 285
LOUIS, Catherine 119
LOURENÇO, Marcelo 315
LÖVKVIST, Jesper 359, 364, 374
LOWE & PARTNERS, London 33
LOWE & PARTNERS, Madrid 254
LOWE BRINDFORS, Stockholm 35, 72, 77, 100, 140, 206, 278, 294, 320, 338
LOWE DIGITEL, Zagreb 151
LOWE FOREVER, Stockholm 309
LOWE GGK, Budapest 52
LOWE PEOPLE, Stockholm 205
LOWE TESCH, Stockholm 356
LOWE, Amsterdam 19, 112
LOWE, Brussels 39
LOWE, Dubai 234
LOWE, Lisbon 163
LOWE, Zürich 143, 144, 145
LÖWENHIELM, Magnus 72, 294, 320, 338
LOYTOKORPI, Jussi 361
LUCAS, Patricia 98
LUCENA, Mercedes 116, 192, 330, 333
LUCKAS, Katja 29
LUDWIG, Florian 255
LUFTHANSA 71
LUIGI LAVAZZA 337
LUIS SANCHEZ, Juan 50
LUKIC, Milos 288
LUNDQUIST, Pelle 292
LUNDSTRÖM, Christoffer 50
LUSTH, Lennart 156
LUTGE, Fred 85, 149
LUTHERAN CHURCH AID 122
LYDEKING, Stockholm 122
M&M'S 29
M.E.C.H., Berlin 71
MAALOUF, Joseph 49
MAC FILM, Stockholm 128
MACCARIO, Antonio 109, 160
MACDONALD, Toby 248
MACDOUGAL, Dan 363
MACKEN, Jan 73, 167
MACLAND, Matthew 193
MADARIAGA, Miguel 215
MADDEN, Shay 292
MADEDDU, Emanuele 281
MADELEINE 168
MADILL, Warren 62
MAEHNICKE, Gert 79, 295
MAES BEER 53
MAGALHAES, Pedro 132, 166, 236
MAGER, Christoph 310
MAGGI 33
MAGGIONI, Sonia 176
MAGIC HAT, London 186
MAGUIN, Thomas 334
MAGUIRE, Mike 48
MAINO, Elisa 170, 252
MAJER, Marko
MAJOROVA, Marika 135
MALA, Anna 90, 238
MALM, Andreas 359, 374
MAMMUT 249
MANISCALCO, Mauro 170
MANIX 180, 181
MANKOPF, Jan 359
MANNHEIMER, Fabian 101
MANOHAR, Syam 168
MÅNSSON, Sophie 122
MANTHEY, Andreas 130
MARCUS, Pierre 26, 56, 57,149, 218
MARIANI, Michele 337
MARIESTADS 52
MARIN, Josep 165
MARINI DOTTI E ASSOCIATI, Milan 170, 252
MARINI, Lorenzo 170, 252
MARINI, Patrizio 281
MARINO, Mary Ann 259
MARKENFILM, Wedel 243
MARKHUS, Rune 148
MARKLUND, Martin 127, 247
MARKOVITCH, Ida 40
MARKS, Stephen 234
MARLOW, Jonathan 177
MARONI, Sune 154
MARQUARDT, Rico 357, 359
MARRAKECH, Stockholm 262
MARRAZZO, Jose Luis 282
MARTEL, Yann 360
MARTELA 229
MARTI, Lorena 283
MARTIN & FROST 314
MARTIN, Aaron 323
MARTIN, Alex 216
MARTIN, David 112
MARTIN, Mark 129
MARTIN, Michael 118, 289, 352
MARTIN, Pete 360
MARTIN, Victor 112
MARTIN-BUITRAGO, Jesús 315
MARTINEZ, Alex 55,187
MARTINEZ, Raquel 164
MARY, Samantha 367
MARZO, Helena 327
MASTERCARD 101
MASTROMATTEO, Giuseppe 237
MATADOR RAZORS 185
MATE, Gabor 52
MATHERON, Eric 173
MATOS E SILVA, Catarina 236
MATOS, Catarina 372
MATTER & PARTNER, Zürich 215
MATTER, Daniel 215
MAUDSLEY, Toby 185
MAURIZIO SANTARELLI, Rome 208
MAWDESLEY, Dan 175, 329
MAYER McCANN, Ljubljana 298
MAZZA, Giuseppe 272
MBR 234
McCANN, Helsinki 305
McCANN, Malmö 36, 244
McCANN-ERICKSON, Amstelveen 44
McCANN-ERICKSON, Dublin 292
McCANN-ERICKSON, Frankfurt 18,140, 264, 288
McCANN-ERICKSON, London 39, 79,179
McCANN-ERICKSON, Madrid 122, 123, 164
McCANN-ERICKSON, Milan 114
McCANN-ERICKSON, Prague 90, 181, 238
McCANN-ERICKSON, Tel Aviv 40, 339
McCANN-ERICKSON, Vienna 189
McCANN-ERICKSON, Warsaw 193
McCLOUD, Andy 208
McDONALD'S 16
McGRANN, Richard 284
McHUGH, Peter 257, 286
McNULTY, Gary 325
McPHAIL, Alan 221
McPHEE, Jamie 355
MEDIAMIX, Maribor 167
MEDICOS SIN FRONTERAS 122, 123
MEDINA TURGUL DDB, Istanbul 201
MEEK, Nick 104
MEHRWALD, Marco 81
MEINKÖHN, Derik 198
MEIRI, Maya 208
MEKANO FILM, Stockholm 127, 156
MEMAC OGILVY, Jeddah 332
MENET, Gilles 63
MENETRET, Benoît 120
MERCATOR 188
MERCEDES-BENZ 205, 334, 358
MERIE, Philippe 160
MERILION, Tom 42
MERONI, Flavio 236
MERZ, Uwe 207
MESSAGER, Pierre Louis 283
METEOR 153
METHOD FILMS, London 134
METROPOLIZ 361
MEUNIER, Thierry 89
MEURISSE, Klaus 29
MEYER, Annabelle 256
MEYER, Kersten 314
MICHALSKI, Julian 350
MICHELIN 224
MICHELSEN, Ulrik 20
MICKA, Ales 115
MICU, Alexandru 166
MIGHALI, Debora 17
MIGROS 84
MIKI EYEWEAR 262
MIKIELS, Michael 73
MIKKELSEN, Mone 154
MIKOLA, Erkki 25, 62
MILCZAREK, Michael 83
MILK, Gothenburg 320
MILLEN, Ian 129
MILLISHIP, Simon 358
MILLS, Graham 50, 130, 323
MINA, Basil 48,106, 107, 118, 289, 290, 291, 294, 352
MINDER, Stefan 43, 135, 299
MINI 357
MINIER, Sylvier 61
MIO 156
MIRON 192
MISIRLIOGLU, Hakki 161
MISKOVSKY, Dominik 135
MISS GAZZOLINE 375
MISSING SPARKY, Barcelona 196
MISSKE, Bernd 189
MITCHELL, Scott 251
MOBILKOM AUSTRIA 149, 305
MODERNA MUSEUM 299
MOESSLER, Olaf 302
MOILANEN, Esko 155
MOINE, Olivier 98
MOIRA, Arno 98
MOLAND FILM COMPANY, Copenhagen 80, 82
MOLAND FILM COMPANY, Oslo 28, 68, 154
MOLAS, Silvia 342
MOLTKE, Rasmus 64
MOMATIUK, Eastcott 195
MONARCH, Bratislava 135
MONDADORI 272
MONDINO, Jean-Baptiste 337
MONINO, Vicky 196
MONKEWITZ, Nicolas 23, 76
MONNET, France 56, 57,149
MONOLA, Milla 276

MONTERO, Antonio 95, 215, 283
MONTES, Manuel 24, 74
MONTGOMERY, Colin 360
MONTGOMERY, Giles 257
MONZINO, Enzo 272
MORA 19
MORABITO, Paola 93
MORAES, Tico 179
MORAN, Paul 241
MORENO COFFEE 55
MORENO MARQUEZ, Manolo 192, 326, 333
MORENO, Luis 66
MORGAN, Richard 376
MORO, Monica 164
MORRIS, Ed 134
MORRIS, Tim 241
MORTEN JANKEL ZANDER, London 33, 48, 216
MORTIER, Jens 32, 67, 102, 103, 152, 182, 270
MOSER, Nathalie 19
MOSQUERA, Virginia 92, 333
MOST, Charlotte 142, 145, 146, 176, 185
MOTHER, London 48
MOTHERCARE 254
MOTION BLUR, Oslo 150
MOULIERAC, Olivier 240
MOUNTNEY, Richard 314
MOURÉ, David 122
MOUZANNAR, Bechara 311
MRM PARTNERS WORLDWIDE, Oslo 319
MUEHLEHALDE HOME FOR THE BLIND 135
MUELLER, Lothar 18
MUENCH, Marc 211
MUGUET, Jérome 367
MULLER, Christine 162
MULLER, Daniel 274
MULLER, Mark 287
MUNILL, Xavier 216
MUNNS, Garry 323
MUNTEAN, Radu 280
MURA 331
MURATOGLU, Ilkay 65
MURPHY, James 321
MURPHY, Paul 196
MURRO, Noam 98
MYSAP 323
NABS 327
NACHTWEY, James 267
NAERLAND, Torgrim 88
NAIRN DUNBAR GOLF CLUB 316
NANA, Poehner 21
NANNAVECCHIA, Camilla 337
NANSO 252
NASCIMENTO, Mário 228
NASTRO AZZURRO 50
NATALE, Giorgio 114
NATIONAL GALLERIES OF SCOTLAND 296
NATIONAL GEOGRAPHIC CHANNEL 277
NATURA ARTIS MAGISTRA ZOO 287
NAUG, Thorbjørn 150, 202
NAUMOVICI, Bogdan 235, 280
NAUTILUS 22
NAVARRE, Christophe 149
NAVILLE, Bernard 57, 149, 218
NAVIO, Rubén 95
NAZER, Fitna 332
NELSON, Jacob 359, 374
NEMAN, Zohar 40
NEMIROVSKY, Orna 208
NERGER, Jürgen 276
NEUBER, Wiltrude 243
NEUE DIGITALE, Frankfurt 364, 367
NEW DEAL DDB, Oslo 34, 38, 68, 148, 150
NEW PARTNERS 237
NHS SUNDERLAND 129
NICHOLAS, Greg 44
NICOLSON, Don 193
NICOTERA, Sandro 89
NIEDERWIESER, Raimund 334
NIELSEN, Joachim 80, 82, 371
NIESSERON, Eric 263
NIEUWERKERK, J-P 328
NIKE 246, 253, 256, 258, 259, 263, 354, 355
NILSON, Greger Ulf 347
NILSSON, Filip 359, 374
NILSSON, Johan 35, 72, 77, 100, 140, 278, 294, 320, 338
NILSSON, Niklas 128
NILSSON, Ulf 326
NIMICK, Colin 322
NIPSTAD, Stefan 60
NISKA-WÓJCIK, Agnieszka 211
NISSAN 195, 216, 225, 302
NISSEN, Tom 280
NITRO FX, Helsinki 361
NITRO SNOWBOARDS 367
NOËL, Rémi 212
NOLAN, Jack 50, 130, 323
NOLTING, Ralf 198
NORDIC LIGHT CARE 324
NORDOFF/ROBBINS 136
NORDPOL+ HAMBURG, Hamburg 233, 365
NØRGAARD, Søren 361
NORGUEIRA, Daniël 72
NORLING, Torkel 320
NORRA, Ville 305
NORRBY, Daniel 147
NOR-WAY BUSSEKSPRESS 68
NORWEGIAN CHURCH AID 124
NOVOTNY, Marek 181
NUROFEN 179
NUTLEY, Colin 40
NYBERG, Håkan 147
NYBØ, Kjetil 124
NYGREN BARRETT, Susanna 353
NYROP-LARSEN, Michael 371
OATLY 60
ÖBERG, Silla 142, 145, 185
OBERWILER, Dominik 100
OBRINK, Johan 368
OCB 260
OCEAN VIEW, Amsterdam 19
O'DONNELL, Damien 153, 292
OFF 179
OFFENBACH, John 79
OFFERMANNS, Frank 228
OGILVY & MATHER, Brussels 118
OGILVY DENMARK, Copenhagen 131
OGILVYINTERACTIVE WORLDWIDE, London 376
OGILVYONE WORLDWIDE, Frankfurt 323, 324
OGILVYONE WORLDWIDE, London 319, 322, 376
OGILVYONE WORLDWIDE, Paris 367
O'HAGEN, John 142, 145
OHLSSON, Magnus 36
OHRT, Mads 131
OLAF, Erwin 105
OLECH, Dariusz 211

OLIVER, Isahac 87
OLIVERO, Johan 375
OLSSON, Magnus 70
OLSSON, Olle 324
OLYMPIC DDB, Bucharest 166
OLYMPIC GAMES 348
OPITZ, Cornelia 253
ORANGE 143, 144, 145, 153
ORANGINA 62, 63
O'REILLY, Brendan 42
ORIAN, Matan 178
ORLIAC, Axel 218
ORRILLO, Jens 223
ORTEGA, Alvaro 122
OSBORNE, Nic 154
O'SHAUGHNESSY, Andy 350
OSSENDRIJVER, Marcel 44
OSTIGLIA, Tomas 267, 268
OTTE, Ingo 237
OTTO FILM, Helsinki 141
OTTO, Mike John 359
OUDAHA, Mohammed 199, 209
OUTSIDER, London 210, 246, 253, 266, 268
ØVERÅS, Håkon 148
ØVERSVEEN, Turid 148
ÖZKUT, Kerem 201
PAATELMA, Heikki 377
PACREAU, Josselin 205
PAGAN FILMS, London 220
PAIVINEN, Jappe 25
PAKULL, Thomas 81
PALACIO, David 317
PALMER, Chris 284, 365
PALOMBA, Siegfried 368
PALYEKAR, Anil 222
PAM, Matt 54
PANCOTTI, Alessandro 71
PANICCA, Andrea 241
PANIZZA, Silvio 297
PAPWORTH, Kim 194
PARSONS, Mike 39
PARTIZAN, Paris 194
PARTIZAN, London 54, 58, 59, 194
PASCAUD, Jean-Guillaume 22
PASECKY, Martin 106
PATERSON, Euan 196, 197
PÄTZOLD, Patricia 198
PAUL WEILAND FILM COMPANY, London 110, 248
PAULIN, Petter 242
PAVESIC, Tieneke 256
PAVLETIC, Bostjan 298
PEARLFISHER, London 343
PEC, Philip 90, 181, 238
PEDERSEN, Jan 93
PEDERSEN, Per 93
PEDRO, Rui 372
PEDROCCHI, Vincent 180, 242
PEJAS, Steffen 83
PEKKANEN, Mimmu 377
PELED, Avner 40
PELLETIER, Jérôme 189
PELUCA 243
PEMBERTON & WHITEFOORD, London 321
PEMBERTON, Simon 321
PENICAUT, Alban 119
PEPSI 56, 57
PERAZZOLI, Luca 114
PEREZ, David 27, 133
PEREZ, Fernando 144
PÉREZ-PAREDES, Juanma 74
PERSSON, Johan 146
PERSSON, Martin 60
PERSSON, Ted 362, 363
PETERSEN, Timothy 155
PETERSON, Niklas 362
PETERSSON, Gunnar 244
PEUGEOT 212
PFEFFERKORN, Gritt 134, 303
PHILIPP UND KEUNTJE, Hamburg 105
PHILLIPS, Jimbo 31
PHS\INTERACTIVE, Helsinki 377
PIEBENGA, Piebe 121, 277
PIEKARZEWSKI, Jacek 164
PIETTE, Eric 281
PIGGOTT, Marcus 263
PILKINGTON, James 54
PILSNER URQUELL 48
PINGUET, Hugues 285
PINKCOMBE, Rik 111
PIOLA, Gigi 208
PIRES, João 163
PIRONET, Pierre 209
PIXSHIFT, Stockholm 362, 363, 370, 371
PLANTROSE, Philippe 285
PLESKOT, Jiri 48, 289
PODRAVKA 24, 332
POETZSCH, Britta 71
POGUNTKE, Arndt 272
POLAT, Demir Karpat 65
POLDERWEG ANIMAL SHELTER 112
POLETTI, Francesco 322
POLIDORI, Mario 281
POLISH SCRABBLE FEDERATION 293
POLLACK, Hans-Holger 29
POPELIER, Paul 53
POPP, Kristina 78, 152
POPPELAARS, Herman 53
POPPETS 341
POREBSKI, Maciek 169
PORRO, Giovanni 157, 322
PORSCHE 209
POST-IT NOTES 227
POSTMYR, Lena 216
POTUGUESE CREATIVE CLUB 236
POULTER PARTNERS, Leeds 241
POWELL, Carol 250
POWER DUCK 166
PRADO MUSEUM 297
PRAGUE MUNICIPAL COUNCIL 115
PRAGUE MUSEUM OF COMMUNISM 289
PRAGUE MUSEUM OF TORTURE 290
PRAGUE ZOO 291
PRATA, Francisco 108, 125, 163, 166, 179, 315
PREDA, Adrian 47
PRELEC, Monika 86
PREMIÈRE HEURE, Paris 117
PRESTO 166
PRIDAN, Ariel 153
PRIMIZIA 252
PRINC, Peter 135
PRIOR, Colin 50, 130

PRISTOP, Ljubljana 188
PROBSTMAYER, Melanie 368
PROJECTOR 362
PROPELER, Ljubljana 101
PROVINCIA DI BRESCIA 108
PRYCE, Cristina 372
PUBLIC SENAT TV CHANNEL 283
PUBLICIS CONSEIL, Paris 44, 98, 151, 189, 260
PUBLICIS DIALOG, Frankfurt 207
PUBLICIS ESPAÑA, Madrid 74, 75
PUBLICIS, Brussels 124, 239
PUBLICIS, Frankfurt 33, 63, 79, 114, 159, 206, 295, 310
PUBLICIS, Zürich 84, 100, 236
PUGLISI, Giandomenico 17
PUIG, Carles 55, 187
PUIG, Joan 342
PUMPKIN FILM, Zürich 84
PUPELLA, Marco 29
PUPULEK, Enis 101, 127
PURGAR, Krezimir 151
PUUMALAINEN, Kari 21
QANTAS 79
QUAD, Paris 63, 218
QUADENS, Catherine 239
QUAGLIA, Stefano 71
QUALITY MEAT SCOTLAND 22
QUEMADES, Ricardo 342
QUINN, Lex 188
RADEKER, Jochen 336
RADICAL MEDIA, London 44, 56, 57
RAETHER, Franziska 41, 136
RAFINERI, Istanbul 65
RAGGIO, Johannes 37, 41, 76
RAKETSPEL 364
RAMALHO, Paulo 228
RANKIN 301
RAUCH, Stephanie 78, 126, 152, 225
RAY, Gordon 222, 227
RAY, Vince 31
RAYMENT, Richard 191
RAYNERT, Benoît 162
REALE, Carlo 129
REBBIN, Oliver 357
REBOLJ, Aljosa 188
RECIO, Ángel 196
RECRUIT IRELAND 235
REDLICH, Andreas 295
REHN, Michaela 23
REICHER, Christoph 149, 308
REID, David 316
REIDINGA, Hesling 329
REILAND, Gösta 184, 185
REIMANN, Christian 230
REIMERSHOLMS 340
REINACHER, Heinrich 84
REINDORF, Olivier 173, 312
REISSINGER, Michael 333
REMINGTON 177
RENAULT 206, 207
RENCK, Elin 338
RENCK, Johan 185
RENCK/ÅKERLUND FILM, Gothenburg 185
REPORTERS WITHOUT BORDERS 141
RETTINGHAUSEN, Peter 23
REUTER, Erich 18, 264
REY, Frank 205
RHEINDORF, Olivier 89
RIBENA 64
RICHARD, Stéphane 262
RICHEZ, Chantal 375
RICHON, Pascal 262
RICKABY, Chris 129
RIEKEN, Torsten 71
RIES, Sabine 215
RIFFAULT, Hervé 62, 63, 117, 217
RILEY, Tim 275
RIMMEL 187
RINGQVIST, Martin 142, 144, 145, 146, 269
RIPOLLÉS, Alex 165
RITTER, Lorenz 113
RIVEN, Tal 178
RKCR/Y&R, London 216, 284
ROBAS, Shira 153, 146
ROBERSON, Susan 110
ROBERT, Michael 80, 82, 371
ROBERT/BOISEN & LIKE-MINDED, Copenhagen 80, 82, 371
ROBERTS, Nigel 31, 275
ROBINSON, Jen 290
ROBSON, Thomas 354
ROCA DE VINYALS, Jose Mª 87, 196
RODRIGUEZ, Sergio 71
ROE, Gerard 49
ROEFFEN, Kai 225, 302, 366, 368
ROEHLING, Jochen 359
ROGERS, Peter 350
ROGINSKI, Szymon 349
ROGUE, London 58
ROHNER, Patrik 299
RØKEBERG, Glen 202
RØKFRITT 128
ROKSVAAG, Ragnar 88
ROLAND, Olivier 32
ROLET, Alex 244
ROMAHANYI, Pedro 61
ROMAN VALENT FILM, Vösendorf 222
ROMSTAD, Bendik 68
RÖNKÄ, Olli 276
RONKKO, Markku 229, 377
ROQUE, João 108
RÖRSTRAND 158
ROSANDER, Mussi 126
ROSEBERRY, Brad 257
ROSENGREN, Michael 128
ROSENKRANZ, Klaudia 52
ROSENTHAL, Oliver 357
ROSET, Vigdis 34, 38
ROSSELLI, Stefano 213
ROSTI, Paula 25, 62
ROTH + SCHMID 83
ROTHWELL, Paul 259
ROUSSEL, Florian 141
ROUX, Walter 140
ROUZIER, Luc 61
ROWNTREES 33
ROWOLD, Katja 33
ROXAS, Edward 332
ROYAL MAIL 319, 322
ROYER, Frédéric 283
RUCKAY, Tomas 135
RUDKIEWICZ, Jan 70
RUDOLF KONIMOIS, Tallinn 25
RUF LANZ, Zürich 96, 135
RUF, Markus 96, 135
RÜHMANN, Lars 233

RUIGROK, Paul 200
RUIZ NICOLI, Madrid 282, 315
RUIZ-NICOLI, Paco 282, 315
RUKI, Jerôme 117
RUOLA, Eka 40
RUSSEL AVIS, Dublin 292
RUSSELL, Russ 292
RUTH, Stockholm 138, 335
RUTHSTRÖM, Magnus 335
RUVEN, Paul 19
S2 INTERNACIONAL 333
SAAB 206, 356
SAATCHI & SAATCHI, Amsterdam 317
SAATCHI & SAATCHI, Frankfurt 204, 304
SAATCHI & SAATCHI, Italy 207, 272
SAATCHI & SAATCHI, London 210
SAATCHI & SAATCHI, Paris 119, 141, 162
SAATCHI & SAATCHI, Vienna 149, 308
SAATCHI & SAATCHI, Warsaw 164, 211
SABRI, Jens 18
SACCO, Jean-François 217
SACKMANN, Uli 336
SADOLIN 167
SAGEM 151
SAHORES, Benoît 51, 306
SALA, Maurizio 337
SALA, Ramón 67
SALATI, Michele 160
SALES, Miquel 216
SALIH, Metin 323
SALINSKI, Szymon 349
SALMINEN, Hanna 21
SALVATION ARMY 132
SAMPAT, Manish 234
SANCHEZ, Mari Luz 75
SANCHEZ, Sergio 268
SANDBERG, Linda 362
SANDELL, Ola 320
SANDER, Henrik 68, 148
SANDERSON, Phil 289
SANDSTRÖM, Mattias 373
SANGDHORE, Rajeev 227
SANITAS 95
SANNUM, Eva 150
SANROMA, Bernat 27, 133
SANZ DE ANDINO, Carlos 215
SANZ, Vanessa 123
SAPTHU, Fabian 265
SARAC, Emanuela 214
SARC, Ayse Bali 65
SAS 72, 77
SASMAZ, Candan 311
SASSMANN, Bernhard 189
SATOMAYOR, Alvaro 256
SAULNIER, Alain 189
SAVE THE CHILDREN 319
SAWYER, Adam 220
SCANDIC HOTELS 70
SCHAAFSMA, Dick 264
SCHACK, Peder 168
SCHAEFER, Eva 78, 152
SCHAEFERS, Holger 113
SCHÄFER, Roland 23
SCHAFFEROVA, Patricia 135
SCHAU-KNUDSEN, Arne 28
SCHAUPP, Wolfgang 204
SCHEFFCZYK, Sonja 264
SCHEIBEL, Tim 356
SCHELLART, Marieke 30
SCHENK, Anke 357
SCHERPENZEEL, Evert-Jan 329
SCHINDLER, Heribert 263
SCHIPPER, Menno 44
SCHITTKOWSKI, Sandra 357
SCHLICHTE, Nadine 228
SCHLUPP, Uwe 100
SCHMID, Martin 208
SCHMID, Max 144
SCHMID, Michael 208
SCHMIDER, Benoît 119, 141, 162
SCHMIDT, Christine 324
SCHMIDT, Jens 21, 334
SCHMIDT, Rainer 225, 302, 366
SCHMIDT, Stefan 134, 249, 288, 303, 331, 366
SCHMITT, Harald 63, 114
SCHMITZ, Ulrich 243
SCHNEIDER, Roger 89, 92
SCHNEIDER, Tim 243
SCHOEB, Thomas 96
SCHOLES, Adam 210
SCHOLZ & VOLKMER, Wiesbaden 358
SCHREGENBERGER, Felix 43, 135
SCHREIBER, Gunther 233, 365
SCHREMPF, Eva 264
SCHREPFER, Urs 92
SCHRÖDER, Daniel 65
SCHRÖDER, Margit 357
SCHROEDER, Simone 228
SCHULZ, Stefan 357
SCHUMACHER, Björn 212
SCHUSTER, Birgit 254
SCHUSTER, Thies 198
SCHWARTZ, Johannes 30
SCHWARZ, Daniel 329
SCHWARZ, Dennis 23
SCHWEIZER ILLUSTRIERTE 277
SCHWEIZER, Daniel 65
SCHWEYER, Carla 71
SCHWIEDRZIK, Boris 249, 331
SCOTONI, Roland 169
SCOTT, Chris 126
SCOTT, Emma 210
SCOTT, Henry 281
SCOTT, Simon 22, 138, 251, 296
SCOTTISH NATIONAL PARTY 309
SCREENBASE, Edinburgh 360
SEA LEBANON 311
SEAR, Rick 319
SEAWARD, Peter 193
SEBASTIA, Jordi 67
SEBASTIEN, Bernard 117
SEELENBINDER, Caren 136
SEELT, Henk 328
SEEMANN, Ali 222
SEGAL, Shahar 40
SEGOVIA, Paco 297
SEHIRLI, Cem Sultan 161
SEIFERT, Alon 40, 339
SEJERSEN, Casper 265
SEK & GREY, Helsinki 25
SELS, Véronique 39
SEÑOR, Rubén 254
SENSILIS 346
SEPPÄLÄ 260
SERETIDE 193

SERON, Pablo 372
SERRA, Henrique 236
SERRANO, Ramón 55
SERVAES, Paul 152, 159
SERVICEPLAN GRUPPE, Munich 351
SETTEBELLO 92
SEZNAMKA 310
SHALMOR AVNON AMICHAY/Y&R, Tel Aviv 153, 178, 232
SHAMIR, Yigal 208
SHAVIT, Asi 232
SHEARER, Paul 246, 253, 256, 258
SHEARLOCK, John 372
SHOTS 234
SIDDHARTA 340
SIEBENHAAR, Dirk 120, 237
SIHVO, Risto 25
SILBURN, Paul 46
SILJA LINE 70
SILVA 292
SILVA DIAS, Luis 108, 179
SILVA, Juan 283
SILVENNOINEN, Timo 260
SIMAKOVA, Svetlana 305
SIMON, Zoltán 16
SIMONET, Matthieu 215
SIMPSON, Alex 153
SINCLAIR, James 134
SITJAR, Xavi 87
SJÖBERG, Lennart 269
SJÖNELL, Mary Lee 40
SKANDAALI/LEO BURNETT, Helsinki 25, 62, 276
SKIP DETERGENT 163
SKODA 208
SKOG, Johan 156, 176
SKRABAL, Philipp 215
SKUDNIGG, Peter 329
SLABBYNCK, Peter 86
SLIVKA, Vlado 64
SLUITER, Cas 264
SMI 353
SMIDT-FIBIGER, Tobias 361
SMIEJA, Jennifer 259
SMIRNOFF 42, 43
SMIT ROETERS, Fulco 121
SMITH, Adam 138
SMITH, Laurie 54
SMITH, Martyn 44
SMITH, Phillippa 58, 59, 256
SMOLDERS, Greg 265
SMOLIANSKY, Gunnar 335
SMOODOO 345
SNCF 312
SNELLENBERG, David 99, 287
SNICKERS 26, 30, 31
SNIDER, Luke 344
SOARES, Rui 132, 166, 236
SØDAL DIETHRICSON, Irene 68
SÖDERLIND, Bitte 212
SÖDERLUNDH, Walter 87
SOLE, Xavi 203
SOLERO, Luis M. 75
SONY PLAYSTATION 171, 172, 173, 174, 300, 331
SOREC-MEDIA, Moscow 336
SOS RACISME CATALUNYA 133
SOTO, Valen 327
SOUCEK, Ondrej 310
SOUTER, Peter 31, 128
SPA REINE 67
SPÄNNAR, Ola 362
SPARKSMAN, Claire 220
SPARRE-ENGER, Pål 150
SPECTRE, London 46
SPEERS FILM, Dublin 42
SPEERS, Johnny 42
SPILLMANN, Martin 76, 249, 299
SPILLMANN/FELSER/LEO BURNETT, Zürich 76, 249, 299
SPIROSKI, Yougo 273
SPORTFIVE 233
SPORTSBLADET 278
SPOTTORNO, Carlos 267
SPRINGER & JACOBY, London 91, 220, 221
SPRINGER & JACOBY, Paris 205
SPRINGTIME, Stockholm 362, 363, 370, 371
SROKA, Ryszard 164
STAAL, Oslo 28
STADHAMMAR, Martin 77
STAGNITTI, Gaia 71
STÅHL, Björn 205
STAHR, Wolfgang 130
STALLAERT, Kurt 152
STAMM, Henning 230, 276
STANISTREET, Jonathan 292
STARCK, Hans 333
STAUB, Simon 143, 145
STAUDINGER & FRANKE 255
STAUSS, Frank 228
STEARNS, Tony 258
STEEG, Thorsten 18
STEEL, Léon 180
STEELE, Leon 91
STEFFEN, Jens 364
STEHLE, Mark 233
STEIN, Matt 259
STEINER, Rob 194
STEINHILBER, Jan 204
STEINIJANS, Katarina 364
STELLA ARTOIS 52
STELLATOS, Athanassios 134, 303
STENCO, Alessandro 272
STEP HALI 161
STERN 132
STEWART, David 54
STILLKING FILMS, Prague 48, 106
STINK, London 162, 208
STINK, Stockholm 101
STOCKER, Christian 345
STÖCKER, Ramona 53
STOELZL, Philippe 98
STOETER, Paul 290, 294
STÖHR, Martina 185
STOIMENOFF Ljubomir 33, 159
STOLETZKY, Judith 136, 230
STOLZ, Calle 279
STONEHAM, Sara 188
STORÅKERS McCANN, Stockholm 101, 127, 247, 279, 299
STRAHM, Barbara 274
STRAVS, Janez 331
STREPFEN 193
STRICHPUNKT, Stuttgart 336
STRID, Steve 362
STRÖM, Jonas 345
STROOY, Marq 317
STUB, Totte 72
STULZ, Martin 143, 145
SUBRAMANIUM, Suresh 168, 227
SUCHET, Bertrand 98, 285
SUCKSDORFF, Susanna 377
SUND,Tosse 138, 335
SUNDBERG, Oskar 362, 363
SUNDEREN, Henrik 38
SUNDIN, David 373
SUPER, Sven 94
SUREK, Eva 357
SURFRIDER ASSOCIATION 117
SUTILA, Ivona 188
SVENSSON, Magnus 122, 370
SVF 366
SWE, SCHUMACHER WESSMAN & ENANDER, Stockholm 212, 347
SWISS MILK PRODUCERS 37, 41
SWISS MOBILIAR 100
SWISS PRESS 238
SWISSCOM 299
SYNNING, Niklas 122
SYNSAM 262
SZABLAK, Darek 137, 295
SZULECKI, Jacek 164, 211
TACEVSKI, Goran 291
TACEVSKI, Nikola 290, 294
TADDEUCCI, Francesco 207
TAFT, John 258
TAFT, Josh 26
TAGES-ANZEIGER 274
TAILDEMAN, Nils 44
TAIRA, Carina 261
TAIVAS, Helsinki 21
TAMBAY, Derya 224
TANDEM DDB, Madrid 24, 27, 74, 87,133 ,196, 203
TANGO 54, 58, 59
TARBARIC, Teo 151
TAROUX, Philippe 313
TARSEM 56, 57
TATARKO, Raffo 64, 135
TAUBES, Nicolas 22
TAURA, Marjo 377
TAYLOR, Christine 174, 331
TAYLOR, Rob 350
TBWA\BRUSSELS 73, 167
TBWA\EL ALJ & PARTNERS, Casablanca 273
TBWA\ESPAÑA, Barcelona 67, 216
TBWA\GERMANY, Berlin 134, 174, 225, 249, 288, 302, 303, 331, 366, 368
TBWA\ISTANBUL 224
TBWA\LONDON 46, 134, 248, 270, 271
TBWA\PARIS 171, 172, 173, 195, 300, 312, 313
TBWA\PHS, Helsinki 229, 234, 252, 377
TDK 175, 329
TEAM/YOUNG & RUBICAM, Dubai 168, 222, 227
TEFAL 159
TEICHNER, Fabien 62
TEISMANN, Ben 368
TEISSEIRE 65
TEIXEIRA, Jorge 228, 315
TEIXIDÓ, Joan 67, 216
TELE2 142, 145
TELENOR 148, 150
TENNIS MASTERS MADRID 317
TEQUILA\PHS, Helsinki 229
TERRES DES FEMMES 126
TESCH, Johan 356
THÁI CÔNG 365
THE BEARDED LADY DDB, Stockholm 368
THE BIG ISSUE 134
THE BORDERS RUGBY 298
THE BRIDGE, Glasgow 298
THE DAILY TELEGRAPH 266, 268
THE ECONOMIST 275
THE FAMILY, Milan 71
THE GLUE SOCIETY, Sydney 301
THE GUARDIAN 325
THE LONDON EYE 376
THE NICOLAS HULOT FOUNDATION 116
THE SPECTATOR 274
THE SWEDISH ASSOCIATION OF HARD OF HEARING PEOPLE 138
THE TIMES LONDON FILM FESTIVAL 284
THE UNION ADVERTISING AGENCY, Edinburgh 22, 138, 251, 296
THE WHITE HOUSE, Reykjavik 192
THE WORD TRANSLATION AGENCY 361
THEIS, Gulliver 205
THEORIN, Magnus 299
THERAPY FILMS, London 128
THERY, Catherine 44
THEUNER, Michael 311
THOMAS, Christopher 304
THOME, Eric 20
THOMPSON, Matt 346
THOMSEN, Robert 355
THONIK, Amsterdam 351
THYSSEN 228
TIBITS 83
TIEDEMANN, Kay-Owe 230
TIGER OF SWEDEN 338
TILKIN, Steven 365
TILLIGER, Tom 63, 114
TIMNEY, John 191
TIMONEN, Mikko 359, 374, 375
TINDALL, Justin 197
TITECA, Grégory 199, 209
TIVINEN, Samuli 377
TJEBBES, Klas 36
TODD, Daniel 128
TODD, Hugh 210
TOKCAN, Deniz 125
TOKKARI, Marjo 260
TOLKKINEN, Mari 377
TOMASEK, Toni 167
TOMPKINSON, James 194
TOO MUCH TOO SOON, Stockholm 373
TOPIC, Marin 332
TOPSOE, Christiern 80, 82
TORRE LAZUR McCANN, London 193
TOSCANA, Agostino 93, 207, 272
TOSTIVINT, Jean-Marc 26
TOTAL 218
TOTH, Andrea 52
TOYOTA 210, 211, 212
TOZER, Jason 197
TRABELSI, Osnat 208
TRAEN, Mick 97
TRAKTOR, Santa Monica 36, 58, 59, 256
TRATBERGER, Christoph 159
TRAUTMANN, Marc 334
TRE VÄNNER, Stockholm 60, 87, 156
TRESCHOW, Stefan 80, 82
TRIBAL DDB, London 373
TRICOT, Remy 45
TRIER, Sara 354, 355
TRIFKOVIC, Vlado 167
TRIGLAV 101
TRILL BIRDSEED 21
TROUVÉ-DUGENY, Christophe 89
TRUCE 344
TUCKER, Adam 197
TUDOR, Micky 58, 59, 266, 268
TUMIATTI, Stefano 237
TUNBJÖRK, Lars 69
TUOMELA, Panu 377
TURCHETTI, Federico 207
TURCONI, Marco 108
TURESPAÑA 75
TURETSCHEK, Gerd 368
TURNER BROADCASTING SYSTEM 322
TURNER DUCKWORTH, London 341, 344, 347
TURNER DUCKWORTH, San Francisco 341, 344, 347
TURNER, Brian 58, 59, 266, 268
TURNER, David 341, 344, 347
TURNER, Debbie 33, 48, 216
TURSMAN, Donald 225, 302, 366
TURTLE, Tommy 56, 57
TVE 267, 268
UAMK 106
UFER, Meike 357
UFNALEWSKI, Lukasz 137, 295
UGGLA, Gabriel 320
ULPANOT, Tel Aviv 40
UMWELT ADVERTISING, Copenhagen 282
UNCLE/GREY, Århus 93
UNESCO 311
UNICEF 124
UNIPI 17
UNIT 9 365
UP A GUM TREE 346
URIBETXEBERRIA, Mikel 255
URL, Martin 33
UTSIKT KOMMUNIKATION, Stockholm 325
UYTTENHOVE, Frank 39, 103, 167, 245, 281
VACATURE 281
VACHEROT, Sebastien 195
VAJGL, Peter 115
VALASTI, Johanna 25
VALENT, Roman 222
VALLISTO, Tommi 252
VAN 'T VELD, Paul 328
VAN BECKHOVEN, Monique 72
VAN BEEK, Kris 231
VAN BERKEL, Carsten 265
VAN DE SANDE, Jeroen 19
VAN DEN BERG, Marloes 94, 102
VAN DEN BERGE, Pascale 94
VAN DEN BROECK, Joeri 211, 245
VAN DEN HOVE, Ivar 307
VAN DER HEYDEN, Machiel 286
VAN DER LAKEN, Richard 99
VAN DER PLOEG, Rogier 102
VAN DER VAEREN, Manoelle 195
VAN DER ZWAN, Ivar 19
VAN DIJK, Darre 121, 277
VAN DIJK, Edo 351
VAN DOORMAAL, Dominique 199, 209
VAN DUYNEN, Phil 118
VAN DUYVENBODE, Michel 30
VAN HEIJNINGEN, Matthijs 210
VAN OEVELEN, Paul 53
VAN RECK, Werner 53, 265
VAN VELSEN, Pieter 19, 112
VAN VIJFEIJKEN, Rob 44
VAN WENSVEEN, Matthijs 200
VANDEN BRANDE, Didier 120
VANDEN BROECK, Eric 217
VANDENBERGHE, Philip 231, 281
VANDERBORST, Maja 375
VANDEVYVER, Iwein 231, 281
VANONI, Roland 97
VAPAASALO, Samuli 305
VARGA, Tibor 16
VARHAUG, Morten 34, 38
VASSELIN, Pascal 141
VAZQUEZ, Samuel 74
VEERMÄE, Kaido 25
VEET 188
VEIJOLA, Jaakko 239
VEKSNER, Simon 196
VELDHOEN, Zwier 19
VELTEN, Patric 334
VENEKAMP, Clarisse 19
VENTILATOR, Bled 340
VENTURA, Joe 246
VENVILLE, Malcolm 128
VERBIST, Muriel 167
VERDON-SMITH, Fiona 342
VERLIC, Vital 101, 331
VERMUS, Oren 153
VERSION HOMME 273
VERVROEGEN, Erik 171, 172, 173, 195, 300, 312, 313
VIBENIUS, Christofer 128
VICKERSTAFF, Guy 296
VIDAL, Oscar 196
VIGLIONE, Guillermo 255
VIGORELLI, Gianpietro 213, 261
VIITANEN, Mirva 25, 62, 276
VIJALAINEN, Sanna 377
VIKINGO, Pedro 97
VILEDA 167
VILLA, Gianluca 114
VILLANUEVA, Javier 66
VILLAR, Alfonso 74
VINCE, Dario 151
VINCENTE, Javier 255
VINCI ARREDAMENTI 160
VINCIGUERRA, Mathieu 116
VINCK, Ole 136
VINIZIUS YOUNG & RUBICAM, Barcelona 66
VINZAVOD 347
VIRPIÖ, Markus 21
VITALI, Max 38
VIZIR 169
VIZNEROVA, Tereza 90
VLADUSIC, Alan 79, 295
VLASMAN, Pepijn 367
VLIEGENTHART, Jaap 155, 307
VOLFE, Tony 365
VOLKSWAGEN 196, 197, 198, 199, 200, 201, 373
VOLVO 208, 332, 359, 374, 375
VON ARB, Christoph 89
VON ESSEN, Fredrik 325
VON KIETZELL, Hasso 79, 295
VON REIS, Christoffer 146
VON VOGELSANG, Henning 43
VON WERDER, Edwin 101, 247
VONIER, Julien 37, 41, 76, 169, 215
VONTOBEL, Nicolas 43
VOSS, Katharina 228
VOSSEN, Jürgen 83, 130, 136, 243
VOUHÉ, Christian 205
WAAGE MOHN, Anette 319
WAAL, Magnus 28
WACHSMANN, Jean-Marc 124, 239
WÄCHTER & WÄCHTER WORLDWIDE PARTNERS, Munich 243
WACKER PAINTS 243
WAGNER LA PIZZA 18
WAGNER, Maw 329
WAHL, Jack 309
WAHL, Nico 28
WAKEFIELD, Paul 50
WAKEMAN, Simon 316
WALCKIERS, Damien 184
WALKER, Ben 194
WALKER, Sam 48
WALLMARK, Anna 40
WÄLSTEN, Magnus 362, 363, 370, 371
WALTER, Anders 156
WANADOO 149
WANDA, Paris 98, 212
WARD, Stephen 271
WARNER, Carl 376
WARNER, Jonathan 344
WASASTJERNA, Kaj 21
WATERKAMP, Hermann 132
WATERS, Mark 341
WATERS, Patrick 278
WEBER, Florian 113
WEBSTER, Rob 46
WEDDLE, Helen 376
WEDENDAHL, Kasper 84
WEEKS, Robin 91, 220, 221
WEGMAN, Dannes 175
WEIGERTPIROUZWOLF, Hamburg 333
WEIHENSTEPHAN 41
WEISS, Stig 93
WEISS, Yair 232
WELCOME TO ORANGE COUNTY, Soller 160
WELL ADVERTISING & PR AGENCY, Budapest 32
WELLHAUSEN, Andreas 357
WELMAN, Karen 343
WENDEL, Albin 36
WENDEL, Anti 247
WENDT, Katrin 323
WENGER SWISS ARMY KNIFE 265
WENTZ, Jan 358
WESTERBEEK, Fleur 175
WESTERDAHL, Patrik 356
WESTERHULT, Annika 128
WESTPHAL, Bernd 105
WETZEL, Patricia 136, 230
WEYMANN, Nico 198
WHISKAS 20
WHITE, Luke 39, 79, 179
WHITE, Paul 188
WHITEMAN, Mo 132, 224
WIDDERSHOVEN, Thomas 351
WIDGREN, Kalle 206
WIED, Holger 200
WIEDEN + KENNEDY, Amsterdam 246, 253, 256, 258
WIEDEN + KENNEDY, London 194
WIEDEN + KENNEDY, Portland 259
WIENERS & WIENERS 237
WIENTZEK, Marc 130
WIGBELS, Sonja 237
WIKSTRÖM, Arne 244
WIKSTRÖM, Mathias 185
WIKTOR LEO BURNETT, Bratislava 64, 135
WILLIAMS, Helen 250
WILLIAMS, Mark 138
WILLIAMSON, Peter 372
WILSHER, David 158
WILSON, Charlie 319
WILSON, Dougal 72
WILSON, Philip 90
WIND 353
WINER, Santiago 215
WING, Bob 191
WINKLER, Thoams 243
WINSCHEWSKI, Anke 23
WINTERHALDER 23
WINTERHALDER, Katja 23
WINTHER, Martin 169
WIRZ WERBUNG, Zürich 83, 89, 277
WIRZ, Dana 76, 249, 299
WIST, Mika 229
WITKIEWICZ, Lukasz 219
WITTIG, Harald 204, 304
WLODARSKI, Janusz 137, 154
WOHLNICK, Lars 254, 272
WOLFE, Art 195
WOLFE, Tim 258
WOLOWSKI, Jacek 193, 211
WOMEN TO WOMEN 126
WOOD, Lucy 271
WOODRUFF, Richard 367
WOODS, Dave 325
WOODWARD, Gary 79
WORLD ATHLETICS CHAMPIONSHIPS 285
WORLD VISION 310
WORTHINGTON, Nick 110, 111, 250
WRANGLER 250
WRETBLAD, Magnus 206
WÜBBE, Stefan 230
WUDTKE, Daniel 159
WUNDERMAN INTERACTIVE, London 358
WUNDERMAN, Vienna 329
WWF ADENA 112
YAHOO 152
YANI 19
YANTUR, Ferit 201
YATES, Bart 72
YEE, Michael 118, 289, 294, 352
YEE, Ruth 22
YILMAZ, Tamer 161
YOGGIE 35
YOP 40
YOPLAIT 39
YOUNG & RUBICAM, Brussels 217
YOUNG & RUBICAM, Copenhagen 168
YOUNG & RUBICAM, Frankfurt 18
YOUNG & RUBICAM, Paris 62, 63, 117, 217
YOUNG ADVERTISING, Dublin 49
YUSTE, Carlos 315
ZACHRISSON, Jonas 16
ZALTSMAN, Shirli 208
ZANINI, Sébastien 65
ZAPATER, Sergi 87
ZAPPING, Madrid 92, 116, 192, 317, 326, 330, 333
ZATORSKI, Darek 137, 154, 169, 219, 295
ZE PROD, Paris 104
ZETTERHOLM, Emma 184, 185
ZIELINSKI, Tomek 219
ZIENGS 264
ZINIC, Nikola 24, 332
ZINIEWICZ, Leszek 219
ZONTAR, Toma_ 151
ZSCHALER, Stefan 132
ZUAZO, Julian 267, 268
ZUERCHER, Hansjoerg 37, 41, 76, 169
ZUIDERVELD, Robin 317
ZÜNKELER, Ulrich 41
ZÜRCHER BROCKENHAUS 89
ZURCHER, Tom 100, 236
ZWART, Harald 150
&Co, Copenhagen 265
.START, Munich 78, 81, 126, 152, 225, 254, 272
141 PORTUGAL, Lisbon 372
1576 ADVERTISING, Edinburgh 316
180 AMSTERDAM, Amsterdam 257, 286
183 CHILD HELPLINE 125
3 SUISSES 85
41/2, Oslo 34, 38,148
4MBO 336
539090 PRODUCTIONS, Hamburg 276
5J CINCO JOTAS 24